Psychology Comes to Harlem

New Studies in American Intellectual and Cultural History
Howard Brick, Series Editor

Psychology Comes to Harlem

Rethinking the Race Question in
Twentieth-Century America

JAY GARCIA

The Johns Hopkins University Press

Baltimore

2 4 6 8 9 7 5 3 1

The Johns Hopkins University Press
2715 North Charles Street
Baltimore, Maryland 21218-4363
www.press.jhu.edu

Library of Congress Cataloging-in-Publication Data
Garcia, Jay, 1972–
Psychology comes to Harlem : rethinking the race question in
twentieth-century America / Jay Garcia.
p. cm. — (New studies in American intellectual and cultural history)
Includes bibliographical references and index.
ISBN-13: 978-1-4214-0519-3 (hbk. : acid-free paper)
ISBN-10: 1-4214-0519-9 (hbk. : acid-free paper)
ISBN-13: 978-1-4214-0541-4 (electronic)
ISBN-10: 1-4214-0541-5 (electronic)
1. American literature—African American authors—History and criticism.
2. African Americans—Intellectual life—20th century. 3. Wright, Richard, 1908–1960—
Criticism and interpretation. 4. Baldwin, James, 1924–1987—Criticism and
interpretation. 5. Harlem (New York, N.Y.)—Intellectual life—20th century. I. Title.
PS153.N5G24 2012
810.9'896073—dc23   2011034757

A catalog record for this book is available from the British Library.

*Special discounts are available for bulk purchases of this book. For more information, please
contact Special Sales at 410-516-6936 or specialsales@press.jhu.edu.*

The Johns Hopkins University Press uses environmentally friendly book materials,
including recycled text paper that is composed of at least
30 percent post-consumer waste, whenever possible.

Where men have always looked around
And searched for secrets never found,
You saw a vision, dark, profound;
You heard beneath a distant sound;
You took the lid off the Underground.

Fredric Wertham to Richard Wright

I could never understand why people think these structural questions were not connected to the psychic, with emotions and identifications and feelings because, for me, those structures are things you live . . . they have real structural properties, they break you, they destroy you.

Stuart Hall

CONTENTS

Many people helped to make *Psychology Comes to Harlem* possible. For their formidable critical talents and generosity I thank my main dissertation advisors in the Program in American Studies at Yale University. Jean-Christophe Agnew's "American Century" course was the challenging and indispensable starting point for the book, and his close attention to the particulars of the project always buoyed my spirits. My work was likewise sustained by Hazel Carby's enthusiasm about the project and the model of her own scholarship. Michael Denning's combination of sound practical advice and exacting questions was essential for seeing the project in new ways at crucial junctures. Several other colleagues affiliated with the American Studies Program and Department of African American Studies at Yale University shaped my thinking in different ways throughout the trajectory of the project. Paul Gilroy, Alan Trachtenberg, Matthew Jacobson, and Jonathan Holloway provided vital insights and leads.

While at Yale, I was lucky to be part of an excellent writing group that quickly became an invaluable resource. Amy Chazkel, Michael Cohen, Mark Overmyer-Velazquez, Tori Lawless, and Fiona Vernal helped me strengthen my arguments. Scott Saul, Becky Ruquist, Leigh Raiford, Lori Brooks, JJ Fueser, and Joseph Thompson were also key interlocutors and made graduate studies a great deal of fun to boot. Shafali Lal's passion for scholarship, as for social change, was another resource as I worked on this study. Questions she posed in her own work were not only relevant to my research, they also led me to conduct more searching investigations. A presentation based on the first phase of my research came about only after Shafali's insistence that we jointly organize an American Studies Association panel. Her humor, vision, and skill in seeing the best in others continue to wend through the lives of those she touched.

While teaching at the University of North Carolina at Chapel Hill, my work on the book benefited from critiques by John Kasson and Fred Hobson and the support of colleagues in the Department of American Studies. For engaging with my work at various points, and for their warmth, I also thank Amy Wood, Jennifer Greeson, Tom Reinert, Eliza Richards, Michelle King, Mark Sheftall, Cynthia Current, and John Sweet. I've had the good fortune of meeting colleagues at scholarly conferences, among them Mari Jo Buhle, Daryl Scott, and Werner Sollors, whose kind words and comments were, probably unbeknownst to them, instrumental in moving the project to its next stages. Conference audiences at meetings of the American Studies Association and seminar participants at the School for Critical Theory at Cornell University led me to give my arguments different and richer inflections. While at Cornell, I profited in multiple ways from conversations with Robert J. C. Young.

Fellowships from the Spencer Foundation, Yale University's Beinecke Rare Book and Manuscript Library, the Carolina Postdoctoral Fellowship Program, and the Institute for the Humanities at UNC–Chapel Hill allowed me to make research trips and devote time to working through key archives. I benefited from the assistance of librarians and archivists at the Beinecke Library, the Schomburg Center for Research in Black Culture, the Moorland-Spingarn Center at Howard University, the Louis Round Wilson Special Collections Library at the University of North Carolina at Chapel Hill, and the Hargrett Rare Book and Manuscript Library at the University of Georgia.

It has been a pleasure to work with the Johns Hopkins University Press and I am especially grateful to Robert J. Brugger for his attention to details large and small. For reading my manuscript and helping me to see my work in new ways, I thank Howard Brick, whose support has been central to my ability to complete the book. I thank Kirsten Bohl for superb editorial assistance. Glenn Perkins and Alison Anderson supplied excellent copy editing.

Rachel Oberter read large parts of this study in its many guises: dissertation, book, and everything in between. Yet she deserves my appreciation for many more things than that. Her steadfast support was essential during the final stages of writing and in our most recent transition. I am once again thankful for her bountiful love and kindness, no small things in a time of great flux.

Psychology Comes to Harlem

Introduction

In 1945, the Wiltwyck School for Boys opened its doors to Richard Wright. While researching a book on youth delinquency, the celebrated author visited the school, which took in and counseled troubled youngsters from impoverished and neglected parts of New York City, including Harlem. Located in a hamlet by the Hudson River, Wiltwyck had come to Wright's attention earlier that year. While at the school, Wright felt "drenched with the conviction that human relations, the daily love that is expressed for one another, trust, devotion, dependence, tenderness, self sacrifice, selflessness, are things all too often missing so deeply that their lack is not even known." In "Harlem Is Human," a sketch about Wiltwyck, Wright described a place where "childhood is known and loved, handled with care, lest an awkward step ruin forever a delicate spirit reaching out for meaning and share of life." To Wright's great distress, the qualities he encountered at Wiltwyck were "greatly missing on the American scene."[1] His comments on Wiltwyck recall what Michel Fabre, author of the classic Wright biography, described as Wright's "wonder before life, his thirst for a natural existence," which nurtured "his courageous and incessant battle against all that prevents an individual from fully belonging to the world."[2]

Tellingly, "Harlem Is Human" focused on the school's psychiatrists, who tracked emotional changes and attempted to understand each boy "inside and out, physical and mental, his relationship to teachers and other boys, his home, his past, his capacity to learn." Indeed, the psychotherapeutic dimensions of Wiltwyck intrigued Wright above all. Written over 1945–46, "Harlem Is Human" described Wiltwyck as a potentially transformational experiment addressing the delinquent behavior of poor urban youth. For readers primarily familiar with Wright through his stark depiction of violence in *Native Son* or with subsequent criticism that interpreted the novel as an exemplar of protest fiction, "Harlem Is Human" offers alternative angles on Wright's literary and intellectual preoccupations. The sketch demonstrates that Wright regarded Wiltwyck's psychotherapeutic function as an institutional variant of the battles he waged as a writer and intellectual. A validation of the significance of psychological explorations of race hierarchy, Wiltwyck deepened Wright's conviction that psychological inquiry carried liberatory and antiracist possibilities.

This book argues that Wright's commitment to psychological inquiry contributed to a distinctive moment in the critical exploration of racial ideology that emerged in American letters beginning in the early 1940s. Although largely minimized, Wright's public role in merging psychological inquiry and antiracism can scarcely be overstated. While scholars have treated psychological themes in Wright's literary works at length, his status as a source of psychological information, even expertise, has been obscured. Yet much of Wright's work was predicated on the belief that psychological inquiry and psychotherapeutic practices represented catalysts of social and cultural transformation, levers necessary for collective reckoning with race hierarchy. The elasticity of psychological inquiry afforded Wright and other critics a range of avenues for devising antiracist cultural politics. The vocabulary of modern psychological thought provided ways to rethink the interdependence of personal investments in racial ideology and institutional practices of segregation and racism. Giving psychological inquiry decidedly antiracist inflections became a key goal of cultural critics determined to reinvigorate the social and political analysis of racial domination and conflict. In the hands of Wright and other antiracist writers, psychological inquiry supplied a means of exposing the material and ideological dimensions of white supremacy and the injuries it inflicted as a technology of domination. The commentary that followed transformed the terms of public discussion around racial ideologies and racial antagonisms.

Emotional distress and psychological maladies generated by racist social environments stood at the center of Wright's work. Moreover, his public intellectual activism emerged in large part via concepts and questions he drew from modern psychological thought, for patterns of psychological harm engendered by racist social environments recurred not only as themes in Wright's literary corpus but also as subjects of his cultural commentary. As Wright wrote, the "emotional deprivation that is found among the black boys of the huge cities is but a reflection of the emotional deprivation that stalks the homes of black boys, that exists in the parents of the boys; and the emotional deprivation that grips black life in America is but a reflection of that which grips the white population in different ways and in various guises."[3] Wright's literary and intellectual contribution involved placing the psychological dimensions of racism and racial ideology on the agenda of American cultural expression and criticism. If African American writers had long turned to themes of interiority, probing emotions and subjectivities created amid racial violence and racial codes, the extensive purview and authority of psychological knowledge created a new dispensation for the articulation of antiracism and psychological inquiry. Wright understood his work in the 1940s in terms of the development and consolidation of new forms of critical inquiry into the bases and power of racial ideology and racial antagonisms. His writings made the investigation of psychological dynamics and cultural logic in accounts of race hierarchy indispensable to national reading practices and thus necessary to the very work of American criticism.

Wright's best-known literary and intellectual achievements took place between 1941 and 1945, the years the critic and journalist Carey McWilliams described as the start of a "racial revolution," a time when "racial issues began to be seen in a new light." The creation of camps for Japanese Americans and the eruption of race riots—events on the domestic landscape, not a distant battleground—made it difficult to ignore the contradictions of a society organized by "race." The beginnings of the modern civil rights movement flickered in several key events from the early 1940s, notably the push for a March on Washington, slated for 1941.[4] The March on Washington movement signaled the arrival of a distinct moment in civil rights activism and followed from vast demographic changes, including the migration of two million blacks to northern and western industrial centers, as well as large-scale migration from rural to urban locales within the South.[5] Among writers and intellectuals, the escalation of fascism abroad and domestic racial antagonisms, especially in urban contexts, highlighted the need for more perceptive and informative explorations of the origins, power, and appeal of race thinking. W. E. B. Du Bois thus created the journal *Phylon* in 1940 to "survey the field of race and culture" and equip readers with a "broad historical, political and psychological grasp of the actions of men."[6] That same year, the editors of another journal, *Common Ground,* began gathering writers to interpret a palpably distinct phase in America's "racial-cultural situation."[7] War and fascism had given the contradictions of the longstanding "racial-cultural situation" in the United States a glaring and global character; the race question could no longer be cordoned off from approved national concerns. As social scientists, cultural commentators, and journalists increasingly described race hierarchy and racism as practices constitutive of the social order as a whole, Richard Wright turned his intellectual and literary lights on the ideological particulars of that order, the dynamics and meanings of America's "racial-cultural situation."

Regarding racial ideologies as part of the overall ensemble of social and political facts of domination, Wright and other antiracist writers in the 1940s became especially interested in the ways varieties of "race thinking" acquired the status of cultural common sense. Attention to "race" as an invidious, destructive, and deadly principle increasingly figured in American social thought and public commentary. In such a context, race thinking emerged as an expanding area of investigation, not a neutral subject but a volatile problem of great social consequence. *Race thinking* in the present study denotes the urgency created by the Second World War context for an active arena of critical analysis—one that interpreted race hierarchy and the material dimensions of segregated social relations as a "racial-cultural situation" involving everyday attitudes, practices, and psychological investments and thus implicating all Americans. To be sure, American commentators and social scientists of the 1940s put forth another phrase for such revamped analysis: the study of *race prejudice*. Although *race prejudice* will appear at times in the study, I regard it as an artifact of midcentury social thought rather than as an analytical term. Although *prejudice* was a particularly important term in and around the Second World War and the postwar period which became infused with a psychological dimension suggesting complex emotional needs, it has undoubtedly lost much of the semantic strength it once conveyed.[8] By the 1960s, the study of "racism" largely canceled out the analysis of "race prejudice," which seemed incapable of addressing the structural dimensions of segregation and discrimination, particularly insofar as the term became linked to an overriding concern with attitudes. *Race prejudice,* despite its periodicity and psychological connotation, does not do justice to the forms of cultural transformation and renewal that animated the investigation of the race hierarchy undertaken by Wright and like-minded critics. Neither *racism,* absent as a term in the 1940s, nor *race prejudice,* is adequate to account for the antiracism of these writers.

Within midcentury U.S. intellectual formation, race hierarchy increasingly surfaced as a complex of problems demanding several questions and angles of vision: a "racial-cultural situation" in which "racialism" writ large—structures, ideologies, feelings, behavior, practices—demanded renewed investigation. Throughout this book, I refer to *race thinking* as the broad problematic within which antiracist critics worked. These terms reflect the ideological dimensions of race hierarchy, a topic ever subject to historical fluctuation and revision. I also mean for the term to implicate the antifascism of the Second World War era; *race thinking* therefore communicates the antipathy toward racism and racial ideologies heightened in the midst of segregation, fascism, discrimination, and racial violence. For the writers at the center of this study, the beliefs and practices of race thinking could no longer be marginalized but that instead called for national deliberation. Investigating the beliefs and practices that bequeathed and sustained the racist social order was a prerequisite to altering that order.

Addressing the complexities and power of U.S. race thinking raised the possibility of arriving at valid assessments of cultural imperatives and psychological undercurrents that nurtured race hierarchy. The use of *race thinking* did not presuppose the rejection of "race" as a social category, but it did indicate that reading racial categories, and the structures and psychological patterns that gave them traction, became a larger critical endeavor, one antiracist writers considered vital for the meaningful analysis of race hierarchy. By focusing their attention on *race thinking* as a constellation of beliefs, habits, and practices, antiracist writers increasingly drew the attention of American readers to the processes by which race hierarchies became part of the social world, the stuff of common sense.

The tremendous acclaim that greeted *Native Son* (1940) and *Black Boy* (1945) turned Wright's books into mass-cultural events that promised "creative thinking and writing about our cultural problems," in the words of southern novelist Lillian Smith. Like Wright, Smith believed that the narrow tethering of public discussions of racial divisions to economy and politics led to an underestimation of the broad reach and import of racial ideologies. In 1944, Smith proposed to Wright that the two "work out some suggestions for other writers" in order to encourage innovative explorations of culture generally and cultural problems in particular. For Wright and Smith, America's cultural problems had everything to do with the persistence of segregation, racist laws, and the racial ordering of everyday life. Wright and Smith agreed with sociologist Horace R. Cayton when he wrote that race hierarchy was as "fundamental a part of our culture as is the belief in free competition, individual enterprise, freedom of worship," and other tenets of American life.[9] They therefore turned to anthropological definitions of culture—culture as common beliefs and a shared way of life—to create narratives and press questions that looked to the entirety of American life to assess the meanings and effects of "race." From such an intellectual starting point, Wright, Smith, and other writers could bring all Americans and questions of "race" within a common analytical space.

Bound up with research in the psychological sciences, mid-twentieth-century definitions of culture thoroughly informed the work of antiracist writers. To contemplate cultural problems meant thinking in the terms of psychological conditions and patterns. To challenge commonsense beliefs about "race," Wright and other critics endorsed more systematic study of the mental habits, dispositions, mechanisms, and practices that conspired to produce and reproduce the racist culture. Different questions than those that had dominated discussions of race hierarchy came into view via analysis that yoked cultural and psychological inquiry. How did psychological maladjustments and common neuroses relate to prevailing racial ideologies? How did racial ideologies enter and remain part of everyday practices? Were there mechanisms in individuals and collectivities that facilitated the drawing of the color line? Such questions animated the work of several writers and followed from the conviction that to explore the deep-seated beliefs, impulses, and psychological patterns that informed behavior was arguably to approach culture at its most crucial points of origin. Within the sphere of antiracist writing, psychological inquiry thus became a means of understanding—and devising paths beyond—the racist social order. Psychological modes of analysis promised ways of rethinking race ideology and racial antagonisms that enlarged the public relevance and political resonance of antiracism.

The "psychological" offered avenues for broadening and deepening the critique of white supremacy and bringing the subject of racism's pervasive harms into public view in dramatic and potentially transformative ways. Many writers became convinced that placing a premium on psychological analysis strengthened the case for understanding the far-reaching effects of race hierarchy as deriving from conditions that were manmade, and thus changeable. Belief in the mutability of human behavior and mental habits, and, by implication, social patterns, became an abiding part of the public profile of psychological thought. As psychological ways of thinking permeated midcentury intellectual life, narratives about the corrosive effects of racism held the promise of comprehending the effects of "race" on all subjectivities within the social and cultural order. Indeed, psychological inquiry seemed to offer expanded means of considering the making of personalities formed amid racial hierarchy and racist ideologies.

Although many writers held that psychological inquiry profitably opened up possibilities for more sophisticated accounts of the impact of racial antagonisms and race thinking on the everyday making of cultural life, they only occasionally invoked psychological experts. More often, literary artists and critics brought words or phrases from the psychological study of prejudice into their writing in non-systematic ways. Unconstrained by disciplinary obligations, writers and critics could give psychological inquiry pointed antiracist valences. A supple resource for the analysis of harms, seen and unseen, deriving from racism and racial ideologies, psychological analysis served antiracist writers, not as a means of relegating questions of race hierarchy to a marginal arena of attitudes and values, but instead as a means of making race hierarchy a matter of domination and contestation.

The history of *Brown v. Board of Education* (1954) provides the leading American narrative connecting racism, psychology, and civil rights. A brief return to the landmark case is therefore a necessary starting point for a study that veers away from official accounts of the civil rights movement and toward the cultural politics of antiracism and psychology by way of writers and intellectuals. The *Brown* story dramatizes the contribution of psychological experts to the fall of the long dominant doctrine of "separate but equal." Lawyers for the National Association for the Advancement of Colored People emphasized the causal link between segregated schooling and inferiority complexes in black subjects by drawing upon social scientific studies about the psychological harm racist structures inflicted on black children. To strengthen the case for desegregation, NAACP lawyers procured and submitted "The Effects of Segregation and the Consequences of Desegregation: A Social Science Statement."[10] Among the works cited in the document were major research projects, including *An American Dilemma, The Authoritarian Personality,* and studies conducted by social psychologists Kenneth and Mamie Clark. The social science statement underwrote the endorsement by the United States Supreme Court of psychological research on prejudice: "To separate [African American children] from others of similar age and qualifications solely because of their race generates a feeling of inferiority as to their status in the community that may affect their hearts and minds in a way unlikely ever to be undone." "Modern authority," the Court continued, superseded what "may have been the extent of psychological knowledge at the time of *Plessy v. Ferguson.*"

Yet *Brown* in many ways offers an inadequate index to the midcentury intellectual labors that interwove cultural criticism, psychological inquiry, and antiracism. To be sure, *Brown* put a national stamp on the association between civil rights activism and psychological experts; that stamp has often meant that the dynamic interplay between such expertise and civil rights appears self-evident, even sui generis. Public perceptions of *Brown* did not easily accommodate interpretive subtleties and qualifications held by psychologists devoted to the study of prejudice, and dominant formulations to emerge from the case relied on a selectively chosen range of the available literature. Kenneth Clark, for instance, had asserted in his work that patterns of "personality difficulties" did "not hold for every child in a rejected minority group."[11] Although social psychological research seemed to indicate that minority children experienced some deviation from a "healthy personality structure," the damaging effects of segregation and ideologies of inferiority were not evenly distributed. While this proviso entered into the social science statement, a condensed set of claims about "damage" took precedence over arguments emphasizing gradation and variation in the story of the effects of segregated social relations.[12] *Brown* furthered a process of conceptual superimposition by which the fact of minority group status and the condition of psychological victimization became difficult to disconnect discursively.[13] Less noticed, but similarly notable, Clark was displeased that the Supreme Court had all but ignored social scientific claims about the adverse effects of segregation on white children.[14] Without a doubt, the significance of these qualifications and disappointments fade alongside the boldness of *Brown*'s demand for desegregation; they also linger as questions and paths not pursued.

A comprehensive reading of the link between *Brown* and psychology requires an exploration of the full range of psychological research in the mid-twentieth century. This study concentrates instead on cultural critics and literary artists—not social psychologists and other social scientists—who made psychological explanation a vital and indispensable part of the analysis of racial antagonisms. If psychological experts supplied the imprimatur for the systematic investigation of race prejudice and its myriad effects, writers outside the social sciences with keen interests in psychology advanced antiracist psychological inquiry as a portentous mode of cultural commentary. Working in the decade and a half that preceded *Brown,* these critics ventured forms of cultural criticism that addressed the psychological dimensions of race hierarchy. Reaching a wide reading public, this corpus of criticism represented the larger critical environment within which psychological knowledge and civil rights activism merged.

The writers I concentrate upon in this study maintained that emotional and behavioral patterns helped sustain racial ideologies and, concomitantly, that racial ideologies were national and cultural problems requiring individual and collective investigation. In much the same manner as their counterparts in social psychology, they chose to explore a range of phenomena—the inferiority complexes of racial minorities, the neuroses that nurtured racist behavior, and, not least, the psychological harms and scars that characterized the workings of segregated social conditions generally—through writing that challenged available forms of public deliberation. Beginning in the early 1940s, African American writers and white allies accelerated efforts to find a searching and accessible idiom with which to analyze the hazards of race hierarchy and expand avenues for antiracism. Major changes in the character of psychological research, especially the demise of scientific racism, along with the antifascism of the 1930s and 1940s, enabled these efforts and led to a period when modern psychological thought reorganized the vocabulary and scope of antiracist cultural criticism.

Reading "race" along a sociopsychological axis, antiracist writers in the 1940s legitimized analysis of the interplay between race hierarchy and the daily making of culture. This collective effort marked a new phase of African American letters, for African American writers figured centrally in the redescription of segregation and white supremacy as psychological domains whose origins and ramifications had yet to be fully investigated.

The public character of psychological thought in the middle decades of the twentieth century provided the critical backdrop for the significant role psychological inquiry came to play in the work of Wright and like-minded critics. As psychology rose to public prominence in the mid-twentieth century, psychological experts, from psychoanalytic thinkers to social and behavioral scientists, were cast as authoritative cultural diagnosticians capable of providing valid recommendations for individual and social betterment through explanations derived from research.[15] While much of the energetic growth of psychology had to do with the needs of government bureaucracies, modern psychology traveled beyond policy-making circles to become a general feature of intellectual life. In cultural commentary, psychological investigation increasingly promised to reveal "self-deceptions which hide the real motive forces behind all great and small events of history." The émigré psychoanalyst Franz Alexander advocated a historically informed modern psychology predicated on the belief that "no individual can be understood without knowing the social scene in which he lives and which has molded his personality," just as "no historical event can be understood without knowing the fundamental principles of human motivation, which are the dynamic driving force behind the ever-shifting scenes of history."[16] In proposing the lineaments of a "cultural approach to history" in 1940, U.S. historian Caroline Ware similarly stressed the value of modern psychology for making sense of patterns of "idea-formation in the mind of the individual."[17] For writers both within the field of psychology and beyond, questions and analytic styles introduced by modern psychological knowledge constituted an indispensable resource for the study of beliefs, behavior, and cultural conflicts.

The rise of psychology buoyed the conviction of many literary artists and intellectuals that antiracist inquiry required theoretical reinvention. Key to this moment of innovation were earlier developments, not least longstanding efforts by Franz Boas and other scholars to dethrone the protocols of scientific racism that came to fruition in the 1930s as researchers turned away from the scientific methods that had lent substance and authority to racial thinking in the social and behavioral sciences. Within psychology, the exploration of race as a category with a fixed, objective standing gave way to the study of "race prejudice"—the patterns, beliefs, and habits that fueled racial antagonism.[18] This transformation gave the subfield of social psychology a more significant place within the discipline and attracted a new generation of students who regarded the social scientific study of racial and religious prejudice as a democratic challenge and imperative. The rise of fascism in Europe provided a second, interconnected context, for the case for regarding racial ideology as a domestic subject with little bearing beyond national borders became difficult to sustain amid a war against fascist powers intent on fomenting and exploiting racial thinking. The antifascism that became central to the Popular Front of the late 1930s and early 1940s promoted fresh assessments of the relation of racial ideologies to destructive, malevolent political cultures. Antifascism became a platform on which to conceive and engender antiracist commentary appropriate to a historical moment defined by war and marked by heightened domestic racism.

For literary artists and cultural critics, psychoanalysis stood as the most important development in the American embrace of psychology. The skepticism regarding civilization and morality that defined Freudian influence provided a commonsensical approach to the structures of "race." To be sure, antiracist sentiment and challenges to racially oppressive practices did not require psychoanalytic terms. Yet, as literary critic Alfred Kazin put it, "Freudianism gave sanction to the increasing exasperation with public standards as opposed to private feelings; it upheld the truths of human nature as against the hypocrisies and cruelties of conventional morality."[19] As cultural adherence to the conventions and practices of race hierarchy increasingly provided the impetus for antiracist criticism, several writers borrowed psychoanalytic terms and drew upon psychoanalytic interpretation. Beyond the antagonistic relation to established social standards, psychoanalytic thought appealed to writers as a counterpoint to readings of race hierarchy that failed to address "unconscious forces that are constantly pulling people apart, both in themselves, and from each other."[20] While the material conditions and deprivations of race hierarchy were real enough, writers grew to see race not simply as the transparencies of segregation but instead as involving cultural practices. The unconscious forces behind those practices needed to be factored into the work of the antiracist critic. The broadest, and arguably most important, value of Freudianism for artists and critics had to do with the primacy it accorded to making discoveries. The conventions of race hierarchy were known to all Americans, but discoveries about its workings, internal complexities, and concealed meanings had yet to be made.

Beyond the arena of psychoanalytic criticism, academic psychology increasingly acquired a public character, implicating many areas of American life. Racial discord on the home front during World War II expanded the relevance and import of the psychology of prejudice, and social psychologists actively researched racial and ethnic conflicts. Depending on the particular psychologist or study, racial prejudice was diagnosed as anything from mild neuroses to severe ailments that resembled insanity. Psychologists challenged myths of racial difference and increasingly investigated individual insecurities and collective emotional disturbance as prime motivators for race hierarchy and race prejudice. Terms such as *community disorders,* emerging from the work of World War II–era psychiatry, provided new categories for the study of social antagonisms, including racial tensions and riots.[21] By the late 1940s, and certainly by the time of *Brown,* the study of psychological dynamics and harms related to race prejudice attained wide legitimacy, in no small part because of voluminous research undertaken by social psychologists and other social scientists.

The antiracist criticism produced by Wright and others contributed to the desegregationist cultural politics that set the stage for *Brown v. Board of Education,* a decision that came to be regarded as a pivotal moment in the public career of psychological expertise. Yet conflating the work performed by psychology in *Brown* and the criticism of Wright, Smith, and Baldwin, among others, conceals more than it reveals. For all its reliance on modern psychological knowledge, *Brown* took a certain angle on race prejudice, reworking the complex field of social psychological research on the subject of race prejudice to emphasize the inferiority complexes endemic to racist social environments. The formulations that came to define *Brown* constituted a translation of the range of psychological inquiry and cultural commentary that preceded the case, and a collapsing of multiple lines of critical investigation in order to achieve discursive uniformity. The authors of the social science statement supplied the basis for this uniformity by concentrating on the mental anxiety displayed by minority-group children, establishing psychological damage as a dominant rubric for the interpretation of African American life.[22] Invoking findings from the 1950 Midcentury White House Conference on Children and Youth, social scientists helped to install "self-hatred and rejection of his own group" as among the chief effects of segregation on the "minority group child."[23]

The scope of antiracist critical inquiry went well beyond a search for damage imagery. In Wright's work, investigating race thinking through psychological and cultural patterns challenged the tendency to evade fuller acknowledgement of the far-reaching ramifications of racism and segregated social relations in American life. The political Left took part in the evasion of these ramifications in its own way, Wright argued, for as a politically mobilized coalition it took pains to "make the Negro problem fit rigidly into a class-war frame of reference" but, in so doing, failed to recognize that the "roots of the problem lie in American culture as a whole."[24] Wright's view led reviewers of his fiction and nonfiction from the 1940s to regard him as a writer who delivered insights into American life as a whole through stories emerging from the situations of African Americans. For literary and cultural critic Lionel Trilling, Wright's autobiographical *Black Boy* recounted a life marked by the "psychic wounds and scars" incurred by a racist social order, but the book told a story that went beyond Wright's youth and even beyond experiences common to African Americans. *Black Boy* helped to lay bare the "moral flaws of the dominant culture."[25]

Recent historical readings of Wright overlook the significance of psychological inquiry to the writing he produced. In one account, Wright's work merely buttresses images of damaged black psyches codified by *Brown* and much liberal postwar social scientific research through literary representations of psyches marked by fear and hatred of whites. Such readings accord a singular importance to Bigger Thomas, the main character in *Native Son,* but reduce the story to an image, setting aside the full range of Wright's artistic production.[26] Scholarly interpretations that assimilate Wright within liberal social science minimize the possibilities he linked to psychological inquiry as a means of positing racist ideologies as changing, dynamic forces, not as historical faits accompli. Indeed, Wright went beyond most social scientific research in his insistence that psychological explanation, psychotherapeutic intervention, and cultural criticism could serve the purposes of antiracist transformation. The fatalistic focus on rage and damage imagery, even where they help to describe aspects of Wright's work, muffles the work of articulating psychological investigation and cultural criticism that he advocated. Moreover, such a focus makes it difficult to understand the earnest disposition that led Wright and others to maintain that investigating the psychological undercurrents of the racist social order could lead to a socially viable and culturally resonant antiracism.

Different accounts locate Wright within traditions of black radicalism, rejecting the view that his well-known departure from the Communist Party signaled clear-cut "movement away from left-wing radicalism into liberalism and literary celebrity."[27] Yet the focus on black radicalism can further the mistaken claim that Wright's vision emerged from and only implicated the sociopolitical status of African Americans. Here, black radicalism becomes a version of black nationalism, and Wright's fiction and nonfiction about African American life are severed from the larger cultural matrix and intellectual influences that sustained him. Advancing such a model effectively makes Wright the proponent of both an African American or black-centered perspective, one the one hand, and a race-centered analytic orientation that serves as the basis for his interpretations of politics and culture in the United States, on the other. Yet "race" is such a charged, problematic, and delimiting category in Wright's thinking that it cannot be regarded as his taken-for-granted analytical constant. Moreover, exploring African American life in discrete, historical terms presented contradictions and problems all its own, especially since black life was indivisible from the "glorious hopes of the West, all of its anxieties, its corruptions, its psychological maladies," as Wright observed.[28] Wright's work follows from the premise of the social and psychological harms of racism, segregation, and racial ideologies, not from the inherent value of a race-centered method. Wright posited a large and varied "Sargasso of racial subjugation" and advocated a capacious antiracist critical idiom that brought analytic attention to, among other things, the effects of racist ideology on whites. Not a small portion of his work involved the problem of why "few white Americans have found the strength to cease being victims of their culture to the extent that they can throw off their socially inherited belief in a dehumanized image of the Negro." The present study rejects the positive valuation of "race" sometimes ascribed to Wright and instead underscores the central importance that Wright and other midcentury critics accorded to the overcoming of the injuries engendered by race thinking and segregated social relations.

This study does not treat at length the story of Wright's complex relationship to the Communist Party, which has been the subject of much scholarly interpretation. The focus on Wright's departure from the Communist Party too often directs a disproportionate amount of attention away from other features of his intellectual trajectory. Paradoxically, even the larger question of Wright's critical encounter with Marxism can fade when his Communist Party alliance and disaffiliation serve as the prime lenses into his literary and intellectual work. As many scholars have demonstrated, much of Wright's work emerged from his engagement with Marxism and from his reflection on its limits.[29] Wright concluded that the psychological dimensions of modern life encompassed literary subjects and thematic domains that the conceptual resources of Marxism approached but did not always satisfactorily explain. Modern life—especially the place of race hierarchy and fascism within the West—did not lead Wright to set aside Marxism as such. Nevertheless, the theoretical firmament that had long sustained Wright did shift as psychological investigation came to stand in for a necessary reckoning with modernity and its racialized character. Even as Marxism retained significance for Wright, psychological investigation emerged in his thinking as a value in itself.[30] This book therefore casts Wright's public endorsements of psychotherapeutic thinking and commitments to psychological inquiry as irreducible dimensions of his work, integral to the radicalism of the projects he undertook.

Not all midcentury critics were prepared to recognize antiracist possibilities in psychological inquiry. Marxist critics such as Herbert Aptheker denounced the work of Gunnar Myrdal and Richard Wright as capitulations to a moralistic orientation that veered away from the material and social dimensions of racism.[31] For Aptheker, arguments that drew attention to psychological dynamics and themes of subjectivity invariably distorted the political and economic character of racism, siphoning off energy needed to fully reckon with the material underpinnings of the racist social order. Wright came under special criticism for his introduction to Horace Cayton and St. Clair Drake's *Black Metropolis,* which Aptheker regarded as merely repeating Myrdal's view that whites experienced the dissonance between national ideals of egalitarianism and the racist strictures of American life as a psychological conflict. For Aptheker and other critics, giving credibility to interpretive models that veered from materialist conceptions compromised antiracist politics. Yet Wright did not see how restricting approaches to race hierarchy served the strategic aim of providing a greater base of knowledge about the effects of racial ideology and thereby expanding the reach of antiracism. Moreover, even where the argument in *Black Metropolis* coincided with Myrdal's point, Wright ventured several other lines of argument that Aptheker ignored in his blanket disqualification of perspectives on race hierarchy that foregrounded psychological inquiry and moral problems.

If Wright's brand of antiracism elicited the ire of certain critics, it also attracted many readers. Wright emerged as the major antiracist writer of the 1940s. Among his readers were other black writers for whom Wright's work became the impetus for their own explorations of psychological harms and dynamics stemming from the racial organization of American life. Especially close readers of Wright's work— Ralph Ellison, Chester Himes, Horace Cayton, and the Trinidadian Marxist thinker C. L. R. James—produced different kinds of writing throughout the 1940s meant to expand the discursive reach of antiracist inquiry.

Wright and fellow writers like Ellison, Himes, Cayton, and James challenged the boundaries of available work on racial divisions. The measure of that challenge can be taken by recalling the response to Gunnar Myrdal's *An American Dilemma,* the most important work on the subject published in the 1940s. Although Wright and other black writers described the book as a milestone in American letters, the study also seemed to fall short of psychologically incisive antiracist criticism. For Ellison, for instance, Myrdal and his team of researchers had undertaken a careful investigation of different aspects of black life, but they had not adequately addressed the psychological complexity of personality formation within the racist social order. Ellison praised Myrdal for characterizing racial antagonisms and racial ideologies in psychological terms, agreeing that the "problem of the irrational" in American culture indeed "took the form of the Negro problem." Yet, lacking subtle ways to explore "Negro perspective," Myrdal had assimilated black life to social pathology: "Negro personality" emerged only in response to dominant and adverse social arrangements. "Can a people live and develop for over three hundred years simply by *reacting?*" Ellison asked.[32] If Myrdal's tome proved informative in its assessments of America's race problems, it lacked the psychological acuity Ellison deemed necessary for the analysis of racial ideology and the worlds created by segregation. Ellison's own cultural criticism provided occasions to direct writing about race along what he envisioned to be more productive, and more explicitly psychological, lines.

The period of Wright's *Native Son* (1940) and *Black Boy* (1945) provides the starting point for this study, which explores the merger of psychological investigation, cultural inquiry, and antiracism from the early 1940s into the early Cold War years. Published and unpublished writings bring to the fore Wright's determination to develop and expand antiracist cultural politics through psychological inquiry. Just as *Native Son,* his sensational narrative of murder, social deprivation, and racial animosity, gave midcentury readers a picture of the "unconscious machinery of race relations" in modern American life, so too did Wright's work as a whole turn on the psychological repercussions of a society structured by race.[33] His contribution begins with the rejection of conventional frameworks devised to describe race problems, notably the "Negro Problem" paradigm.[34] Wright's exploration of alternative paradigms led him to consider psychotherapeutic models as means of addressing the pressures of racist social environments. Moreover, his readings in psychological literatures and his dialogues with psychiatrists and psychoanalytic thinkers worked dialectically to strengthen his belief in the intellectual and political promise of psychotherapeutic resources. He even put his commitment to antiracist applications of psychotherapeutic resources into institutional practice by helping found Harlem's Lafargue Clinic, an interracially staffed, low-cost treatment center organized to aid neighborhood residents with psychological problems, and by supporting the Wiltwyck School for Boys, mentioned above, where psychotherapists worked with poor urban youth.

African American writers and cultural commentators who shared with Wright the desire to alter antiracist criticism also figure in this study. The writings of Ellison, Himes, Cayton, and James, among others, actively fused radical political visions with psychological inquiry and collectively served to strengthen the case for understanding racial ideology as a topic that required a larger purview within American cultural criticism. The remarkable career of the southern white writer Lillian Smith, Wright's contemporary, provides another key perspective on the rethinking of race through psychology. Smith similarly turned her analytic lights to the "minds and hearts and culture" created within segregated social conditions.[35] Her work on the interplay of culture and psychology in the context of segregated and racist social relations provides a fascinating parallel to Wright's intellectual trajectory. The two writers, sometime correspondents, read and knew each other's work well. Through the commentary of antiracist critics of the 1940s generally, but in Smith's work in particular, "whiteness" became an increasingly invoked analytic object within U.S. cultural criticism. Smith made the exploration of the histories and vicissitudes of whiteness the defining feature of her fiction and nonfiction. I argue that the radical character of her writing and its divergence from the gradualist politics of much racial liberalism stemmed in part from her determination to interpret southern cultures through the prism of psychological dissonance and conflict.

James Baldwin's evocative early essays—collected in *Notes of a Native Son* (1955)— bring this study into the early Cold War years and the period of *Brown v. Board of Education*. Baldwin, influenced by Wright, yet stylistically divergent from him, furthered and reformulated the antiracism Wright did so much to establish within

American cultural criticism. I demonstrate how the proficiency in psychoanalytic thought that characterized the cultural criticism of the New York intellectuals supplied a rich arena for Baldwin's first efforts in fiction and nonfiction and provided the basis for nurturing antiracist cultural politics within the world of modernist prose and the postwar literary avant-garde. Exploring Baldwin's work through this frame furnishes an opportunity to revisit the critically burdened relationship between Baldwin and Wright. The friction between the two notwithstanding, this book makes a case for *Notes of a Native Son* as a complex prolongation of the brand of antiracist criticism Wright and like-minded writers had begun to bring forth in the early 1940s.

The analysis of race as an ideological terrain, and thus the basis for a range of cultural patterns, historical preoccupations, and recurrent antagonisms, comes to something like full fruition with James Baldwin's essays in the late 1940s and early 1950s. Baldwin transmits the concern with the psychological character of racism into an idiom informed by the New York intellectual milieu that found in Freud a pivotal figure for the investigation of the making of cultures. As cultural interpretations always already doing the work of psychological reading, Baldwin's essays ratified the kind of thinking Wright deemed vital if antiracism were to become a constitutive part of American criticism.

Beyond the postwar U.S. context, critics of colonialism increasingly drew from psychoanalytic frameworks to unravel the effects of empire and its attendant race hierarchies. Frantz Fanon and Albert Memmi analyzed the affective investments of colonizer and colonized alike, making psychological questions central to the consideration of colonial situations. The critical inquiry that Fanon and Memmi, among others, developed has been regarded as an *existential psychoanalysis,* that is, writing broadly, if also at times contentiously, in dialogue with Jean-Paul Sartre. Yet existential psychoanalysis also communicates something beyond twentieth-century existentialist thought. It communicates a political-intellectual disposition connected to, but finally different from, Freud's empirical psychoanalysis, especially insofar as it privileges the figure of the philosopher or critic capable of interpreting and thinking beyond negative historical forces.[36] *Existential psychoanalysis* emerges periodically in this study as a valuable general description of the bodies of writing I address. I do not employ it to reference intellectual interactions between Sartre and Wright, as important as these were, but instead to emphasize the interventionist and curative character of Wright's work as he grappled with ways beyond the negative forces of racism and segregation.[37] As a version of existential psychoanalysis, Wright gathered terms and inspiration from empirical psychoanalysis but did not see fit to trace its analytic procedures precisely. His cultural criticism involved investment in modern psychology, yet it gained cultural relevance by way of its distance from empirical psychoanalysis.

A vision of psychological pathologies as universal and latent features of all human mentality informed Wright's work. Such maladies—in the form of neuroses and psychoses, often expressed in patterns of fear and anxiety, and more pathogenic in some individuals than in others—served as recurrent themes for all the antiracist writers I discuss in the chapters that follow.[38] My approach in this study draws on critics who regard racial categorization as an "ideal container"—a container for a multiplicity of practices and beliefs, including disparate ideologies, and desires—in the context of the universal mechanisms of psychological maladies. This analytic starting point dovetailed with the rise of modern psychological thought, leading, among other things, to the reading of racism as a social pathology that became widespread in African American intellectual life in particular. To the writers at the forefront of midcentury antiracism, evading the psychological dimensions of racial antagonism inevitably meant minimizing the damage and pain of racial proscription and segregated social arrangements. Implicitly following an "ideal container" model, African American critics in particular recast racism as a social pathology, arguing that failing to make sense of the psychic roots of racist practices ensured the persistence of the social and psychological ailments bequeathed by race hierarchy. The existential psychoanalysis of Wright and other critics involved decoding in race those ideological and affective commitments instrumental in producing and reproducing the racist social order.

In recent years a rich scholarly literature has demonstrated the depth and range of antiracist writing and thinking in mid-twentieth-century American intellectual life by focusing on black radicalism as a locus of activity and theorization.[39] This study describes features and figures in antiracist criticism without recourse to the "black radicalism" descriptor. Although in many ways useful, that category fails to account for the fact that the work of certain writers reached large audiences, and that these writers therefore entered the historical and cultural imagination of their time as convincing interpreters and commentators, not radical outliers. The black radicalism template may also at times discourage analyses of consonant, parallel, or otherwise comparable antiracist criticism emerging from other quarters, including the work of white writers. Although the account presented here focuses largely on black writers, descriptions of the work of antiracist white writers and psychotherapeutic thinkers who worked to recast racial antagonisms, often in collaboration with black writers, indicate, among other things, the intellectual desegregation to which the protagonists in the book aspired.

Historical investigations of black radicalism tend to minimize the psychological character of much of the commentary that marked midcentury antiracist thought, preferring instead to emphasize the valuable analyses of political economy that appeared at the time. By discounting or marginalizing the psychological questions, scholars have ignored a critical dimension of the reasoning that defined much of midcentury antiracism. This book recognizes the entangled nature of the interpretations of political economy, psychological inquiry, and cultural commentary devised by leading antiracist critics by exploring the analytical and political promise attached to psychological and cultural idioms.

Wright and like-minded critics found in psychological investigations of racial hierarchy not only valid and constructive avenues for the expansion of antiracism but also, more specifically, possibilities for describing and narrating the entrenched character of white supremacy. Of course, they were hardly the first to pose questions about the emotional patterns, values, and interpersonal dynamics of a society organized by race hierarchy. Concerns with the interiority of African Americans, for instance, explicitly entered the writings of African American intellectuals early on, and they were certainly on display in W. E. B. Du Bois's *The Souls of Black Folk* at the beginning of the twentieth century.[40] Yet the mid-twentieth-century antiracist critics entered an intellectual scene that differed markedly from the one that received *The Souls of Black Folk*. Expanded psychological sciences and mass cultural forms of storytelling meant that Wright and others could draw upon growing literatures on psychological conflicts and neuroses, many of them informed by the antifascism of the 1930s and 1940s and focused on the hazards of racial ideologies.

Wright expressed a belief held by several critics when he wrote that psychological inquiry provided ways to "study the conflict of cultures as they are reflected in personalities," and therefore a means of arriving at the "tissue and texture of human experience."[41] This study argues for the distinctive dimensions of a moment in critical commentary in which psychological vocabularies acquired a cultural momentum that could be nurtured and redirected for antiracist ends, a period when literary artists and cultural critics collectively searched for a "new language to express the nature of race relations."[42] The midcentury growth of a range of analytic perspectives within psychology, such as social psychology, brought an emphatically public character to the overall field of psychology, pluralizing, if also complicating, its meanings. Psychology retained associations with experts, but so too did it become a common resource for all manner of discussions about the sociocultural world. Figuring race antagonisms and racist ideology as problems of culture, Wright, Smith, Baldwin, and others raised the possibility of an American cultural criticism organized around the analysis, and overcoming, of race hierarchy.

CHAPTER ONE

Richard Wright Writing
The Unconscious Machinery of Race Relations

Richard Wright regarded himself as "something, no matter how crudely, of a psychologist."[1] He offered that designation in 1960, the last year of his life, as a means of understanding his literary achievements and larger intellectual contribution. Many of Wright's contemporaries were inclined to agree with his assessment and cast his impact on American letters in terms of psychological insights. Midcentury readers and fellow writers habitually identified Wright as an expert in psychology. Ostensibly idiosyncratic, Wright's act of self-naming in fact brings into view a neglected component of the cultural and intellectual history of twentieth-century antiracism. Especially after 1940, Wright's work pivoted on psychological inquiry to such an extent that adopting the designation of psychologist fit within the terms of his commitments and, moreover, communicated the expansive reach he envisioned for his antiracist criticism.

None other than Kenneth Clark, the most prominent African American social psychologist of his time, located Wright under the umbrella of psychological expertise. Clark, whose research famously figured in the strategies of civil rights lawyers who argued against educational segregation in *Brown v. Board of Education*, believed that the antiracism underpinning the landmark case had intellectual roots in narratives by cultural critics who wrote in psychologically perceptive ways. Recognizing writers versed in, but outside the official contours of, social scientific or psychoanalytic knowledge, Clark constructed a literary and cultural genealogy for the case that began with *Native Son*, a book that made Americans "aware of the high costs of racial prejudice" in strikingly new ways. Clark noted the work of novelist and critic Lillian Smith, too, for she had discovered that the "major forces responsible for the development of prejudices in American children are the anxieties and pressures that parents impose on their children in order to foster the values of respectability and conformity." Clark also included James Baldwin in his account of the cultural matrix of *Brown*, citing his writings from 1945 to 1955 as among the most perceptive contemporary analyses of American race problems. To be sure, psychological experts working on problems of racial antagonisms had arrived at their findings "more systematically" than artists and cultural critics, Clark argued.[2] Yet Wright, Smith, or Baldwin, as psychological experts of a kind, had incontrovertibly brought literature and criticism to bear on the story of *Brown*. Wright, Smith, and Baldwin were not the first to bring together psychological inquiry and the analysis of race hierarchy. Yet Clark linked them to a distinctive intellectual conjuncture defined in large measure by the authority that psychological expertise had acquired during and after World War II. Works that undertook psychological investigations of racial domination existed in a continuum with research on race prejudice from within the psychological sciences.

The intellectual developments that made *Brown* possible involved many years of research on the psychology of prejudice, much of it presented and summarized in Gordon Allport's *The Nature of Prejudice* (1954), *The Authoritarian Personality* (1950), and elsewhere. These works affirmed the importance of psychological expertise for the investigation of racist social environments. Yet, for Clark, the psychological expert category could be elastic and inclusive. He chose to place literary artists alongside social scientists and psychoanalytic thinkers in the story of *Brown* because he regarded many kinds of intellectuals as compatible and interconnected actors in the cultural politics of the decision. Wright, Smith, Baldwin, and other cultural critics had helped establish the terms of a viable antiracism that energized civil rights activism and, more broadly, legitimated the aim of decomposing the racist social order.[3]

Michel Fabre has argued that Richard Wright's conception of the role of the artist involved a "technique directed at bringing the reader, through poetic ecstasy or shock treatment, to acceptance of a new consciousness."[4] Along these lines, I argue that Wright's investment in new forms of consciousness had everything to do with a primary desire to nurture greater psychological literacy with regard to the effects of race hierarchy. In this chapter, I read several of Wright's works from the early-to-mid-1940s as intensifying efforts to generate psychological literacy, to bring the antifascism of that period to bear on his interpretations of American life, and to give intellectual substance to an existential psychoanalysis that brought segregation and race hierarchy within the conceptual arena of psychological maladies.

Something, No Matter How Crudely, of a Psychologist

African American intellectuals had addressed the psychological meanings and repercussions of race hierarchy long before Wright's rise to prominence. In 1927, African American sociologist E. Franklin Frazier ventured an analysis of "The Pathology of Race Prejudice," a work that anticipated inquiries into problems of racial antagonism. Frazier defined *race prejudice* as an abnormal behavior deserving of greater study as "an acquired psychological reaction." The abnormal character of race prejudice, he continued, revealed itself in fixed ideas ascribed to African Americans and held so absolutely that they obviated the "assimilation of new data."[5] Working along parallel tracks in the late 1920s, sociologist Robert E. Park understood race prejudice as a "phenomenon of status," irreducibly connected to a "universe of discourse."[6] Scholars like Frazier and Park challenged the racist logic that informed much social scientific research by investigating personalities and collectivities shaped by race hierarchy. Along with a growing cadre of social scientists, including many social psychologists, Frazier and Park legitimated the study of psychological dynamics that underwrote segregated structures and racial conflict.

African American philosopher Alain Locke also defined racial ideologies in terms of psychological dynamics. In 1915–16, while lecturing at Howard University, Locke called the intense "color prejudice" of early-twentieth-century America "a strange sort of aberration that seems peculiar to the modern mind."[7] Like Frazier and Park, Locke believed that the social sciences had yet to fully explore the complex origins of modern racial antagonisms. Much more work in this direction was needed because in the realm of racial conflict, Locke claimed, the "psychological factors are the [controlling] ones." Studies of the kind Locke intimated only began to emerge in substantial numbers in the 1930s, when, amid the rise of antifascism, "race prejudice" became a growing and recognizable area of psychological research.[8] Such work consolidated the view that psychological theory provided valuable information about, and intrinsically important perspectives on, race hierarchy and social environments organized by racial ideologies.[9] By the late 1930s and early 1940s, influential works, such as John Dollard's *Caste and Class in a Southern Town* (1937) and Allison Davis's *Deep South* (1941), brought together social scientific methods and psychoanalytic concepts in ways that reset the intellectual investigation of racial antagonism.

During the war, the focus social psychologists and psychoanalytic thinkers placed on the racial ideologies underlying fascism helped align psychological inquiry with antiracist aspirations. Psychological investigation became a vehicle for making sense of race hierarchy and the situation of African Americans in particular. "What new values of action or experience can be revealed by looking at Negro life through alien eyes or under the lens of new concepts?" Wright began to ask with increased frequency.[10] Locating "new ideological excursions, many heretofore unimagined tangents of thought" for the understanding of racial ideologies and conditions of racial domination became a priority for antiracist critics generally.[11] Especially important to Wright were psychoanalytic readings that posited the "psychological study of the human being, not only as an exponent of a biological specimen or of a social group, but as an individual person molded by . . . specific personality influences."[12] Such an orientation would give rise to the range of questions that Wright considered central to a viable and effective antiracism. He anticipated commentators asking, "What peculiar personality formations result when millions of people are forced to live lives of outward submissiveness while trying to keep intact in their hearts a sense of the worth of their humanity?" In psychological literatures, Wright found several avenues of investigation for interpreting disparate social settings and political cultures.

Readings in the modern psychological sciences did more than offer Wright ways into the problem of racial domination and the effects of such domination on cultures and personalities. The psychological and psychiatric interpretations of modern life that Wright encountered confirmed his sense of the analytic limitations of much economic and social theory. The psychologist William H. Sheldon's *Psychology and the Promethean Will* (1936), a book Wright read in the early 1940s and recommended on at least one occasion, expressed dissatisfaction with dominant forms of social theory and social planning. According to Sheldon, there had been "too much gross, overt, social bustling about things, and in the great business of educating one another 'for citizenship' [we] have overlooked the fact that the final destiny of citizenship cannot be other than building of human minds and developing personality for human consciousness." Sheldon did not discount economic, political, or social analysis, but he did urge a move "from the era of economic interpretation of history to the era of the psychological comprehension of conflict." Wright, long intrigued by the inner and outer conflicts displayed by criminals, delinquents, and other social actors beyond normative socioeconomic frames, pursued models of analysis along the lines Sheldon proposed.[13] Wright was especially dissatisfied with economic and political approaches that directed attention toward, but failed to proceed beyond, the facts of segregation and racial antagonisms.

In Wright's estimation, psychological investigation gained special relevance in the context of the rapid urbanization and attendant transformations affecting African Americans. He tethered his affirmative evaluation of psychological inquiry to a forecast, expressed in 1942: the "next quarter of a century will disclose a tremendous struggle *among* the Negro people for self-expression, self-possession, self-consciousness, individuality, new values, new loyalties, and, above all, new leadership."[14] Urbanization and the migration of southern blacks to cities supplied the basic historical backdrop for Wright's work, which explored the critical consciousness required to meet the challenges of urban life, segregation, and migrant dislocation.[15] He directed attention to the modernity of America's segregated urban landscapes, meditating, in particular, on the alleys and kitchenettes that marked the South Side of Chicago.[16] As the first to bring the concept of modernity to bear on degraded metropolitan settings, Wright identified areas for the investigation of urban life that made race hierarchy and social deprivation features, rather than aberrant characteristics, of the modern world.[17]

In Wright's view, the urban settings African Americans occupied as residents and workers demanded perspectives on modern racial ideology that looked at the interplay of material conditions and psychological undercurrents. Wright shared with sociologist Horace R. Cayton a desire to contribute toward a "theoretical framework in which to study the Negro population of large urban localities."[18] Drawing inspiration from Wright's work, Cayton conceived of urban life as structures inseparably connected to symbolic meanings and psychological dynamics. In particular, Cayton's research explored the "contradiction between the ideology of democracy and free competition" and the "fixed status" assigned to African Americans by dominant social practices. Much like Wright, he analyzed the broad "realm of sentiments" that activated racial antipathy so as to continually "preserve the color line."[19]

"Complex Consciousness" and the Chicago School

Wright never contested his biographical and intellectual debts to the Communist Party. "Communism had not been for me simply a fad, a hobby; it had a deep functional meaning for my life," Wright told his editor, Edward Aswell, in 1955. It had "been the only road out of the Black Belt for me."[20] Wright joined the Communist Party while living in Chicago, where John Reed clubs, cultural organizations named for the American militant activist, proliferated. Associated with the International Union of Revolutionary Writers in Moscow, the clubs provided a forum for Wright's early efforts in poetry and fiction.[21] The Communist Party expressed opposition to racism and segregation more vocally and persistently than any other organized body in the 1920s and 1930s.[22] In the late 1920s, "Negro self-determination" became a component of Communist opposition to capitalism and imperialism; it expressed a policy of "self-determination for the black belt" that served as an acknowledgment of nationalist sentiment among African Americans.

Wright's work from the late 1930s sought to bring Marxism and investigations of psychological patterns together as critical enterprises capable of producing valuable new forms of writing. Wright described the configuration he advocated as "complex consciousness," a dialectical aim that might redefine African American writing. He urged writers to develop a "deep, informed, and complex consciousness" that investigated the interplay of material conditions and subjective life.[23] Interspersing Marxist formulations and reflections on the sociopsychological character of African American life and its "nationalist" dimensions, Wright delivered a "Blueprint for Negro

Writing" (1937). The essay explored African American writing from the early decades of the twentieth century and ventured a reconfiguration of African American literature. Surveying Harlem Renaissance and other African American literary artists, Wright controversially claimed that "Negro writing in the past has been confined to humble novels, poems, and plays, prim and decorous ambassadors who went a-begging to white America."[24] Wright's assessments ignored overlapping artistic tendencies and shared associations that stretched across the Harlem Renaissance and the African American social realism that followed.[25] Indeed, his insistence on the need to break with preceding literary practices did not prepare him to acknowledge such interrelationships. Yet, despite his essay's analytic limitations, Wright's determination to demote past literary practice did prompt a dramatic reformulation of approaches to the investigation of African American life. The key to that reformulation was a thorough assessment of "Negro nationalism." The "Negro church, a Negro press, a Negro social world, a Negro sporting world, [and] a Negro business world" represented a material "way of life" generated by the dominant social and political order, Wright argued. "The Negro people did not ask for this and, deep down, though they express themselves through their institutions and adhere to this special way of life, they do not want it now."[26]

Yet if Negro nationalism involved institutions and specific settings, its workings could not be reduced to the social facts of segregation. For Wright, "Negro nationalism" entailed psychological dynamics, not least the "emotional expression of group-feeling" and a "reflex expression whose roots are imbedded deeply in the Southern soil." Beginning with the premise that "psychologically, this nationalism is reflected in the whole of Negro culture," Wright encouraged writers to treat the ramifications of Negro nationalism more deliberately and thus to nurture a "deep, informed, and complex consciousness" that depicted "Negro life in all of its manifold and intricate relationships."[27] Wright understood the primary purpose of working though the "nationalist implications" of African American life as the consolidation of a cultural politics that would finally transcend the limitations of nationalist positions. He encouraged literary artists to heighten awareness of the historical conditions and emotional undercurrents that gave rise to nationalist formulas in the first place.

Although he urged writers to turn to Marxism to help reimagine the content and possibilities of African American literature, Wright was careful to call Marxism "but the starting point" of the transformation in literary culture he envisioned. "No theory of life can take the place of life," he wrote, as he recommended that writers train upon "the complexity, the strangeness, the magic wonder of life that plays like a bright sheen over the most sordid existence."[28] In "Blueprint for Negro Writing," Wright situated nationalist positions within the history of segregation and racial domination and intimated that psychological perspectives on "Negro nationalism" furthered a much desired political revisioning. Anticipating later work, "Blueprint for Negro Writing" proposed the interdependence of antiracist aspiration and attentiveness to psychological dynamics and patterns.

During the war, heightened racial tensions and political mobilization, notably the NAACP's "Double-V" campaign, which put the eradication of domestic racism and the defeat of fascism on equal political footing, reinvigorated antiracist criticism. It was in this context that Wright officially left the Communist Party. By the early 1940s Wright had come to believe that race problems had exceeded the conceptual reach—and political imagination—of the Communist Party. He described his departure as above all an intellectual challenge to himself, a way of reckoning with a "race situation [that] was a far harder matter than the Communist one."[29] Wright's membership had prevented his involvement in the March on Washington movement, the antidiscrimination initiative started under A. Philip Randolph in 1941, which was not endorsed by the party. His final break with the party came when Cayton told him that Communists had chosen not to support court battles against governmental discrimination during the war.[30] Ralph Ellison, with whom Wright discussed the limitations of party policies, regarded Wright's work as a fuller exploration of Marxism than that allowed within party intellectual circles. Indeed, Ellison interpreted Wright's work as a counterpoint to the failure of "Marxist-Leninist literature to treat human personality," and therefore as an improvement on existing socialist criticism. Impressed by Wright's meditation on African American history in *12 Million Black Voices,* Ellison wrote that the book had made him a better thinker in general and a "better Marxist" in particular.[31]

While Wright's time in Chicago involved immersion in Marxism, it was also marked by encounters with social scientists researching migration, urbanization, and racial ideology. Over time, he came to know sociologists such as Louis Wirth and gained wide familiarity with the work that emerged from "Chicago sociology."[32] The appeal of sociological writing flowed from his desire to comprehend and contend with the behavioral problems and mental distress of urban blacks.[33] Wright was especially attracted to Chicago sociology's focus on urban life. The Chicago school's study of cities involved political economy, social organization, and psychological currents, a mix already evident by the time of *The City* (1925), a work by Robert E. Park, Ernest Burgess, and Roderic McKenzie. *The City* emphasized patterns of subjective life and human behavior, often subsumed under the term *mentality,* which soon emerged as a distinguishing feature of Chicago sociology.[34] The analytic import the Chicago sociologists ascribed to psychological mechanisms stimulated Wright's own questions about the nexus of urban life, racial ideology, and behavioral patterns.

Studying the patterns and complex features of urban landscapes resonated with Wright, whose own experiences, first in Memphis and then in Chicago, convinced him of the need to theorize cities and their impact on migrants.

In *The City,* Park and his colleagues argued that the key to making sense of urban life was acknowledging that it was a product of "human nature." The result of the "vital processes of the people who compose it," the urban environment amounted in many ways to a "state of mind." By "human nature," Park did not imply that such behavior was immutable but that it grew from the malleable character of all human activity. Thus, Park viewed the city as a whole as "a kind of psychophysical mechanism in and through which private and political interests find not merely a collective but a corporate expression." Chicago sociology's approach to urban life emphasized combustive energy and conflict. Park called every city an "unstable equilibrium," in which various populations experienced "a chronic condition of crisis." The instabilities and crises of cities required analyses of collective behavior and special attention to the ways mobility and population density generated tensions that spilled over into veritable "psychological moments," reverberating beyond sites of origin to urban environments at large.[35]

Wright acknowledged the role Chicago sociologists had in his intellectual development. "The huge mountains of fact piled up by the Department of Sociology at the University of Chicago gave me my first concrete vision of the forces that molded the urban Negro's body and soul," he wrote.[36] He hoped such work on the rapid changes brought about by African American migration might engage more laypeople. At times, Wright even made the case that his work and the sociological literatures were intellectually contiguous efforts to account for patterns in racialized urban formation.[37] Beyond the longstanding focus on urbanization and migration, Park and other Chicago sociologists often pointed precisely to those aspects of social environment that Wright wanted to grasp in all their complexity. In addition to studying the technologies of communication and transportation, "which enable individuals to distribute their attention and to live at the same time in several different worlds," Park regarded "immigrant and racial colonies" as key features of the urban landscape.[38] Wright, too, wanted to understand the multiple subjective dimensions that shaped the everyday lives of urban dwellers and the effects of racial patterns and ideologies on urban environments. The work of Chicago sociologists convinced him of the substantive character of the questions he posed about urban life, inspiring him to explore them in fiction and cultural criticism. Readings in Chicago sociology encouraged Wright to understand his work, more and more, as efforts to account for social environments and their effects on personality formation. A corollary to that larger aim, the impact of racial ideologies on the personalities of minorities and majorities alike, became the pivotal subject matter of Wright's cultural work.

Native Son's "Unconscious Machinery of Race Relations"

Soon after *Native Son* was chosen as a Book-of-the-Month Club selection, Wright garnered national and international audiences. Sales for the novel significantly exceeded those of any other black writer in American literary history. The publication of *Native Son* was a mass cultural event, and many commentators promptly attempted to explain why. "The book deals with an important present-day situation which is deeply rooted in the past and the success with which the book has met the test is epoch-making," wrote J. D. Jerome in the *Journal of Negro History*. The dramatic portrayal of urban racial oppression led many critics to address the perceived and potential impact of Wright's work. Americans had been "shaken once and for all from our complacency" by *Native Son,* according to one critic, for the novel showed that "it is no longer we whites who are in a position to grant equality if we please, but the Negroes who are wresting it from us whether we please or not."[39] Alain Locke praised Wright for working outside the strictures "both of the squeamishness of the Negro minority and the deprecating bias of the prejudiced majority." In Locke's judgment, Wright had demonstrated "artistic courage and integrity of the first order." The novel's main character, Bigger Thomas—youth, dreamer, tenement dweller, suspect-turned-murderer, and prisoner—entered the American cultural imagination and confirmed Wright's ability to narrate stories about segregation and racial discord that delivered scenes at once distant and all too familiar. In the view of many readers and commentators, Wright had created the "most significant probing of the lower-class Northern urban Negro in contemporary American fiction," acquiring in the process a "nation-wide prominence as a literary diagnostician of racial and economic ills."[40]

Critics and readers who praised *Native Son* often applauded both Wright's powerful prose and what they regarded as the psychological character of the book. Although Wright would go on to write "How 'Bigger' Was Born," an essay that described the psychological concerns informing his writing, reviewers and readers did not need an authorial explanation to recognize the psychological dimensions of the story. Many began with the premise that the novel amounted to a psychological study. "Negro Writes Brilliant Novel, Remarkable Both as Thriller and Psychological Record," announced the *Chicago Tribune.*[41] In the pages of the *Modern Quarterly,* Melvin B. Tolson stated matter-of-factly that Wright's approach in *Native Son* was that of a "psycho-analyst" attempting "get at the roots of motivated personality."[42] Reader Jacque Frederick of Los Angeles was impressed with how Wright conveyed the "deep, emotional indignations we would all like to be able to express so comprehensively." The basis of Wright's success had to do with his facility with "psychological reactions and analysis," Frederick added.[43] Roy Wilkins, then assistant secretary of the NAACP, said that Wright had "set down with great skill and insight the inner feelings of the vast majority of Negroes."[44]

Wright's novel departed from his previous work and evinced a determination to deliver information about the psychology of race hierarchy. Reflecting on the reception of the stories collected in *Uncle Tom's Children,* Wright famously wrote that he made a "naïve mistake," for he had authored a "book which even bankers' daughters could read and weep and feel good about." Future work, he resolved, "would be so hard and deep" that readers "would have to face it without the consolation of tears." The claim presents a gendered picture of the sentimental reader, and the reference to the world of banking surely evokes the anticapitalist thinking so much a part of the world of proletarian storytelling to which Wright belonged. Beyond these implications, however, his account of *Native Son's* genesis invites another, more generic interpretation. Wright indicated a pervasive feeling that he had not yet written fiction he considered a counterpoint to social and economic configurations prevalent in American life. The stories in *Uncle Tom's Children,* powerful though they were, had not diverged from conventional means of addressing racial antagonisms. He imagined work that decisively veered from familiar paths in interpreting race hierarchy. After *Uncle Tom's Children,* he wanted not only to refute racism and racist ideologies but also to depart unambiguously from established ways of understanding them.

Wright's statement suggested that after *Uncle Tom's Children,* working actively against conventional reading and writing practices related to race hierarchy became a distinct priority. He envisioned his work proceeding along an alternative route, or through what Edward Embree called a "strategy of rupture." "Richard Wright wanted to write not a book but a bomb," wrote Embree in a 1944 profile.[45] In the context of a strategy of rupture, Wright's reluctance to facilitate "the consolation of tears" takes on further meanings. Forms of writing that provided consolation constituted conciliatory acts that failed as catalysts for social transformation. Wright considered consolation an ineffectual end point that obstructed new thinking about race hierarchy. In *Native Son,* by contrast, Wright attempted psychological exploration of racist social environments as a means of stimulating further antiracist critical inquiry. When Boris A. Max, Bigger Thomas's lawyer, delivers the closing argument that he hopes will spare his client the death penalty, psychological discourse assumes the dual status of interpretive resource and technique of contestation.

Max's speech, long regarded as a literary error on Wright's part, produces a flattened, sociological explanation for Bigger's actions—perhaps even one to which Wright did not give his full assent.[46] Yet reading Max's speech against the grain of its explanatory zeal, one finds an appeal to unconscious governing systems and practices of race hierarchy that lend the novel's conclusion greater intellectual intricacy. In the final part of his work, Wright turns directly to the psychological meanings beneath rituals of "race." The unswerving and punishing speech calls up terms and analytic directions that reveal less about Max's social judgments and more about the psychological and therapeutic concerns that animated Wright's thinking. The final part of the book registers both the environmentalism of social psychological thought and psychoanalytic interpretations of the unconscious that had become part of Wright's overall intellectual lexicon.

Max's speech is replete with psychological terminology and turns on Bigger's "mental and emotional life." We learn in short order that Bigger's "psychological distance" from the society he lives in will provide Max with his main conceptual starting point. Bigger's life experiences afford a symbol for "our whole sick social organism" and therefore make possible an analysis of the socially produced and simultaneously "unconscious machinery of race relations."[47] Yet exploring both the psychological conditions engendered by Bigger's environment and the unconscious structures of the racist social order does not amount in Wright's narrative to an unqualified endorsement of psychological explanation. A "psychiatric attaché" for the police department publicly links Bigger's denial of the charge of rape to the likelihood of other, unknown crimes. Similarly, professional psychologists emphasize the purported "fascination" of white women for black men in ways that inflame the tensions surrounding Bigger's trial. Thus, the claims of psychological experts are in no way beyond criticism. As Wright draws the novel to a close, it is clear that the value of psychological inquiry derives from the alternative it can provide to the calls for mob violence directed at Bigger from the streets and within the courthouse. The psychological exploration of racist social environments becomes important as a critical disposition, without making psychological explanation an unqualified good. That disposition is invoked in different ways throughout the novel but acquires the status of cultural criticism in Max's presentation before the court.

The process of understanding Bigger Thomas's life, Max submits, inevitably leads toward a cultural reckoning that can be likened to the "thawing out of icebound impulses." Max moves beyond Bigger as an individual and looks more broadly at the totality of sociopolitical and cultural life and the impact of racialism and racist patterns upon them, as when he argues that reflecting on Bigger's life brings about an "unveiling of the unconscious ritual of death in which we, like sleep-walkers, have participated so dreamlike and thoughtlessly."[48] Wright narrates Bigger's responses to the circumscribed conditions of African American life through themes of guilt, resentment, and estrangement from the world around him. A "people who have lived under queer conditions of life," Max later states, attempt to realize "personalities and to make those personalities secure," for these goals are synonymous with conceptions of the nation as such. Yet the rejection of attempts by African Americans to carve out a satisfying space for themselves in the nation generates a dynamic of fear and hate, feelings "we have inspired in him," indeed "woven by our civilization into the very structure of his consciousness," as Max puts it. Registering both the physiological and psychological impact of these social and ideological constraints on the "hourly functioning of his personality," Max claims that "every movement of [Bigger's] body is an unconscious protest."[49] Max's words bring to the fore what Wright once called "that psychological area of tension and depression consequent upon social exclusion."[50] The story Max unfolds involves the signifiers "black" and "poor" and "what we have made those things mean in this country."[51] As in Wright's cultural criticism, Max's speech connects acts of naming to the physical, psychological, and social reproduction of racist social structures. The scrutiny of racial designations emerges in the novel as part of the overall investigation of the "unconscious machinery of race relations."

The Fascist Scene and the Rise of Antifascist Common Sense

Native Son introduced readers to Bigger Thomas through a narrative of dispossession, fear, murder, and imprisonment. A saga beginning in the tenements of Chicago's South Side brings Bigger, a twenty-year-old African American, into a world of communists, luxurious homes, and a mob fueled by race hate. Yet *Native Son* first and foremost connects Bigger's mental conditions to segregation and isolation. The death of the white Mary Dalton and Bigger's murder of the black Bessie Mears afford the novel's treatment of something no less concrete: the "unconscious machinery of race relations" in American life.[52] The effects of racial ideologies become so deeply patterned as to take on the power of an unconscious force impinging on all of Wright's characters. *Native Son* presents Bigger's trajectory as one of degradation and debasement within a narrative in which the main character does not receive, or provide readers with, much respite from a pervasive sense of dislocation and terror.[53]

The antifascist politics nurtured by the Popular Front informed Wright's thinking, furthering his conceptualization of Bigger Thomas as "an American product, a native son of this land, [carrying] in him the potentialities of either Communism or Fascism."[54] According to philosopher Harry Slochower, *Native Son* unmistakably brought to life a story that shed light on the social conditions of protofascist societies. Slochower's *No Voice Is Wholly Lost* (1945) belonged to a body of writing from the 1930s and 1940s drawing on both psychoanalytic and Marxist thought for the study of fascism. In "Clash and Congruence between Marx and Freud" and other essays, Slochower treated fascism as a phenomenon that precluded exclusive applications of Marxist or Freudian analysis. Accounts of fascism describing social determinants alone too often failed to touch its "psychic aberrations," which, according to Slochower, led "a more or less autonomous existence." At the same time, Marxist frameworks correctly located the "fascist myth in a material context which conditions and limits its form." An advocate of more "cross-translations" between Marxist and Freudian thought, Slochower understood the politics and culture of fascism as the central problem of modern industrial societies.[55]

In the pages of the *Negro Quarterly,* the short-lived journal started by Ralph Ellison and Angelo Herndon, Slochower held that *Native Son* acquired proper resonance when seen in the light of the "fascist scene." In his reading, Bigger emerges as a specific kind of victim of fascism, the "product of racial demarcations," even as he accepts his state of alienation as an unchanging condition and converts his own state of exclusion into a brutal sense of status. A counterpoint to pastoral representations of African American life, Bigger is made up of powerful impulses: "*suppressed* fear, anger, and hate, *suppressed* impatience and tension." Slochower sees Wright's story as a search for freedom within a fascist scene that designs forms of "warped participation" within the social order for racialized minorities. For Slochower, Bigger's murderous acts play a creative, if perverse, part within a larger social world shot through with fascist tendencies. Indeed, the novel pictures Bigger coming to "regard himself as a part of the world he lives in, a sharer in its mode of behavior."[56] Wright portrayed dispossessed blacks as possible agents of fascism amid hopeless social conditions even as he described domestic racism and terror—in lynching, segregation, and long-standing forms of exclusion—as emblems of a fascist order.[57] In Slochower's view, Wright had delivered an evocative exploration of the American scene as a variant of the fascist scene through a novel about the combustive power of vitriolic racist ideologies and social marginalization.

The emergence of Popular Front antifascism, precipitated by changes in Communist Party policy, united left and liberal organizations in a social-democratic movement centrally based in opposition to fascism. Popular Front antifascism brought psychoanalytic thinkers and artists, writers, and intellectuals together in a shared political moment in late 1930s and early 1940s. In 1941, when the Popular Front merged with war mobilization, broadly shared and commonly invoked antifascism became a recognizable feature of American life.[58] Popular Front antifascism would play no small role in setting the stage for alternative forms of writing on racial ideology. The movement brought political vigor and urgency to social scientists intent on challenging Nazi race theories and varieties of scientific racism more generally. Many of the intellectuals who actively turned to psychological inquiry to reinterpret racial ideologies were influenced by the changes within intellectual life set in motion by the Popular Front, the strength and scope of which had particularly lasting effects on research in the social sciences.

The intellectual content of antifascist politics followed largely from psychological and psychoanalytic work. The difficulty of understanding the origins and manifestations of fascism through traditional categories of political analysis supplied the central premise for Franz Alexander's *Our Age of Unreason: A Study of Irrational Forces in Social Life* (1942). According to Alexander, the psychological sciences had discovered that "in all human behavior intellect plays a role subordinate to that of the blind and irrational emotions." The moment of fascism and war indicated that in the "course of human development new questions arise determined by the specific cultural problems of any given period." Just as antiracist writers endeavored to remake antiracism through new questions, so too did psychoanalysts see a range of analytic challenges thrown up by the modern world. More generally, a shared sense that traditional questions about social life offered limited intellectual guidance united many psychoanalysts and antiracist writers.

If psychological research expanded the intellectual investigation of antifascism, the platform provided by antifascist politics facilitated questions about the psychological dimensions of fascism and racism. Intellectuals, such as the anthropologist M. F. Ashley Montague, recognized that antifascism had quickened the work of eradicating scientific racism. The "monstrous unfolding of the Nazi racist policy" and the "mounting racial tensions in this country" meant that the "very real seriousness of the problem at last broke in on many scientists." Montague voiced a common view when he held that the eradication of racist doctrines had to be supplemented by work on the problem of "race prejudice." For a large cross-section of sociologists and psychologists, the work of researching the complex dynamics of race prejudice had to proceed on "an ever widening front." Antifascism accelerated the end of scientific racism in the social sciences, drawing attention to lacunae in current understandings of racism and racial ideology. The intellectual response to fascism led to the consolidation of race prejudice as a social scientific subject, and in turn fortified the view that social and economic explanation did not by themselves always supply satisfying accounts of the complexity of race prejudice. Moreover, according to Montague, policies of racial betterment designed to transform racist social environments remained insufficient "for the simple reason that race prejudice stems from sources these remedies, for the most part, fail to reach . . . These sources are the internalized basic structures which determine the social functioning of the personality."[59]

The interdependence of antifascist politics and psychological inquiry informed both Wright's literary explorations and the questions he brought to his rethinking of antiracism. In conceiving *Native Son,* Wright wrote, "I made the discovery that Bigger Thomas was not black all the time; he was white, too, and there were literally millions of him, everywhere . . . As a writer, I was fascinated by the similarity of the emotional tensions of Bigger in America and Bigger in Nazi Germany and Bigger in old Russia [because all] Bigger Thomases, white and black, felt tense, afraid, nervous, hysterical, and restless."[60] Casting Bigger Thomas merely as a stand-in for African American life did not appeal to Wright, who instead regarded his literary creation as a "type" that could provide a "springboard for the examination of milder types" across geographical and national lines.[61] He envisioned his literary work furthering the investigation of a range of fascist conditions and tendencies that arose amid patterns of social dispossession and exclusion. In was in this context that Wright described *Native Son* as a narrative about the "psychological reaction of the Negroes to the law and the relation of that contact to the wider contents of American life." To write about African American life in such a way called for willingness to treat subject matter not typically seen as within the purview of "Negro writing." It meant considering the specificity of African American situations while also thinking comparatively across different social and national contexts. A writer prepared to undertake such work, Wright said, "has to be his own research worker, his own psychologist, he has to do the whole job himself."[62]

Not all critics were inclined to see *Native Son* in terms of antiracism or antifascism. In the pages of the *Atlantic Monthly,* David L. Cohn rejected what he called Wright's objectionable call for "not only complete political rights for his people, but also social equality."[63] For Cohn and likeminded observers, Wright's work was strident, politically dangerous, and based in hatred of whites. When Wright responded to Cohn's charges in a subsequent edition of the magazine, he refused to reduce the novel to political formulations. In words echoing the formulations in "Blueprint for Negro Writing," he explained his literary construction of Bigger Thomas as the "process of objectifying emotional experience in words," a process that demanded that he use "his feelings in an immediate and absolute sense." To Cohn's assertion that Wright failed to "understand that oppression has harmed whites," Wright countered by returning to the novel. He wrote, "Did I not make the mob as hysterical as Bigger Thomas? Did I not ascribe the hysteria to the same origins? The entire long scene in the furnace room is but a depiction of how warped the whites have become through their oppression of Negroes."[64] Wright's response emphasized his desire to bring the psychology of racial antagonisms into American literature in more thoroughgoing ways and communicated his understanding of the effects of race hierarchy as multiple hazards that worked across the entire social order.

Wright's response communicated his immersion in modern psychological thought, as when he described the responsibility of writers to represent the "effects of our civilization upon the personality."[65] His *Atlantic Monthly* piece was culled from a much longer draft that pivoted, like much of his work, on problems of personality formation amid racist social structures. In his review, Cohn claimed that *Native Son* was a "blinding and corrosive study in hate," but in the draft Wright argued that the novel was not a study with a "thesis." Instead, "it is my communication, in words, of an emotional experience of Negro-American life . . . Its aim is to illuminate the psychological core of Negro life in this country." To this end, Wright regarded Max's speech as an "effort to overcome hate"—not engender it—through "meaning and explanation."[66] The writer Lillian Smith also described Wright's work in ways that contradicted Cohn's characterization. Wright "creates not dehumanized figures that never existed but men and women involved in a struggle larger than their own small lives," she wrote. Far from a study in hate, Wright's work created a forum in which the "concept of human freedom grows complex and ambiguous."[67]

A concerted focus on the pathologies of fascism allowed Wright to venture a rethinking of American race problems and attempt "new ideological excursions." Wright thought of these excursions and "heretofore unimagined tangents of thought" in largely sociopsychological and cultural terms. He envisioned an expanded analytic terrain that included the study of "personality formations" emerging "when millions of people are forced to live lives of outward submissiveness." For Wright, among the most urgent questions about the racist social order were ones that delivered as-yet-unavailable psychological insights. "What are the personality mechanisms that sublimate racial resentments?" he asked.[68] Moreover, how did the repression carried by exploited minorities affect everyday cultural life? Such questions had recently entered Wright's *Black Boy,* and he put them forth as problems of theoretical and political urgency for readers and writers alike.

To pursue "new ideological excursions" and press a kind of existential psychoanalysis into antifascist service, Wright increasingly targeted the nemesis of "race." Indeed, Wright asked readers to revise their reading practices in order to see race as an opponent in *Native Son.*[69] Writing a novel against race hierarchy and the corruptions underwritten by invidious deployments of race allowed Wright to work in concert with antifascist political sentiments and simultaneously to make the antagonistic relation to racial ideology in antifascism amenable to critical redeployment in U.S. literary culture.

Defying the Negro Problem:
12 Million Black Voices and *Black Metropolis*

If with *Native Son* Wright wished to depart from earlier modes of African American literary production, with *12 Million Black Voices: A Folk History of the Negro in the United States* (1941), the photodocumentary for which he supplied the narrative text, he explicitly pursued a corresponding task: the active discrediting of conventional constructions of the "Negro Problem."[70] The social scientific veneer of the Negro Problem discourse hid its nineteenth-century origins and connection to notions of black inferiority.[71] Wright had long expressed ambivalence about the vast energies that had been deployed within the intergroup relations movement and the many committees gathered to assess racial antagonisms under that banner. Most efforts to reckon with matters of racialized discord had paradoxically helped to strengthen "fierce resistance" in both whites and African Americans to understanding the "Negro question . . . in all of its hideous fullness," he wrote.[72] *12 Million Black Voices* demonstrated his distance from standardized accounts of racial conflict.

Not only the proverbial Negro Problem but the category Negro required scrutiny, according to Wright. If segregation and discrimination defined the parameters of everyday life for most African Americans, forms of cultural exclusion sealed the status of African Americans in part through categories of racial difference. The term *Negro,* he wrote, "by which, orally or in print, we black folk in the United States are usually designated, is not really a name at all nor a description, but a psychological island whose objective form is the most unanimous fiat in all American history; a fiat buttressed by popular and national tradition, and written down in many state and city statutes; a fiat which artificially and arbitrarily defines, regulates, and limits in scope of meaning the vital contours of our lives, and the lives of our children and our children's children."[73] Wright effectively argued that the discursive power that attached to the Negro category, and by extension to the Negro Problem, naturalized racial divisions. Any attempt to work comprehensively toward the transformation and overcoming of race hierarchy had to address the scheme of categories and designations by which racial difference emerged as the common sense of social and cultural life.

12 Million Black Voices presented a counterpoint to parochial constructions of the Negro Problem by bringing the psychological harms engendered within racist social environments to the center of his narrative. Wright's notes for the book confirm his vision of the project as a conduit for more work on the psychological effects of racial ideologies and racist structures within antiracist criticism. He understood his writing in *12 Million Black Voices* as a set of descriptions of common patterns of migration and social organization among African Americans and the common psychological characteristics and reactions that often followed from them. Wright endeavored to create a coherent account of African Americans as a "form of modern refugee . . . fleeing the terrors of the plantation and seeking desperately to gain a footing in our highly complex and impersonal cities." The story of the "migrant Negro" was both old and new. It was a tale repeated throughout history in the countless instances in which the "desperate fold of the farms are forced to seek refuge in the noisy cities."[74]

In other ways, however, the situation of African American migrants represented a break with the larger history of migrations, and it was in marking the specificities of African American migration to the urban North that Wright made his boldest claims for moving beyond the Negro Problem framework. He stressed that "whereas with other peoples the process of urban adjustment is long and drawn out, with the Negro it is concise, compact, volatile, brutal and compressed within a historical space of time." The exclusion of African Americans from the "American Way of Life" was another difference from other migrant trajectories and led to the emergence of the "so-called Black Belt areas of our Northern industrial cities like Chicago, Detroit, Pittsburgh, and St. Louis," concentrations of African American migrants that Wright called "the black, undissolved lumps and cods in the quickening, life-giving fluid we call democracy."[75]

To characterize the world of African American migrants, Wright pointed to both the resilience and "blasted" personalities bequeathed by the history of slavery and its aftermath. The story of migration to the North involved "complex sensations," encompassing "more strangeness than going to another country," even "living on a new and terrifying plane of consciousness." If the central contradiction of African American migration was displacement within yet another system of exclusion and discrimination, Wright chose to narrate that displacement as a politico-psychological crisis featuring, among other emblems of containment and deprivation, decaying urban "kitchenettes." "The kitchenette injects pressure and tension into our individual personalities," Wright wrote, adding that the "unbearable closeness of association" often led to "quarrels of recrimination, accusation, and vindictiveness, producing warped personalities."[76] The sometimes dark picture that emerged from Wright's words intimated patterns of psychological tension within the racialized urban environments of modern American life that Wright was determined to bring into American writing.

The relation of *12 Million Black Voices* to social science intrigued several reviewers, who regarded Wright as having taken on the "task of a specialist in the social sciences" while infusing the project with fervent and effective writing. The "objective mood" of the book meant that it was full of "facts that are invaluable to the student, sociologist or psychologist."[77] H. C. Nixon reported that *12 Million Black Voices* "comes close to etching the mind of the Negro for the white man."[78] Beyond the link between Wright's work and social science, reviewers reflected on the powerful effects of the book's descriptions of the psychological pressures of southern oppression and northern racism alike. "This is one of the most emotional books it has ever been our experience to read, but it is naked emotion rigidly controlled and never veering from its purpose," wrote Cara Green Russell in North Carolina's *Charlotte Observer.* For many, *12 Million Black Voices* was a "new kind of book."[79] Wright's words and Edwin Rosskam's photo-direction were seen as a unique and cogent merger that vividly presented stories of antiblack racism and the material deprivation encountered by African American migrants. This "black 'J'Accuse' " stood as a powerful counterpoint to commonly held beliefs in the intractability of racial problems.[80] In the *New York Times,* readers were told that "Wright speaks as a rebel," delivering a "stinging indictment of American attitudes toward the Negro."[81] For another reviewer, Wright's prose was the "impassioned, intimate language of an abolitionist" that would "place another powerful weapon in the hands [of those] who are striving to obtain the defeat of Hitlerism everywhere."[82]

Letters describing *12 Million Black Voices* as a storehouse of psychological insight poured in from readers. One African American woman called the book the "most profound piece of Negro psychology it has ever been my good fortune to read."[83] Although Wright rejected any notion of a singular and static "Negro psychology," this reader's response captured the widely shared sense that Wright had succeeded in attaching historical and analytical significance to the psychological repercussions of migration, racism, and segregation. Another reader wrote, "I cannot recall any book which has moved me as deeply or which has aroused such a feeling of anger within me as has this one." "Portions of your book, Mr. Wright," the reader continued, "made me so god damned mad, especially those sections dealing with life on the Southern plantations and the even more degrading existence of the black folk in the cities."[84]

If Wright's major books revealed the increasingly important place of psychoanalytic concepts and psychological inquiry in his thinking, the introduction he supplied for St. Clair Drake and Horace R. Cayton's *Black Metropolis: A Study of Negro Life in a Northern City* (1945) arguably offered the most informative picture of the antiracism he advocated. Wright returned to the subject of fascism and the "unconscious machinery of race relations" in American life he had invoked in *Native*

Son. Although he regarded the "dominant hallmark" of the book to be its "combination of sociology and anthropology," Wright considered the study a work motivated by key psychological questions. The book's ability to deploy sociological concepts, such as industrialization and urbanization, rendered it a "scientific report," but its descriptions differed from those of most other social scientific studies because of its singular focus on the "state of unrest, longing, and hope among urban Negroes." Having become a writer who refrained from providing ameliorative narratives about American life, Wright found Drake and Cayton praiseworthy as social analysts who similarly refused to "soothe or quiet" readers. The authors had explored black Chicago through a number of lenses—"psychological, political, racial, moral, spiritual and economic"—that Wright also understood as critical dimensions of his own literary and intellectual work.[85]

Drake and Cayton held that World War II had set in relief "contradictions in our culture," transforming the status of African Americans into a global question "almost overnight" (xxv). More and more, racial antagonisms and the wartime context precipitated "subjective" changes in the "attitude of the Negro himself." One could discern a "new mentality" that involved the displacement of a "purely racial point of view" in favor of an emboldened identification with the world's oppressed populations. Drake and Cayton warned readers about the possibility of an "emerging American Fascism" that would latch onto black Americans as "a symbol around which the frustrations of a frustrated society can be organized" in the context of potential postwar unemployment.[86] Wright would develop a divergent view that looked upon alienated and dispossessed African Americans as possible recruits for a homegrown fascist movement. Nevertheless, fascism served as the shared problematic. Indeed, he cast the study of "Bronzeville" as part of the larger discussion about the fascist tendencies of modernity. He cautioned readers not to "hold a light attitude toward the slums of Chicago's South Side" as they prepared to read Drake and Cayton's study. "Remember that Hitler," Wright continued, "came out of such a slum" and that "Chicago could be the Vienna of American Fascism" (xx). For capitalists, Hitler revealed the "shaky, class foundations of their society" pointing up their "hypocrisy" and heightening racisms of their society "to a degree that they had never dared" (xxiv). Indeed, for Wright, the larger frustrations that Hitler exploited in Germany were not dissimilar to those that characterized much of African American life. In the U.S. context, African Americans shared "all of the glorious hopes of the West, all of its anxieties, all of its corruptions, its psychological maladies," as well as the disposition "toward surrendering all hope of seeking solutions within the frame of a 'free enterprise' society" (xxv–xxvi). Wright took the introduction as an opportunity to link the analysis of fascist social tendencies and racism and thus to "show that there is a problem facing us, a bigger one than that of the Negro, a problem of which the Negro problem is a small but a highly symbolically important part" (xxi). In forgetting the "millions of exploited workers and dissatisfied minorities," Americans courted fascism on their own soil (xxiii).

Building on antifascist politics, and supported by other antiracist thinkers eager to generate fresh interpretations of race hierarchy, Wright adumbrated an antiracism in his *Black Metropolis* introduction that made psychological concerns central and implicitly cast the longstanding Negro Problem paradigm as a less relevant, even anachronistic, mode of inquiry. The case of many African Americans, Wright held, demonstrated how processes of social rejection put in jeopardy the ability of individuals to develop a "social self" (xxxii). By evoking William James's notion of the "social self," Wright claimed that patterns of racial exclusion in American life threatened to solidify a "kind of rage and impotent despair" endemic in fascist cultures (xxxii). In an argument that yoked the social self concept to the everyday workings of the racist social order, Wright began by conceding that there "can be, of course, no such thing as a complete rejection of anybody from society; for, even in rejecting him, society must notice him." Yet, any viable antiracism had to concede that "the American Negro has come as near being the victim of a complete rejection as our society has been able to work out, for the dehumanized image of the Negro which white Americans carry in their heads, the anti-Negro epithets continuously on their lips, exclude the contemporary Negro as truly as though he were kept in a steel prison, and doom even those Negroes who are as yet unborn" (xxxii–xxxiii).

If he sometimes presented arguments that differed from those of Drake and Cayton, Wright nevertheless appreciated that the authors of *Black Metropolis* simultaneously internationalized race problems and enacted a search for alternative vocabularies for interpreting the material *and* symbolic work performed by racial ideologies. Wright thus understood *Black Metropolis* as a counterpoint to most thinking about racial divisions, especially social scientific literature that "diluted the proverbial Negro problem, toned it down," offering the public something far from the "totality of its meaning" (xxviii). Moreover, composing the introduction to *Black Metropolis* gave Wright the opportunity to expand upon an idea central to his thinking in the early 1940s: that of the historical and symbolic resonance of African Americans in the West. African American life had in many ways become the repository of hopes and frustrations throughout the West, suggesting to Wright that African American life offered ways into the complexities that marked the West generally. This idea would only grow in significance in Wright's work, and it acquired special resonance when he relocated to Paris in the late 1940s. For Wright, analyzing urban African American life meant reckoning with an "anatomy of Negro frustration" and demonstrating the relationship of that anatomy to larger patterns of human thought and behavior (xxvi). The power of such work would hinge on showing "how *any* human beings can become mangled, how *any* personalities can become distorted when men are caught in the psychological trap of being emotionally committed to living a life of freedom that is denied them" (xxvi). Wright posited that "today the problem of the world's dispossessed exists with great urgency, and the problem of the Negro in America is a phase of this general problem, containing and telescoping the longings in the lives of a billion colored subject colonial people into a symbol" (xxv).

Wright may have had *Black Boy* very much in mind as he composed the introduction. Although the Book-of-the-Month Club helped Wright gain a wide readership, his involvement with the club came with certain costs.[87] Prompted by a mix of guidance and pressure from club editors in the form of subtly articulated objections, Wright made some changes to his original versions of *Native Son* and *Black Boy*. After the changes, the books were more palatable to white readers. In the case of *Black Boy,* the last third of Wright's manuscript, originally titled "American Hunger," was excised. With the entire section devoted to Wright's experiences in Chicago removed, the book ended with Wright's departure from the South. Pressure to alter the ending, which Wright submitted to only in part, resulted in a finale that invited readers to picture Wright escaping the southern racial order for a hopeful northern landscape— a simpler resolution than his original manuscript had provided.

Even though Wright removed the Chicago sections of *Black Boy,* the *Black Metropolis* introduction provided a pointed and incriminating statement on the breadth of northern racism. Wright reported that Chicago migrants were "driven and pursued, in the manner of characters in a Greek play, down the paths of defeat." He described migrants living in Chicago with the "extremes of possibility, death and hope," within an "environment that battered and taunted" (xvii). Commentators made frequent mention of Wright in discussions of *Black Metropolis.* NAACP director Walter White considered the introduction "one of the most thoughtful analyses of the malady of race prejudice." Wright was especially adept at showing "the extent to which the so-called Negro problem has shifted from the agricultural South to Northern industrial centers since World War I."[88] Thomas Sancton, in the *New Republic,* reprinted a lengthy quote from the introduction, calling it the "the best single essay in [the] field of race relations."[89]

The most prominent critique of Wright's introduction came from the historian Herbert Aptheker, who considered *Black Metropolis* as a whole a capitulation to moral argumentation and a regrettable restatement of Gunnar Myrdal's formulations in *An American Dilemma.* Aptheker felt that Myrdal had presented an unmistakably moralistic argument—that white Americans were conflicted about the disparity between professed egalitarian ideals and the facts of the racist social order. For Aptheker, the moral charge of Myrdal's study, which allowed for psychological harms engendered by racism, constituted the work's greatest flaw. Aptheker's antipathy toward Wright's introduction followed from his conviction that the masses, black or white, were not finally affected by oppression.[90] "The basic integrity of the masses will be untouched," Aptheker once wrote.[91] If such a critical sensibility had ever attracted Wright, its allure had faded by the time he wrote his *Black Metropolis* introduction. Where Aptheker criticized *Black Metropolis* for sharing the inclination toward moral argument that he associated with *An American Dilemma,* Wright claimed that the two works were linked in a different way. Both works provided avenues for considering the impact of race hierarchy on the "Negro's conduct, his personality, his culture, his entire life" (xxv). Wright expressed little patience for social analyses and organizations that "injected foggy moral and sentimental notions into" understandings of race problems (xxviii). For Wright, moral concerns did not in themselves nullify valid social and psychological analysis, and to the extent that moral questioning yielded new insights involving racial antagonisms, they offered important intellectual challenges.

According to Wright, Myrdal's *An American Dilemma* had added to an investigative terrain he and others had already begun to create. Myrdal's notion of dissonance in American consciousness held the potential of expanding the reach of antiracism, especially insofar as it challenged the conventional "Negro Problem" framework. Although the Negro Problem designation remained a feature of public discourse into the late 1940s and beyond, the notion of an "American dilemma" helped articulate an expanding awareness of race problems as coextensive with the social life and politics of the nation. The central ideas in *An American Dilemma* quickly entered the popular lexicon, prompting even mainstream magazines like *Life* to proclaim: "The dilemma, of course, is this: the basic tenets of the American creed make all men free and equal in rights. Yet in fact we deny equal rights to our largest minority, and observe a caste system which we not only criticize in other nations but refuse to defend in ourselves. This makes us living liars—a psychotic case among the nations."[92] The insistence on a divided national consciousness in Myrdal's study represented a powerful and valuable construction. Like others, Wright subscribed to a view of *An American Dilemma* as one lever in the cultural politics of midcentury antiracism.

Wright understood *Black Boy* in similar terms. Intermittent yet strategic psychological terms introduced in the book recoded race hierarchy as mental malady and simultaneously strengthened midcentury links between psychological inquiry and antiracist cultural politics.

Psychological Truths in Political Terms: *Black Boy*

Wright published *Black Boy* in 1945, again with assistance from the Book-of-the-Month Club. The two parts of the autobiography—the story of his southern upbringing and the story of his experiences once he arrived in Chicago—were written in the 1940s. The Chicago portion remained unpublished for decades. Nevertheless, its midcentury provenance reveals Wright's intellectual concerns and provides ways of reading his prose throughout the book.

In *Black Boy*, Wright describes African Americans "transferring" hatred to other African Americans and explores problems of "adjustment"—a common term within midcentury social psychological thought—in a racist social order.[93] Wright's inability to "adjust to the white world" begins to destabilize the "structure of [his] personality" to the extent that "inner barriers to crime" begin to fall. The condition to which Wright temporarily succumbs involves accepting "the value of myself that my old environment had created in me" (258). Beyond his repeated and marked concern with personality formation, Wright employs the concept of self-hatred, a term derived from psychoanalytic research, in the second part of his autobiography. "Hated by whites and an organic part of the culture that hated him," African Americans experienced patterns of "self-hate," according to Wright, that led to a constant "war with reality" involving the attitudes of the majority and, above all, the emergence of volatile internal feelings and simultaneous efforts to shield them from public view (312–13). Although Wright at times adopts the position of the analyst in the narrative as he observes the behavior of blacks and whites around him, he directly implicates himself in the condition of self-hate he describes: "I loaded the empty part of the ship of my personality with fantasies of ambition to keep it from toppling over into senselessness." But over time, he comes to the realization "with the part of my mind that the whites had given to me—that none of my dreams was possible." Subsequent feelings of hate followed from the energy devoted to unworkable hopes, whereby the "circle would complete itself" (237).

If Wright used terms like *personality* and *attitude* to provide his readers with a kind of social scientific commentary on the narrative itself, *fear* and *anxiety*—the province of much psychoanalytic theorizing—occupied an even greater place in the book. Beginning with the insularity of his upbringing and the difficulties it wrought, the management of fear and anxiety within racialized environments defines the entire arc of Wright's narrative. The circulation of fear becomes the basic dynamic of racial conflict, especially during and after World War I, when clashes and tensions flared, and a "dread of whites [came] to live permanently in my feelings and imagination." The psychological burden of racial antagonisms means that nothing "challenged the totality of my personality so much as this pressure of hate and threat that stemmed from the invisible whites." The tensions, fears, and anxieties that mark the racial order transfer hostility into the domestic environments of Wright's upbringing. "I would stand for hours on the doorsteps of neighbors' houses listening to their talk, learning how a white woman had slapped a black woman, how a white man had killed a black man . . . [filling] me with awe, wonder, and fear" (85).

In *Black Boy,* Wright ascribes his ability to objectively analyze patterns of racial antagonism and the effects of racial ideology to his having directly encountered whites later than others did. "I had begun coping with the white world too late . . . I could not make subservience an automatic part of my behavior" (231). Wright's narrative delivers a behavioral account of his simultaneous sense of belonging and distance from the experience of other southern blacks. Later, he learns to "contain the tension I felt in my relation with whites," finding that a "measure of objectivity entered into my observations of white men and women." This explanation cements the narrative focus on behavior and psychological detection. As it unfolds, the narrative renders psychological observation the basis of antiracist reflection and activity.

Working at a hotel in Memphis, Wright recalls his fellow black workers, and his descriptions evoke scenes indebted to his broadly existentialist and psychoanalytic disposition. "I began to marvel at how smoothly the black boys acted out the roles that the white race had mapped out for them." In order to account for figures he views as not "conscious of living a special, separate, stunted way of life," Wright concludes "that in some period of their growing up—a period that they had no doubt forgotten—there had been developed in them a delicate, sensitive controlling mechanism that shut off their minds and emotions from all that the white race had said was taboo." The hotel workers "lived in an America where in theory there existed equality of opportunity," all the while knowing "unerringly what to aspire to and what not to aspire to" (232). Wright's explanation simultaneously imparts psychological dynamic and social indictment.

Soon after *Black Boy's* publication, such descriptions came under attack as relentlessly negative representations of African Americans. Some argued that African American aspirations for social change were conspicuously missing in the narrative. Yet such criticism left untouched Wright's interest in psychological theory. In sketching the psychological conditions of the personalities he encountered and in occasionally deploying clinical categories, as in "controlling mechanism," Wright sought to enlarge the picture of the effects of racial subjugation. Such a narrative practice held the possibility of opening up systems of racial logic and exclusion to more acute forms of analysis and commentary. For Wright, psychological explanation created valid and effective means of investigating racism and the power of racial logic in

everyday life, ways of approaching the "whole race problem." Wright's specific geo-
graphic coordinates notwithstanding, the environmentalism and existentialist psychoanalytic character of the narrative implicated U.S. national culture as a whole.

For Wright, the investigation of "white psychology" figured prominently in assessments of the "whole race problem." The environments presented in *Black Boy*
exact psychological costs—albeit different kinds and in different ways—that stretch
across the color line. At another workplace, Wright's inability to conform to the
forms of social exchange expected of blacks disrupts the patterns of the established
social order. In his desire to look them "straight in the face," Wright inspires fear in
whites. Indeed, many "Southern whites would rather have had Negroes who stole
work for them than Negroes who knew, however dimly, the worth of their own
humanity," Wright surmises. "Hence whites placed a premium on black deceit; they
encouraged irresponsibility; and their rewards were bestowed upon us blacks in the
degree that we could make them feel safe and superior" (236). The ideological
interdependence Wright finds among blacks and whites involves differential psychological needs that emerge from and buttress racist social arrangements.

Although segregation remains a feature of everyday life in Chicago as it had in the
South, the urban flux of the northern metropolis brings Wright into more contact
with whites, leading him to reflect on the ways whites are mired within, and afflicted
by, racial ideologies. In the second part of the autobiography, Wright records his
experiences in Chicago and resorts more readily to psychoanalytic terminology.
Sociological and psychological literatures that Wright encounters help him assess his
own "chronic anxiety" as he assimilates terms for "relating various forms of neurotic
behavior to environment." Wright feels licensed by the studies he reads to become an
analyst of the myriad "racial insecurities" he observes among blacks and whites alike.
Invoking a formulation that would recur in his work, Wright concludes that the
analysis of race problems must account for the "psychological distance that separated
the races" (327).

Through the notion of psychological distance Wright recodes race hierarchy and
racial ideologies in national terms, for the formulation authorizes his description of a
nation incapable of "examining its real relation to the Negro" (320). Psychological
distance, for Wright, does not connote cross-cultural misunderstanding. Examining
American life via the concept of psychological distance dramatizes a social crisis in
which the strictures of race hierarchy circumscribe and deform the lives of individuals and collectivities.[94] Thus the psychological distance between blacks and whites
to which Wright aims to bring narrative coherence does not conform to pluralist
paradigms. Moreover, because it is a defining feature of racist institutional structures,
the psychological distance of which Wright speaks cannot be bridged without great

upheaval. Thus, he argues that "if, within the confines of its present culture, the nation ever seeks to purge itself of its color hate, it will find itself at war with itself, convulsed by a spasm of emotional and moral confusion" (273). Rather than offer facile, ready-made answers to challenges of race hierarchy and the social pathologies of white supremacy, Wright's formulations render those challenges far more complex and intellectually demanding. *Black Boy* delivers stories and claims but, finally, many more questions about role of race hierarchy in American life than it can plausibly answer.

Within the autobiography, and through the use of terms such as *psychological distance,* Wright adumbrates lines of inquiry for an emergent antiracist criticism. Wright's own experience of psychological distance involves racial insecurities in his everyday interactions. He develops a "terse, cynical mode of speech that [rebuffs] those who sought to get too close to me." Such a "protective mechanism," Wright claims, offers a measure of security but also means that he is split from his "deepest feelings" and "withdrawn from the objective world" (328). The maladies he calls forth through terms such as *psychological distance* and *protective mechanism* give *Black Boy* both an analytical cast and a dynamic tension that supplies a somber picture of a world defined by racial hierarchy.[95]

Black Boy and the Critics

Black Boy prompted reviews from both prominent and small newspapers and journals. For many readers and reviewers, the forceful prose and political charge of the book did not capture the key thing about Wright's achievement: *Black Boy* constituted a political act undertaken via psychological investigation. The critic Isidor Schneider wrote of *Black Boy* as a powerful and important "document of the psychological patterns of race tension." For Schneider, Wright's focus on hostility and violence led to "explorations not attempted before." Wright's insights regarding the "neurotic behavior patterns and thought patterns produced by the race tensions in America" conferred prominence on his work. His "conscious interest in psychopathology" had served him well, allowing for "keen observations of the neurotic behavior patterns and thought patterns produced by the race tensions in America."[96] Edward A. Laycock of the *Boston Morning Globe* praised Wright's insights into "mental processes" and told his readers that *Black Boy* surpassed "many a psychological novel."[97] The historian Henry Steele Commager read the book as "an implicit call for social and economic change."[98] In *Commonweal,* George Seaton called *Black Boy* "another milestone on the road to emancipation."[99] In "This Too Is America," an appraisal of the book that appeared in *Common Sense,* one reviewer deemed *Black Boy* both a description and analysis of "psychological and external facts" about racial oppression.[100] In a series of letters, one psychotherapist, Mrs. Joseph Miller, congratulated Wright on the autobiography by referring to him as a "good psychologist" and calling the prose of his book "one of the rare experiences one encounters in a lifetime."[101]

Writing for the *Yale Review,* Raymond Kennedy noted that Wright continued in the tradition of sociologist John Dollard and anthropologist Hortense Powdermaker, scholars who had shattered the "Southern myth of Negro happiness" through ethnographic and psychoanalytic lenses.[102] Moreover, Wright had presented a story about "awful horror of insecurity, fear and frustration."[103] A student from the University of Chicago wrote to notify him that *Black Boy* had been assigned as part of his second-year social science curriculum. For all manner of readers, Wright had imparted analyses that justified the moniker "psychologist." Another reviewer noted how effectively Wright had presented the process of producing subservience in the Jim Crow setting, so much so that readers could begin to understand how racial practices became naturalized, even "automatic, a reflex action."[104]

The psychological content of *Black Boy* prompted one psychologist to send Wright an unsolicited manuscript that praised the "scientific objectivity" of his narrative. In "*Black Boy:* A Value Analysis," psychologist Richard K. White speculated on the psychoanalytic tenor of the book: "There is no psychoanalytic terminology in its pages, but from the nature and extent of its frankness one might almost suspect that the author had recently been through an analysis." *Black Boy* provided scenes and stories that had a "direct bearing upon the psychology" of African Americans, demonstrating the role of physical intimidation as the "most important single source of the Negro's accommodation to their caste position."[105] White's analysis demonstrated that many psychologists found Wright's work rich in its implications for the study of American and African American life and considered his subject matter directly relevant to questions and research agendas in the psychological sciences.

Horace Cayton admired Wright's ability to "express certain psychological truths in political terms" and considered violence—physical and psychological—the main subject of *Black Boy.*[106] In "Frightened Children and Frightened Parents," Cayton credited Wright with offering acute observations on the "brutalization of Negro personality." Much as psychological experts were called upon during World War II to identify and alleviate the conditions war imposed on soldiers, so too did Wright analyze patterns of racial hierarchy in terms of psychological impact. Cayton referred explicitly to *Black Boy*'s "psychoanalytic frame of reference," going so far as to claim that the "central theme of *Black Boy* can be summed up in the fear-hate-fear complex of Negroes." "Like the psychoanalyst who discovers fear and hatred in his Negro patient, Wright performs this painful surgery on himself."[107]

Ralph Ellison published his thoughts about *Black Boy* in "Richard Wright's Blues." The 1945 essay likened Wright's autobiography to the lyricism of the blues. Ellison held that the book revealed "to both Negroes and whites those problems of a psychological and emotional nature which arise between them when they strive for mutual understanding."[108] In direct response to critics of Wright's autobiography who regarded the book as an overly bleak picture of African American life, Ellison countered that although *Black Boy* "presents an almost unrelieved picture of a personality corrupted by brutal environment, it also presents those fresh, human responses brought to its world by the sensitive child." The particulars of individual development, Ellison believed, "link backward into the shadow of infancy where environment and consciousness are so darkly intertwined as to require the skill of a psychoanalyst to define their point of juncture."[109] Ellison thus endorsed the existential psychoanalytic disposition that marked Wright's book. One of the key conceptual insights that *Black Boy* prompted in him was the recognition that stories of individual development foretold aspects of later life. For Ellison, *Black Boy* brought this insight to the fore by merging an unsparing account of the effects of racist environments and racial ideologies with a concerted focus on childhood development.

Wright's status as a writer capable of imparting valid psychological insights to mass reading audiences became a feature of his public profile as psychological questions and terms increasingly found their way into his thinking and projects. The politics of antifascism informed his move to reevaluate available ways of accounting for race hierarchy. He saw the segregation and deprivation of African Americans as a possible springboard for the consolidation of fascist, antisocial sentiments. Understanding the dangers of race thinking and domestic forms of fascism required more explicit attention to the "unconscious machinery of race relations," the social and psychic patterns set in motion by the making and remaking of America's segregated sociality.

By the early 1940s, both established writers and students who would go on to become well-known authors believed that psychology and allied disciplines provided a basis for progressive politics. Betty Friedan, for instance, studied psychology while a student at Smith College and arrived at the conclusion that the field offered people the confidence and practical information needed to shape the world around them.[110] Moreover, the association of psychological research in these years with antifascism emboldened intellectuals to pursue psychology as a form of critical commentary alert to developments in political culture. For not a few writers, the political possibilities of psychological inquiry led to expanded consideration of psychotherapeutic practices. As the next chapter shows, Wright played a substantial part in giving intellectual credibility to an antiracism that enacted psychiatric knowledge and psychotherapeutic models. His investment in psychological inquiry led to relationships with psychiatric experts, who nurtured his understanding of psychotherapeutic services. More and more, Wright understood his intellectual work as the theoretical undoing of the "Negro Problem," a project he linked to practical endeavors, including efforts to bring psychiatric knowledge directly to bear on the lives of racialized minorities.

CHAPTER TWO

Richard Wright Reading
The Promise of Social Psychiatry

Psychiatrist Fredric Wertham's *Dark Legend: A Study in Murder* (1941), a clinical account of a matricide, had a powerful effect on Richard Wright. More than a case study, *Dark Legend* offered a primer on psychoanalytic inquiry. When "any organized forces in mental life come into diametrical opposition," Wertham wrote, "we speak of a conflict." In the event that such conflicts reside primarily below consciousness, "open manifestations" take the form of "strange eruptions in consciousness—impulses, fears, inhibitions and unstable compromises."[1] Wertham did not believe that psychiatry alone could resolve crises and social contradictions. Yet a "dynamic, not dogmatic" psychiatry could provide the "courage to draw conclusions" about intractable and difficult conflicts.[2] "Psychiatry is the art of listening," Wertham wrote in *Dark Legend,* and "real understanding must be based on knowledge of the person's inner life history."[3] After becoming familiar with Wright's work, Wertham concluded that Wright's capacity to recognize and record the effects of race hierarchy on modern subjectivities had much in common with the life histories involving psychological abnormality that defined his training and clinical background. Wright, for whom psychiatric expertise and psychotherapy became increasingly critical subjects, concurred.

Wright's strongly held conviction that psychological inquiry could engender more incisive and informative understandings of race hierarchy is nowhere more evident than in the connections he developed and sustained with psychotherapeutic thinkers. In his estimation, psychotherapists and writers who wove psychological theory into their work were especially well equipped to demonstrate the arbitrary nature of race thinking. Beginning in the early 1940s, Wright explored institutions that modeled alternative forms of socially conscious psychotherapy. By the middle of the decade, his reading practices and activities often coalesced symbiotically with his psychoanalytic concerns. This chapter explores Wright's readings and institutional affiliations in terms of the merger of psychotherapeutic knowledge and antiracism he attempted to enact.

In 1941 Wright wrote a letter in support of parole release for an African American man named Clinton Brewer, who had been convicted for killing a woman who had refused to marry him. Wright had learned about the skills in music composition Brewer had developed during his eighteen years in prison. He seemed to be rehabilitated, capable of living in society and supporting himself through his talents. But, to Wright's astonishment, Brewer committed murder again a few months after his release, in circumstances not altogether different from his first crime. At a loss to understand the shocking turn of events, Wright contacted Wertham.

Wright wanted to know what psychological abnormality had led to the second murder, for which Brewer faced the death penalty. Persuaded to provide expert testimony, Wertham cited pathological obsession as the defining feature of Brewer's mental condition, which helped to nullify the death penalty threat, giving Brewer a sentence of life imprisonment. Wright and Wertham began a long friendship defined by shared interests in literature, the figure of the criminal, juvenile delinquency, and, not least, the antiracist potential of psychological investigation generally and psychotherapeutic resources in particular.[4]

Bavarian-born, Wertham studied in London and Munich before coming to the United States. He had grown familiar with American race hierarchy while working in Baltimore at the Johns Hopkins Hospital. Unlike most of his peers in clinical psychiatry, he sometimes testified in court on behalf of African Americans when his psychological expertise proved relevant. Moving to New York, Wertham widened his knowledge U.S. race hierarchy and worked with black youth while serving as director of psychiatric services at Queens General Hospital in New York. "The exploitation of the Negro in the South is a very direct and brutal one," he commented. "In the North, it is very insidious—half-concealed—and in the long run really much more ruthless and deadly."[5] In the mid-1940s, when he began to conceive of a psychiatric clinic in Harlem, he conferred with Wright and asked for his support.

Yet even before the establishment of Harlem's Lafargue Clinic, Wright and Wertham were engaged in public dialogue. One of the most intriguing results of the friendship formed between the men was an article by Wertham titled "An Unconscious Determinant in *Native Son,*" based on a paper given at the 1944 meeting of the American Psychopathological Association. Wright had agreed to participate in an experiment in the association of ideas led by Wertham. While the session apparently led to a range of insights about the origins of *Native Son* and the psychology of its author, the paper itself concentrated on one finding. A "literary creation is not a translation but a transmutation of human experience," Wertham told the gathered psychotherapists.[6] Wertham linked the scene in which Bigger is discovered in Mary's room by the blind Mrs. Dalton to an experience in Wright's teenage years, when he worked for a white family before and after school. The Wall family employed Wright and treated him well, even offering something of a "second home where," according to biographer Michel Fabre, "he met with more understanding than from his own family."[7] Yet Wertham recovered a disquieting incident of "great emotional power" that he called a "determinant" in the novel. While carrying out routine duties in the Wall house, Wright received a severe reprimand when he apparently opened a door and encountered Mrs. Wall before she had dressed. Elaborating briefly on the meanings in Wright's associations, Wertham closed with the claim that he had discovered "proof in a specific instance" of the role played by the unconscious in literary creativity. Only "unconscious factors with a high emotional value are significant in literary creation."[8]

Not long afterward, in the *Journal of Clinical Psychopathology,* Wertham turned to *Black Boy,* calling the book "an essential foundation of knowledge for the psychiatrist who wants to understand the Negro child or adult." Contradicting the view that Wright's narrative did not typify African American life, Wertham argued that *Black Boy* told the story of a "social inheritance" involving "anxiety and insecurity in the family structure" in ways that were indeed true to the lives of many African Americans, African American children in particular. Wright's ability to attend to both the social inheritances bequeathed by history and the emotional structures exhibited by individuals made him, for Wertham, a perceptive observer of the modern world. For Wertham, the claim of atypicality rang false, as did the assumption that the autobiography only implicated African American life, for *Black Boy* provided insights into "American civilization" and "modern civilization in general." As a work relevant to "the experience of too many people all over the world," Wright's narrative offered ways of understanding aspects of modernity across many national settings.[9] *Black Boy* carried "revolutionary implications."[10]

Psychoanalysis and Culture

A large measure of the attraction of psychoanalytic thought and psychiatric expertise for antiracist writers had to do with their applicability in cultural analysis. Indeed, the impact of psychoanalytic investigation on midcentury social science and intellectual life had everything to do with the idea of culture. Many regarded the concept of culture as the analytic core of the psychoanalytic enterprise. What Freud meant by *culture,* one writer surmised, was nothing less than "the vast and intricate complex of psychological and institutional devices by which society is held together and man converted into a human being." Freud, in the estimation of many midcentury intellectuals, had identified the far-reaching character of the "superstructure of culture" more painstakingly than other theorists and provided ways of "interpreting its social function."[11] As the concept of culture became increasingly important to writers actively working to generate alternative and resonant forms of antiracism, the contributions of Freudian thought to cultural analysis figured more and more in writing about race and racism.

Social scientists also placed psychoanalysis squarely within the terrain of cultural analysis. According to sociologist Talcott Parsons, Freud provided the "entirely correct" argument that culture represented an "essential *component* of any system of human action." The individual and "his attachment to objects, especially other human beings, and most obviously his 'cultural' interests, his ideals and values"— these stood at the center of both social scientific and psychoanalytic inquiry. Social scientists and intellectuals turned to psychoanalytic investigation to reveal the "relations of the personality to social systems and culture." Looking back on twenty years of psychoanalysis in U.S. intellectual life, Parsons wrote that the "psychoanalytic procedure has immensely widened our observational knowledge of the subtle dynamics of human motivation, and psychoanalytic theory has given us what so far is our most sophisticated conceptual scheme for the analysis of personality as a system."[12]

Although there were no psychoanalytic institutes in the United States in 1930, psychoanalytic thought became a pervasive feature of American intellectual life over the next decade and a half. The arrival of émigré psychoanalysts from Europe between 1933 and 1941 would make psychoanalytic concepts and research a feature of American intellectual life. Émigré psychoanalyst Franz Alexander endorsed the study of cultural factors in personality development, arguing that the dynamic nature of any social order involved a "cultural structure" that allowed for an "immense range of individualities as represented by the different personalities of the parents in their relation to each other and to their children." Thus, arguments about the effects of culture provided the basis for the investigation of specific personalities. For Alexander, the persuasiveness of such a framework led to the transformation of the case study into a veritable cultural form. Amid these developments, psychoanalytic and psychiatric thinkers expanded their reach by turning to the entire personality in works aimed at academic and lay readerships. No human activity, however mundane, seemed beyond the understanding of the psychoanalytic or psychiatric expert. Psychoanalysis, in particular, by positing mental mechanisms held to be common to all, offered a theoretical reach that encompassed the everyday, including myriad maladjustments across different social environments.[13]

Psychoanalytic institutes initiated scholarly meetings on race prejudice and the relationships between minorities and majorities. At the Institute for Psychoanalysis in Chicago, Franz Alexander focused on the conflicted motivations of majorities, for whom participation in racist social structures offered material compensation even as it induced a sense of humiliation. Within the discussions of psychologists and psychoanalysts, race prejudice became widely understood as socially sanctioned and learned and, indeed, as a "ready-made and culturally normal outlet" for hostilities and fears throughout much of American social life.[14] Sociologist John Dollard's frustration-aggression theory posited at its most basic level that aggression followed from frustration and became the basis for analyzing a range of social phenomena, not least the fascist and racist social environments much on the minds of wartime researchers.[15] Daring psychoanalysts undertook inquiries into sexuality, encouraging many cultural critics, not least Wright, to recognize the field as a resource for alternative and dissident interpretations of the racialized social order.

Psychological and psychoanalytic conceptions of personality provided a way to bring attention to the "whole of one's behavior traits as expressed in social relations."[16] Thus, social scientists analyzing racist social environments relied on psychological conceptions of personality. In the late 1930s, the American Youth Commission published several studies to elevate awareness of the specific personality conditions of African American youth. Studies such as *Color, Class, and Personality* (1942) collected the views of social scientists, psychoanalytic thinkers, and literary artists alike and asked readers to consider the effects "upon the personality development of Negro youth of their minority racial status." Like other midcentury publications, the book put forth accounts of the harms and mystifications of race thinking—the "shadow of race"—by making personality and minority status analytically central concepts.[17] Within the social sciences and beyond, psychoanalytic concepts informed and furthered research that defined conflicts as intricately linked cultural structures and processes of personality formation.

Cultural Criticism as Modern Psychological Thought

Literary theorist, philosopher, and psychoanalytic thinker Kenneth Burke read *Native Son* not long before publishing *The Philosophy of Literary Form* (1941). Burke believed that Wright had supplied a "whole new avenue to follow" in assessing the "ambiguities of power."[18] Although Burke did not explore that avenue in *The Philosophy of Literary Form,* his later books discussed the theoretical implications of Wright's work. In *A Grammar of Motives* (1945), Burke reflects on *Native Son* to present a general theory of narratives in which two kinds of "epitomizing" are at work: "one imagistic and the other conceptual." If one kind of epitome, or narrative essence, emerged in Boris Max's closing argument and social philosophy, Burke finds in the opening scene of the novel—when Bigger Thomas kills a rat—another narrative essence, the imagistic core of the novel. From the outset, Burke argued, Wright indicates how "Bigger's rebirth will be attained through the killing of the 'rat' within himself."[19] The novel accommodates two narrative essences, and in the case of *Native Son,* Burke implies, they exist in tension.

To explain that tension, Burke draws attention to Wright in relation to Marxist criticism.[20] In *A Rhetoric of Motives* (1950), Burke continued to reflect on the conditions of possibility for *Native Son,* finding in the novel both an appeal to a generalized Marxist terminology and the representation of particularity in the form of "Bigger's criminal protest *as a Negro.*" Burke saw doctrine and concept vying for supremacy in Wright's work, making for a volatile narrative mix of "Marxist critic" and "Negro novelist." Wright's verbal maneuvers registered the predicament of the minority writer who wishes to "confront the world at once specifically and generically by placing his problem in a graded series that keeps transcendence of individual status from seeming like disloyalty to one's group status."[21] Later, Burke turned to *Black Boy* to develop an analysis of the absurd. In the South, Burke wrote, insofar as African Americans could show earning capacity equal to whites, the constant renewal of double standards in wages and jobs had to undergo constant rhetorical reinvention. *Black Boy* afforded a close examination of the intrinsic instability of forms of racial lore in a society organized by monetary norms, where doctrines of superiority and inferiority were subject to impairment. Indeed, for Burke, the book demonstrated "the sullenness and thoroughness with which this 'order' can be imposed," and in the process provided a way of broaching the larger subject of the absurd.[22]

Sociologist Louis Wirth, Wright's guide in the literatures of Chicago sociology during the 1930s, considered Burke a skillful social psychologist, whose work in the area of motives exceeded in sophistication much of what his profession had produced. Wirth endorsed Burke's innovative approaches to "cultural structures," which put forth a "larger frame of meaning" than most social scientists allowed.[23] Burke was especially effective in his consideration of motives, which in his interpretive framework "turn out to be complex subjective aspects of correspondingly complex situations that invariably reflect the culture."[24] From early on, Burke proposed psychological inquiry that departed from orthodox procedure, and his concern for social totality led him to conceive of motives in terms of capitalist formation. He wrote in *Attitudes Toward History* (1937) that while "savants were concerning themselves with child psychology, abnormal psychology, primitive psychology, and animal psychology, and out of them inventing one-man vocabularies of motivation to chart human complexities with the help of simplifying laboratory conditions, we were ignoring the most ingenious and suggestive vocabulary of all, the *capitalist* vocabulary of behavior."[25]

Burke located many possibilities in Marxism but complained that the "psychological problem" was something that the "Marxist vocabulary slighted."[26] Wright likewise did not always find Marxism capable of posing and exploring psychological questions in satisfying ways. Burke's theories encouraged Wright to consider an American social order in which "the 'meanings' of our symbols has become a problem for us."[27] As a literary artist, Wright considered motives in the broad context of human activity, the very scale Burke tended toward in his various investigations of the ways "all motives and all conflicts express themselves in language."[28]

When Wright did not turn to psychoanalytic cultural criticism, he often read writers who shared his appreciation for the intellectual challenges posed by modern psychological thought generally. He also gravitated toward writers who, like Burke, identified cultural conflicts in the workings of language. Such was the case with Philip Wylie's explosive *Generation of Vipers* (1942). Primarily remembered for its antifeminist arguments, especially the notorious caricatures of mothers that underwrote his descriptions of the perils of "Momism," *Generation of Vipers* resonated with many contemporary readers for whom it was an attempt to make sense of a rapidly changing wartime American culture. The forcefulness of the prose style and the relentless flouting of convention in *Generation of Vipers* made the book a bestseller. Wright never identified the arguments in the book he found most convincing, but he did consider the work a courageous endeavor and wrote Wylie to tell him so. Wylie's motivations for writing *Generation of Vipers* recall Wright's insistence on the democratic value of cultural criticism. "I believe we can neither fight at our best nor win lasting peace unless we employ that part of our liberty we call criticism even though, at times, its function is exhumation and autopsy," Wylie wrote in his preface.[29]

Familiar with Freudian theories, Wylie throughout his book criticized institutions that diminished the significance of the subjective reality of the human psyche. Wright shared Wylie's frustration with experts and policy makers who "are so busy promulgating the marvels they have uncovered in the single category with which they concern themselves that they never admit the possibility of another."[30] A sermonlike work on the moral condition of contemporary America, *Generation of Vipers* represented Wylie's response to what he perceived as shallow thinking about the war among Americans. Amid what he considered selfishness and lack of seriousness in a time of crisis, Wylie took it upon himself to diagnose the social types and cultural patterns that allowed for such a state of affairs.

Wylie's approach often involved undermining taken-for-granted categories and beliefs, as when he critiqued the phrase "common man," a standard feature of left-liberal political discourse. "People who should know better melt into a dither of sentimentality at the mere utterance of 'common man,'" wrote Wylie. He did not merely reject the common man as a category but denounced specific figurations of the common man that he considered especially objectionable. The common man, in Wylie's view, responded to the war with complacency and unhindered selfishness but also took form in previous historical periods. Wylie rejects the common man of the historical past who "keeps down his slaves, if he has any, by savage persecution; even as we keep down our half-slaves, the Negroes."[31] His willingness to mar a popular term in American political culture, connecting it not only to the history of slavery but also to contemporary forms of racial oppression, likely appealed to Wright, who decried the inadequacy of much commentary related to race hierarchy and racial antagonisms. Wright's picture of an American metropolis as a potential ground for fascism in his introduction to *Black Metropolis* resonates with Wylie's sense that the dangers of American life outstripped the political visions licensed by appeals to the common man. The convention of the "Negro Problem" frustrated Wright much as the "common man" frustrated Wylie. The Negro Problem, as Wright and others would increasingly argue, obstructed rather than nurtured fresh interpretations of American life. "Because it is an American convention to adore common people," Wylie wrote, "I elect here to criticize them, as a lesson." Dispensing with the phrase "common man" carried important implications for American cultural criticism, which, for Wylie, was too reliant on sanctified terms. "A society that cannot criticize its masses is hamstrung—as is ours," he asserted.[32]

Wylie considered modern psychology, for all the "failures and gaps in its practical knowledge," an important means of escaping the current impasses whereby the individual failed to master his personality. He envisioned a "society with better individual integration arising from a general knowledge of psychological truth and law." Like Wright, Wylie praised psychiatry that dealt directly with human misery and mental disease; he even described his book as merely an "invitation to extend [the] frontiers" of modern psychology. Wylie saw the problems of psychology in the context of modern medicine, and he skewered the idea of modern cities as pinnacles of health, where hygiene and well-being prevail: "Nothing could be farther from the truth." In much the same way that Wright would denounce institutionalized forms of negligence within modern medicine in "Psychiatry Comes to Harlem," Wylie invokes the case of Miami, where within a square mile "are packed forty thousand Negroes, who live in wooden shanties, airless and crowded." A few nurses and doctors do what they can for those living in a veritable "Hadean goatyard."[33] Wylie's sketch of disease and dilapidation graphically surpasses even those images and descriptions of deprivation presented in *12 Million Black Voices*. Wright's letter to Wylie did not refer to particular episodes in *Generation of Vipers* but instead commended the "moral indignation" of the book as a whole. Wylie's "blasts" served as a reminder of the staid nature of much American cultural criticism, prompting Wright to ask: "Why is it no longer 'nice' to be real and react honestly?"[34]

Wright was encouraged that the honesty and "passionate questioning" he identified with Wylie's writing increasingly marked African American letters, which responded more and more to the longing among African Americans for "self-possession, self-consciousness, individuality, new values, new loyalties [and] new leadership."[35] Wright considered J. Saunders Redding's memoir *No Day of Triumph* (1942) a prime example of the new dispensation. Redding's membership in the black middle class spared him the challenges of working-class life, but it introduced another set of problems. According to Wright, Redding's narrative moved "on a high, sensitive plane," portraying "how one man, surrounded by falsehood and confusion, groped toward truth and dignity and understanding."[36] Where most representations of African American middle-class life hewed closely to what Wright considered a defensively and falsely constructed "ideology of the 'Talented Tenth,'" Redding paved a different narrative path. His memoir records a "perverted feeling of fighting alone against the whole white world" as the only African American in his college. "I hated and feared the whites," Redding recalls.[37] For Wright, the candor and vivid prose of Redding's work represented a "manifesto to the Negro and a challenge to America" that set out to "expose, exhibit, [and] declare." If Redding's work was not psychoanalytic in vocabulary, it nevertheless shared the temperament of psychoanalysis by bringing to light dissonant psychological patterns that characterized modern African American life.

By the early-to-mid 1940s, Wright may be said to have begun reading psychotherapeutically: he mined texts for psychological and psychotherapeutic insights. The mix of cultural acumen, moral indignation, and honesty that Wright prized appeared in many kinds of writing and in various prose styles, but, more and more, they shared a debt to modern psychological inquiry. Of all the books he encountered in the 1940s, *Wasteland,* a 1946 novel by Jo Sinclair, was among those Wright considered the richest in psychotherapeutic insight. Wright's strong public endorsement brought attention to the novel and helped Sinclair win the prestigious Harper Prize for Fiction. In *Wasteland,* the psychiatrist who counsels the protagonist, Jake, figures prominently in the narrative and presides over therapeutic sessions that move the story along. Wright took particular interest in Sinclair's decision to bring out Jake's internalized anti-Semitism through the convention of the therapeutic encounter. Jake is lost in a "wasteland" of self-hate, for he has inadequately recognized the pressures and effects of anti-Semitism in his own life. Poverty and the social marginalization of his family exacerbate the inner and outer versions of his predicament. For Wright, *Wasteland* amounted to nothing less than a "monumental psychological study in family relationships, and something of a masterpiece in its ability to evoke the emotional frustrations of Jewish life in America."[38]

Based in New York and set contemporaneously in the 1940s, the story deals with conflicts between working-class Jewish immigrants and their children. Wright gives a brief outline of the plot: "Jake, a neurotic photographer on a metropolitan newspaper, has reached a point of despair that interferes with his ability to function and, for some time, he has been using alcohol as a crutch for his crippled emotions . . . He is determined, however, to end his suffering by laying bare his life before the analyst and, consequently, as he gropes, stammers, weeps and sweats out his confessions, the story of his entire family is overheard by the reader."[39] What was it about Sinclair's debut as a novelist that so captured Wright's imagination? What did he see in the story of a second-generation son of immigrant Jews that led him to describe Sinclair's novel as a major literary work? In a review titled "*Wasteland* Uses Psychoanalysis Deftly," Wright characterizes the novel as a stirring account of immigrant Jewish family life, one that displays skepticism toward sanctified notions of family and morality. Wright on *Wasteland* recalls *Black Boy,* published just one year earlier, which painted a critical, at times dark, picture of his own family. Much of *Wasteland* involves recurring scenes in which the protagonist recounts episodes from his past and present with a psychotherapist, who guides him to pause over key emotional junctures in his biography.

The novel capitalized on the relative newness of psychoanalysis as a cultural force in the midcentury United States, and on the considerable authority accorded to the psychological expert. Rather than allude to psychoanalysis by inserting some of its concepts into her novel, Sinclair places the psychoanalytic encounter itself at the very center of her story and personifies it through a psychiatrist, who offers a space in which Jake can explore the real and perceived anti-Semitism around him. The psychotherapeutic orientation of *Wasteland* is one that refuses to present individual neuroses that can be divorced from the larger social world. For Sinclair, the psychoanalytic encounter provided artistic resources for investigating the social location of her characters. Importantly, psychotherapeutic discourses were not sacrosanct for Wright. He did not believe that the use of a psychoanalytic technique automatically made a novel a success. "Many writers are led astray by thinking that they can easily use the seemingly easy device of the psychoanalyst in novelistic structure," he wrote. Yet he believed Sinclair had produced a compelling story about the social and psychological reproduction of racist ideology by approaching the psychoanalytic device with "discernment."[40] Writers, like Sinclair, who rendered the psychoanalytic encounter a powerful one encouraged Wright to further strengthen the links between psychological investigation, advocacy of psychotherapy, and antiracism in his intellectual and cultural work.

Wright considered *Wasteland* important as a forecast of how psychoanalytically informed literature and antiracist psychological criticism would fare in the United States. "I am anxious about the reception of so nakedly honest a novel, for it can be said that if *Wasteland* fails to win an appreciative audience, that will indicate a failure in our reading public rather than a failure in the novel itself." Wright's anxiety hinged on whether Americans would take advantage of the value of modern psychological thought and its concomitant role in the social and intellectual reckoning with race hierarchy and segregation. Because Sinclair's novel explicitly worked with the psychotherapeutic discourses of its day, Wright believed that a poor reception for *Wasteland* could signal a public unable or unwilling to respond meaningfully to the antiracist possibilities of psychological inquiry. Wright wanted *Wasteland* to succeed because it was a good novel; he also wanted its intellectual innovation and critical ramifications to receive recognition. Wright thus touted it as a "monumental psychological study" able to "evoke the emotional frustration of Jewish life in America."[41] For Wright, psychological insights into the potent social contests of the day, including the powerful effects of race hierarchy, entered cultural politics, and acquired relevance, through literary works such as *Wasteland*. Yet such insights had to be actively developed beyond the written page, including in psychotherapeutic settings.

A Clinic for the Masses

The intertwining of psychoanalysis and psychiatry and the successes of early psychosomatic medicine suggested imminent cures for war neuroses.[42] Many young psychiatrists worked in the military during the war and emerged from that experience increasingly convinced that the chief causes of mental illness and nervous disorders were psychological and interpersonal.[43] At the same time, the psychoanalytic psychiatry that had grown into a robust force during and after the war became a destination for further inquiry for antiracist thinkers interested in underlying factors in long-standing patterns of racial conflicts and antagonisms.

One result of the interaction of psychiatry, psychoanalysis, and antiracism was the Lafargue Clinic. A product of the intellectual and personal bond between Wright and Fredric Wertham, the clinic was an institutional counterpart to the antiracism Wright had helped establish in American letters. Named for Paul Lafargue, the socialist journalist of French and Creole background and son-in-law to Karl Marx, the clinic opened March 8, 1946, as a part-time psychiatric service organization to assist Harlem residents. Consultations were available for nominal fees, which were waived when individuals could not pay. An interracial team of accredited psychiatrists volunteered their time in the basement of St. Philip's Episcopal Church. Because Lafargue was an experiment in bringing psychiatric services to poor New Yorkers without the benefit of philanthropic support, its small scale meant that it easily escaped public notice. Yet the clinic did play a role in the intensification of civil rights battles when a group of children from Delaware, eight black and five white, came to the clinic and served as subjects in research on the effects of school segregation. Previous studies of the effects of race prejudice had looked exclusively at black children. Wertham's work with white children demonstrated that "segregated conditions tended to sanction and make more durable prejudices that derived from several sources in a community."[44] The study would lead Wertham to testify in the Delaware desegregation case, a prelude to *Brown*. His testimony amounted to a reformulation that classified segregation as a public health problem: "Now the fact of segregation in public and high school creates in the mind of the child an unsolvable conflict, an unsolvable emotional conflict, and I would say an inevitable conflict."[45]

Wright's most significant statement about the Lafargue Clinic appeared in the essay "Psychiatry Comes to Harlem" (1946), where he describes the work of the clinic in unequivocally antiracist terms. Indeed, the essay demonstrates how inseparable Wright's interest in the psychological sciences had become from his public profile as a literary artist and cultural critic. Wright began the essay by placing psychiatry in the context of American medicine as a whole. He argued that the postures of neutrality struck by the medical establishment meant that pressing social needs were left unaddressed, and such studied indifference led institutions effectively to serve antisocial ends. Wright's critiques of institutionalized medicine and dominant psychotherapeutic practice formed part of a more general argument within the essay: racist societies and environments produced particular psychological strains. The clinic responded by making those environments and strains its starting points and prioritizing the "powerful personality conflicts engendered in Negroes by the consistent sabotage of their democratic aspirations in housing, jobs, education, and social mobility." Wertham's "social psychiatry"—the philosophical orientation that informed clinic practices—concentrated on people who negotiated an "environment of anxiety and tension which easily tips the normal emotional scales toward neurosis."[46]

The literatures and projects that attracted Wright stressed the socially imposed and environmentally produced nature of many psychological problems. When he referred to the "artificially-made psychological problems in Harlem," Wright pointed to both the social fact of segregation and the effects on individuals of a racialized social order. "(It is neatly overlooked that Harlem is itself an artificially made community!)," Wright wrote in response to the medical establishment's stated concern that bringing psychiatric services to Harlem would reinforce patterns of racial segregation. Wright's essay pointed to the joint racial containment and class oppression that marked much of life for Harlem residents, and it described Lafargue as an implicit critique of the medical establishment and customary distribution of psychiatric services. The clinic's "*sub rosa* methods amount in the main to a complete reversal of all current rules holding in authoritative psychiatric circles." Moreover, Wertham's idea of "social psychiatry" shared nothing with "philanthropy, charity, or missionary work." Since organized medicine seemed skeptical of social psychiatry, the work of the clinic was a direct refutation of the canons of official medical practice. Wertham's social experiment in psychiatry was an effort to create the passion to identify and meet "human need" and the "artificially-made psychological problems in Harlem."[47] By "artificially-made psychological problems," Wright emphasized the social facts of segregation and suggested that the clinic provided ways of countering and redirecting the social processes of racialization.

Lafargue "proved that Harlem's high rates of delinquency and nervous breakdown stem not from biological predilections toward crime existing in Negroes, but from an almost total lack of community services to cope with the problems of Harlem's individuals."[48] In Wright's view, psychiatric work and clinical observations effectively refuted varieties of scientific and popular racism by redirecting attention to the environmental factors and political economies that nourished psychological problems. "Harlem Is Nowhere," Ralph Ellison's essay devoted to Lafargue, echoed Wright's piece, calling the clinic "perhaps the most successful attempt in the nation to provide psychotherapy for the underprivileged." The lack of a race barrier immediately made it more than a valuable psychotherapeutic center: Lafargue amounted to something like "an underground extension of democracy." Harlem, the "scene of the folk Negro's death agony," needed institutions such as the Lafargue Clinic that were alive to the specific situation of African Americans as not "quite citizens and yet Americans"—what Ellison regarded as the "obscene absurdity" of their predicament. Ellison's "ultimate hope was that Harlem might be seen as the world . . . [for] the world itself had become a madhouse."[49] As Ellison biographer Arnold Rampersad has observed, if "Harlem is nowhere, as the title proclaims, then Harlem is everywhere."[50] The social psychiatry conducted at Lafargue presented in miniature a process that needed to unfold at a wider scale.

Nearly as soon as its doors opened, the Lafargue Clinic garnered significant public attention, in no small part because of Wright's involvement and advocacy. In the *New Amsterdam News,* Earl Brown did not restrain his enthusiasm, calling the clinic "one of the most democratic places on earth," a claim not dismissible as overstatement, he insisted, given the "tremendous need for mental hygiene clinics for the masses of citizens."[51] Brown characterized the need for therapeutic services for dispossessed segments of the nation as equivalent to the need for housing, jobs and schools. Many regarded the opening of the clinic as a dramatic sign that large-scale interventions into the problems of racist social environments might soon be devised. For psychologist and *Chicago Defender* columnist S. I. Hayakawa, the clinic represented a "radical new step," for the Lafargue staff demonstrated the relevance of psychiatry for those met "with impossible living conditions, with uncertainty of status, [and] with an environment full of contradictions of democratic precept and undemocratic practice."[52] Hayakawa emphasized the lack of psychiatric services for children as a result of racist practices and linked the problem of juvenile delinquency to "the outward manifestation of dangerously unresolved conflicts within." The tensions that led to juvenile delinquency were aggravated within racist social environments by the "corrosive discovery of the facts of Jim Crow." The critical difference between Wertham's social psychiatry and conventional psychiatric services, Hayakawa wrote, was an understanding of the economic and social lives of patients, in addition to the more typical observation of internal processes within them. Hayakawa expressed enthusiasm for Wertham's experiment and advocated the broad replication of Lafargue-style social psychiatry "not only in Negro communities, but in all communities where social friction and social frustration are intense."[53]

Robert Bendiner, an editor at the *Nation,* profiled the clinic in "Psychiatry for the Needy" and emphasized how Wertham differed from his mainstream colleagues, especially in his insistence that psychiatrists had to overcome many of their own social prejudices in order to recognize the interplay of personal, economic, and cultural circumstances in the lives of patients. Attending to their own social prejudices enhanced the ability of therapists to explain to patients that discrimination, though mired in the idea of race and notions of inferiority, centrally involved unjust economic structures. Such explanations helped Lafargue therapists to challenge the guilt induced by "feelings of alleged inadequacy." Based in the conviction that "mental hygiene should be more than a luxury reserved for those who may need it least," the clinic directed public attention toward and emphasized the social specificity of psychiatric interventions. Wertham summarized his approach when he told Bendiner that "you can't talk about psychotherapy for all time," as one must always discuss psychotherapy "at *this* time and at *this* place."[54] For other commentators, one lesson from Lafargue was that African Americans living in segregated urban conditions did not require therapies that differed in kind from those available to others. According to

Time, Lafargue, in bringing services to a poor and segregated setting, verified that "Negroes are no more happy-go-lucky—or neurotic—than other people."[55]

According to a profile of the clinic that appeared in the *New Republic,* Wright was present when the idea for Lafargue came to Wertham. Demoralized by the lack of available public funding for psychiatric services in Harlem, Wertham dreamed of a day when "psychoanalysis and psychotherapy are not the private property of the rich but the common property of the people" and discussed the urgency of a center organized around his method of social psychiatry with Wright and other friends. Exasperated, Wertham finally said, "If we can't get the money to do it, let's do it without money." Wright and the others looked at him: "Well, why not?"[56] Yet another profile, "Human Salvage in Harlem," presented a picture of a Harlem youngster quickly becoming a delinquent through truancy. His mother brings him to the clinic, where the thirteen-year-old is soon "talking his heart out to his new friend." Wertham, the first person ever to be sincerely interested in his problems, describes his patient in terms of a "pattern born out of frustrations of exploitation and prejudice," while also counseling his mother to refrain from the "unthinking strictness" that has only heightened the appeal of disobedience. Many commentators agreed that through the work carried out with individuals at Lafargue, Wertham's ideal of social psychiatry emerged as a "living gesture against discrimination."[57]

A rethinking of psychotherapeutic services along antiracist lines, Lafargue became a pioneering laboratory for social change. To be sure, the journalistic plaudits came primarily from left-liberal publications. Yet the broad discussion of psychotherapeutic models of social transformation registered a feature of the intellectual life of the 1940s, when writers and commentators undertook public discussions of institutions and resources that could play a role in the demise of the racist social order. In 1947, the Veterans Administration (VA) designated the Lafargue Clinic an "official agency for the psychiatric treatment of white and colored patients alike." The VA acknowledgment of the work of the clinic stood in contrast to the clinic's lack of official standing within the medical establishment and led Wright to predict that the designation would "enable the Lafargue Clinic to offer its help to wider masses of people who cannot at present obtain psychiatric services." He hoped that the "action of the VA" would lead "other communities to learn how to cut through red tape and grapple with the needs of the people directly."[58]

Wright was instrumental in the establishment of the Lafargue Clinic, effectively a co-founder. This fact has not often led scholars to concentrate on the psychotherapeutic dimensions of the cultural politics of antiracism that Wright envisioned. Yet the vision of a transformative antiracism that Wright advocated was predicated on the reimagining of the institutions of medicine and psychotherapeutic expertise. The antiracism Wright adumbrated gave psychotherapeutic institutions a role in widening the political determination to dissolve the power of race hierarchy and racist ideology.

The Wiltwyck School for Boys

Even before the establishment of the Lafargue Clinic, Wright had been searching for agencies that introduced psychological methods in work with minority youth— efforts that brought him to the Wiltwyck School for Boys. Like his connection to the Lafargue Clinic, his relationship to the Wiltwyck School seldom figures in considerations of his work. Yet his association with Wiltwyck reveals a great deal about his commitment to psychological thought and psychotherapeutic methods and directly impinged on his literary and intellectual work. In 1944, Wright wrote to Edward Aswell, his editor at Harper and Brothers, to propose another documentary book on the model of *12 Million Black Voices*. The everyday life and social institutions that shaped the experiences of Harlem youth would stand at the center of an exploration of racial exclusion not "quickly forgotten."[59] Wright hoped to explore the appeal of juvenile delinquency and the roles played by home life and schooling, as well as children's courts and reform schools, in the lives of Harlem youth. These same themes became the basis for a work of fiction he called "The Jackal." In "The Children of Harlem," a working essay for the documentary book, Wright rejected stock answers about the high rates of juvenile delinquency among Harlem youth. Understanding the problems of delinquency would mean moving toward observations and analysis "unavoidably couched in terms more or less alien to popular American thought." It would mean thinking through the "influence of environment on personality formation." The reorientation Wright proposed for interpreting high rates of juvenile delinquency among Harlem youth looked broadly to the social and historical patterns of American life and at the "artificial environment" Harlem represented. Making sense of juvenile delinquency required an acknowledgment of the residential segregation that set the limits of Harlem as a geographical space, some parts of which were the "most densely populated on earth." The segregated formation of Harlem, though made to seem natural and timeless, had to be understood in terms of its powerful consequences, for it compounded a key fact about its residents: most had "never been allowed, on the whole, to act upon the commonest assumptions and aspirations which most Americans take for granted and hold dear." The boundaries that made Harlem seem distant from the rest of New York reinforced the distance residents felt from the common store of values that circulated throughout much of the urban environment. Wright recognized that the complex historical and ongoing social forces that created Harlem could be baffling to many observers, who all too often concluded that "what happens there must be natural, racial, biological." Yet there was nothing "inherently racial" about the "personality disorganization" that followed from segregation and its economic and social effects on families and individuals.[60]

In keeping with the possibility of social transformation he linked to psychotherapeutic knowledge of racialized environments, Wright placed a premium on understanding the "plastic, malleable personalities of growing youth." Yet where were the institutions that could provide Harlem youth with alternatives to the tragic predicaments in which they found themselves, that could help them conceive of their lives in ways beyond racialism and patterns of segregation? For Wright, the Wiltwyck School for Boys was one of the few places that met this charge, in part because it represented a counterpoint to a national culture in which African Americans were "popularly regarded as possessing a super-abundant fund of laughter and song and rhythm." Wright visited Wiltwyck and learned about the cases of many of the children there, eventually writing about the center in "Urban Misery," an essay based on "Children of Harlem." Among the discoveries of the Wiltwyck staff, and the one that Wright emphasized in his essay, was the unique nature of the "emotional deprivation" that characterized the personality of each child. Wiltwyck benefited from a staff "too wise to feel that merely spanking a boy, petting him, giving him a petty job, or making him go to school can heal the ravages inflicted by a brutal Harlem environment." Wright applauded Wiltwyck's willingness to address the specific pressures of racist social environments. He also believed that the work undertaken at Wiltwyck carried implications beyond "Negro children alone," for it related to children undergoing emotional disturbance across different settings. Wiltwyck made a contribution to the concept of child care by providing "a new notion of the frailty of children, anybody's children, everybody's children, white as well as black."[61]

The antiracist aims and universalism Wright identified as the guiding principles of Wiltwyck convinced him of the significance of its mission. The work around emotional disturbance carried out by staff members focused on youth, but to separate such psychological dynamics from American cultural patterns was misguided. The problems explored at Wiltwyck reflected the "emotional deprivation that grips black life in America" and the "white population in different ways and in various guises." The school experiment represented a bold response to the ravages of racism and simultaneously held lessons for everyone in the racialized social and political economy of modern American life. Wright reflected on the antiracism at the core of the Wiltwyck experiment in "Harlem Is Human," a chapter he drafted for the proposed book on Harlem youth. The staff, black and white, and the presence of white juvenile delinquents, helped to break down for black youth the "concept of a solid wall of whites against a solid wall of blacks." Problems "deeper than those of the home are being settled here," he concluded. At stake in the small-scale successes achieved at Wiltwyck was the "entire fabric of American society." Spending time at Wiltwyck inevitably led Wright to conclusions about American life writ large, for the school's approach to human relations, which involved trust, devotion, and self-sacrifice, was in large measure recognizable by the absence of such qualities "on the American scene."[62] Wright was moved to advocate on behalf of Wiltwyck. Among other things, he attended a 1945 fundraising event where Eleanor Roosevelt served as guest of honor.[63]

Like Wright, the leadership at Wiltwyck saw their efforts in expansive terms, as relevant to American culture as a whole. Robert L. Cooper, the director, came to understand the work of the school as the pursuit of "a living situation in which culturally conceived and culturally sustained frustrations do not exist." The experiences of minorities, Cooper wrote, were paradigmatic of cultural proscription and subsequent frustration. "Imagine, if you can," he wrote, "the tragedy of the diffused and dissipated energy that is lost in the process of having constantly to think of one's designated and specifically limited minority role." Cooper believed that Wright's fiction furthered collective understandings of the tensions that accompanied minority status. Wright's *Native Son* had brought the "limiting and restricting implications of caste" into view through a harrowing tale about the "emotionally damaging burden" of minority status. Just as Wright argued that racial categories worked to obfuscate rather than illuminate conditions and aspirations of minorities, Cooper's work at Wiltwyck was predicated on the desire of minorities to "experience democracy" and enter everyday cultural life as persons, "not as a social category."[64] Setting aside the dominant cultural interpretations of juvenile delinquents as hopelessly antisocial figures, the school adapted mental hygiene concepts regarding positive personal relationships to serve marginalized youth confronting sociopsychological injury.

From Wiltwyck to *Rite of Passage*

Wright composed drafts of a story he called "The Jackal," which eventually became the novella *Rite of Passage,* during 1945, commenting on his progress in his journal.[65] The story brings together several themes of long interest to Wright: the experiences of youth, the social origins of criminality, and the effects of segregation and social marginalization on the personality formation of minorities. The Harlem setting of the story prefigures the support that Wright would lend to the Lafargue Clinic. Yet the story also owed much to what he learned through his involvement with Wiltwyck.

Wright recorded his progress on "The Jackal" regularly, describing his narrative of a Harlem youth as the possible "seeds of a damn good psychological study." An early outline of the story involved a youth gang that kidnaps a woman, holding her for fear that she will betray them. That structure, Wright anticipated, would permit him to "deal with these boys' emotions, their relations to their families, their friends, their ultimate hopes." In order to register the emotional patterns of Harlem youth, Wright visited several schools, courts, and institutions over four months. On many of these trips, Wright was accompanied by Ira L. Gibbons, a social psychiatric caseworker at Wiltwyck, who expressed enthusiasm for Wright's new literary endeavor. Wright considered Gibbons, originally from the British West Indies, one of the best psychiatric caseworkers he had met. Gibbons, who would go on to teach at the School of Social Work at Howard University, helped Wright to think through the sociopsychological experiences of Harlem youth, supplying observations from his professional vantage point. Gibbons, like Wright, connected the status of poor and troubled Harlem youth to the challenge of creating and extending democracy in modern America. Indeed, he regarded the group interaction among youth and staff at Wiltwyck as a kind of laboratory for thinking about both the precariousness and possibilities of democracy. "Voluntary group life and freedom to participate are integral parts of the democratic structure," wrote Gibbons. Yet such a democratic structure had broken down in a "society with dual standards" that discounted the "social and emotional needs of Negro children and youth."[66] Wright looked forward in particular to a plan he had arranged with Gibbons to "look into the problem of juvenile delinquency in Harlem," including the "gang life there," elements of which he hoped to bring into "The Jackal."[67]

Wright's story pivots on a single event that transforms the life of Johnny Gibbs, a fifteen-year-old African American youth and successful student. Early in the novella, Johnny discovers that the family he has lived with all of his life is in fact his foster family. Bureaucratic policies lead to Johnny's relocation with another family. This central conceit, though on one level nonsensical, triggers a sense of existential threat that quickly become the main thrust of the narrative as Wright tracks the mental convulsions that ensue from Johnny's shaken sense of belonging. Johnny must move into a new home that has been selected for him, and there is no possibility of returning to his family. The gangs in the neighborhood feel distant in their alienation from the generally nurturing figures that surround Johnny. That distance closes with dramatic speed once Johnny is removed from the only home he has known. The narrative moves swiftly from that initial shock, affording nothing in the way of a return to Johnny's prior sense of safety. The opportunity to join a local youth gang, a community in miniature, offers one alternative to his acute sense of dislocation, allowing him to keep feelings of existential threat at bay: When Johnny is given his gang name, "Jackal," he becomes part of a world that promises communal life but only at the price of rapid dehumanization. Acquainted with the protocols of other violent groups, the gang regularly robs men and women in and around Central Park, and Johnny, who initially balks at such violence, soon realizes that he will need to habituate himself to violence and feelings of hostility toward all those outside the closed social world he has entered. "Yes, this was his passport to his new life, to the new and strange gang of boys upon whom he would have to depend for his food, for friendship. If, for any reason, they rejected him, he would once again be on the windswept streets."[68]

Johnny's internal turmoil stands at the center of much of *Rite of Passage*. As he moves with the others toward the park one evening, Johnny peers with longing at the homes he passes, which recall the "warmth of a home where people lived with smiles and trust and faith." Even though he has taken on some of the superficial characteristics of his new social group, he imagines that he might "flee to the shelter of one of those dark, looming houses," gaining entry to a different social environment with a mere "knock on the door."[69] The story ends with another mugging. This time, however, Wright adds a haunting element that brings Johnny's divided self into even sharper relief. In the distance, a "Negro woman" who appears to have witnessed one of the muggings moves in Johnny's direction with determination. In tones of alarm and condemnation, she calls out, "You boys! You boys!" The voice is inaudible to all but Johnny.

"You boys! You boys!" provides the final refrain for a story that refuses to locate Johnny in any space other than a moral netherworld. The refrain, coming from afar yet close by, become a plaintive cry emerging from no one person or place in particular, suggesting a common condition of dislocation and estrangement. Though in one sense intended specifically for Johnny and the gang, the refrain, by its very directness and urgency draws attention to youth obscured by minority status and an antagonistic world. Johnny's rapid fall into a world of violence and moral self-recrimination provided Wright with another way to consider the psychological fragility and social instability engendered by the racist social order and the psychological fissures and maladies associated with juvenile delinquency, in particular.

The estrangement on display in *Rite of Passage* recalls the sense of social isolation among African Americans that Wright described in his *Black Metropolis* introduction. Not an uncritical admirer of pragmatism, Wright nevertheless found pragmatist philosopher and psychologist William James's concept of the social self valuable for thinking about minority youth and racialized minority status generally. According to James, "a man has as many social selves as there are individuals who recognize him and carry an image of him in their minds." Because such recognition was a vital part of everyday life, patterns of social exclusion derived their invidious character in large part from their rejection of the social self. Thus, "no more fiendish punishment could be devised, were such a thing physically possible, than that one should be turned loose in society and remain unnoticed."[70] For Wright, the rejection of African Americans involved multiple mechanisms, including dehumanizing imagery and other forms of social alienation. Together, these mechanisms made the process of composing a social self that could identify with the nation deeply contradictory. In place of identification, "atomized and despairing rebellion" often held sway.[71] The rebellion that often ensued from the hazards of maintaining a social self amid a racist social order emerges as pivotal theme of *Rite of Passage,* a work that flowed from Wright's philosophical reflections on the forms of estrangement created by modern race thinking, his interactions with minority youth at Wiltwyck, and his commitment to representing the psychological effects of segregated social environments.

The Case of Benjamin Karpman

The number of psychiatrists practicing in the United States grew from 2,295 in 1940 to 4,700 by 1948.[72] The profession's rapid growth created a sense of indeterminacy as to the character that psychotherapeutic work would assume. Wright's conversations and collaborations with psychiatrists took place within this context of expansion and indeterminacy. Given the momentum in the growth of psychiatric services and Wright's efforts to bring psychological expertise to bear on problems of race hierarchy, it is not surprising that his connections to the psychotherapeutic community were not limited to the Lafargue Clinic and the Wiltwyck School for Boys. Wright's relationship to psychotherapist Benjamin Karpman, who was not connected to either institution, expands the picture of his determination to make psychotherapeutic services a more decisive part of antiracist criticism. The relationship with Karpman also reveals tensions that emerged as the work of psychotherapists came more and more to figure in Wright's thinking.

In 1942, Karpman, who worked at St. Elizabeth's Hospital in Washington, DC, and for a time taught at Howard University, requested a meeting with Wright to discuss his plan to "write a book that will take up from the psychoanalytic point of view various aspects of race relations." A correspondence between the two ensued. "When you state in your letter that you 'do not see why there should not be a psychoanalytic volume on the subject of black-white relations' you are echoing an idea which I have been carrying in my mind for over twenty years," Karpman wrote.[73] The publication of Wright's novel quickened Karpman's long-standing interest in the subject of race antagonisms. *Native Son* brought together subjects around which Karpman had built his professional life: the criminal mind and the psychology of the racial minority. For his part, Wright was attracted to Karpman's extensive work on criminal behavior because of his lifelong interest in criminal cases. Karpman and Wright communicated frequently between 1942 and 1945. The volume of the correspondence underscores the shared assumption that brought the two together: psychology could illuminate as yet dimly understood truths about the persistence of race hierarchy.

Wright and Karpman met on a few occasions. There are no records of their meetings, but the letters do reveal something about the nature of the affiliation. "The last year I was at Howard I asked some 15 students of mine to give me their reflections on 'Native Son.' You can imagine the great variety of opinions and viewpoints expressed. I have tried to melt it altogether into something like a coherent whole." The project on Wright's novel was in many ways the culmination of research on race that Karpman had undertaken over years. "In the course of my 20 year connection with Howard," Karpman wrote, "I have collected an immense amount of material on the racial problem . . . I have accumulated enough material to publish a good-sized volume, perhaps two, taking up the Negro-White problem from a large number of viewpoints . . . I believe that if all this could be published it could be the scientific parallel to 'Native Son' as Carey McWilliams's book was to Steinbeck's 'The Grapes of Wrath.' "[74] In pointing to McWilliams's *Factories in the Field,* which recounted the history and conditions of migrant farm labor in California, Karpman voiced a desire to produce a study that complemented Wright's novel by way of methodical psychoanalytic argumentation.[75]

In proposing the "scientific parallel" to *Native Son,* Karpman both affirmed the novel's psychological richness and implied its scientific limits. For all of his enthusiasm for Wright's novel, Karpman communicates anxieties about bringing imaginative work and professional psychological investigation alongside one another. Referring to an article on *Native Son* published by one of his students, Karpman wrote to Wright: "You told me in your first letter that you had been conscious of the feelings of Bigger Thomas, it is Charles's article that gave all of these things a label."[76] Without the work of psychoanalytic investigation, he suggested, the psychological dimensions of *Native Son* and other such works would go unrecognized. Wright's insights into racial antagonisms, powerful though they were, required the explication that only psychoanalytic experts could provide to acquire the status of scientific material.

If Karpman maintained that his credentials enhanced Wright's work, he was also eager to draw on Wright's literary artistry to transform his own research. Karpman envisioned Wright novelizing the psychoanalytic materials he had gathered, thereby giving readers an appreciation of those "true motives" and psychological processes seldom satisfactorily elaborated in fiction.[77] The desire to influence spheres outside of psychotherapy reflected Karpman's attempt to depart from what he considered orthodox psychoanalysis. In a letter written in 1937 to his friend and Howard colleague Alain Locke, Karpman complained that most "psychiatrists see the patient only as a particular individual and having a particular type of sickness, but do not stress enough the cultural setting in which the sickness is precipitated and in general the social import of this phenomenon in relation to the other phenomena of similar nature."[78] Yet Karpman's desire to make "cultural setting" and "social import" analytical priorities in his research and thus separate himself from orthodox psychoanalysis existed in tension with his wish to protect psychological expertise as a privileged, professional form with clear limits. Even as he sought greater attention for his work, he wrote of the necessity of staving off wide public appeal. "I personally do not hope to ever achieve a wide public appeal," he wrote to Wright. "Indeed if some of my writings were to achieve a wide appeal, I would immediately begin to suspect, even question, the soundness of my scientific presentations." A wider cultural purview for psychotherapeutic experts appealed to Karpman, even as he worried about the impact of heightened public exposure on his research. Ultimately, Karpman believed that collaborations between psychiatrists and novelists promised powerful analytical narratives that overshadowed the risks of public intellectual life. He urged Wright to consider a cooperative venture in which he developed story based largely on Karpman's psychoanalytic evaluations of African Americans. The "intuitive insight of fiction writers aided by the intellectual insights of psychiatrists could perform wonders," Karpman wrote.[79]

The collaboration between the two correspondents never materialized. The publication of Gunnar Myrdal's *An American Dilemma* made it difficult for studies of race relations to find willing publishing houses, since Myrdal's book was widely regarded as definitive.[80] Nevertheless, for a time, Myrdal's study provided Karpman with an opportunity to better define and promote his own research. "I can envision two solid volumes of the type that Myrdal published but with entirely different content. I would begin where he left off . . . He gives you factual material. I am searching for motivation . . . It is my idea to produce a two-volume work dealing with the psychology of minority-majority relationships in the same way as Myrdal did on social relations . . . I believe that since I will be continuing where Myrdal left off, the work will be far more spectacular and its impact on our racial relations greater."[81]

Karpman solicited Wright's help in seeking funding from foundations for his project, which he tentatively called "The Many and the Few: Psychogenetic Studies in Race Relations."[82] Although funding sources were not in the end procured, Wright did meet with a representative of the Marshall Field Foundation on Karpman's behalf.[83] His endorsement of Karpman was of a piece with his aim of expanding the public profile of psychotherapeutic perspectives on race hierarchy beyond the focus on social structures Myrdal had emphasized.

Wright's dialogues with psychotherapists and psychoanalytic thinkers extended to the Chicago-based Institute for Psychoanalysis. The psychotherapist Helen V. McLean, who considered *Black Boy* a tremendous intellectual achievement, wrote to tell Wright that she planned to present on his book during a seminar at the institute.[84] Yet even before *Black Boy,* Helen Ross, one of the institute's directors, had communicated with Wright and urged him to return to Chicago and speak at the institute, which he did in 1945.[85] Wright was invited to join a discussion with Franz Alexander, the institute's director, the African American social scientist Allison Davis, and others.

Beyond Psychoanalysis

In letters to Gertrude Stein, Wright described his existential psychoanalytic intellectual orientation while also revealing how his readings in the 1940s extended beyond psychoanalysis to yet broader interests in semantics and rhetoric. Although he had known Stein's work since the 1930s, Wright did not meet the famous modernist writer until he arrived in Paris in 1946. Reading Stein gave Wright the confidence that he could "tap at will the vast pool of living words that swirled around me."[86] A correspondence between the two writers developed during the war, when Stein's article about American soldiers in Europe appeared in the *New York Times Magazine.* "The New Hope in Our 'Sad Young Men'" recorded Stein's sense of the downhearted and hardened mood among soldiers who, having seen firsthand how tensions between majorities and minorities could escalate, expressed hopelessness about returning to a "country divided against itself." Attempting to reassure soldiers with signs of changes afoot in America, Stein invoked Wright's work. So long as "the Negro was just a native race, the white man's burden point of view" obtained, Stein told them, and the continuation of racial antagonisms seemed inevitable. "But now when one Negro can write as Richard Wright does writing, writes not as a Negro but as a man, well the minute that happens the relation between the white and the Negro is no longer a difference of races but a minority question."[87]

Stein became one of Wright's prized interlocutors. "There is no doubt that this race problem in our country cuts deep to the bottom of the lives of both whites and blacks," he wrote her. "We are wonders when it comes to making machines; we are marvels when it comes to selling things. But when it comes to just talking to each other, we get scared and reach for our guns." Because Stein had been in Paris during the war, Wright found it especially valuable to discuss the question of fascism with her. He tried from his perspective in America to describe what the effects of the war had been and expressed pessimism that Americans seemed to have forgotten the war in Europe by the fall of 1945. It "has been tied up in a neat psychological package and stored away in a bureau drawer." For Wright, as for Stein, problems of fascism and race hierarchy belonged to the present, not the past, and required a great deal of work to address. Few were willing to reflect on the danger of America "collapsing in a panic when she faces the problem of the Negro—as she really must one day—just as Europe collapsed when she faced the problem of the Jew," as Wright put it.[88]

Wright sent Stein books and articles, including articles about the work of the Lafargue Clinic. Stein had studied with William James when she attended Radcliffe College and had been a student for several years at Johns Hopkins Medical School before turning to writing, and Wright knew of her background in neurology and physiological psychology. As he prepared to leave for France, Wright carried books that he hoped to discuss with Stein, including Alfred Korzybski's *Science and Sanity,* which brought together semantics, psychology, and neurology. The major lines of thought in *Science and Sanity* provide a window on Wright's thinking about psychology, science, and cultural analysis.

Korzybski, a philosopher and scientist known for his theory of general semantics, proposed ways of addressing what he called a "neuro-semantic environment"— spaces made up of beliefs, creeds, and knowledge. Korzybski's book posited the identification of semantic environments as a prelude to the eradication of the "delusional worlds that all of us, in some respects at least, inhabit in our evaluational habits," a kind of space-clearing for "new knowledge and new orientations."[89] Korzybski stressed the relationship of his ideas to the fascism and totalitarianism flashing throughout the modern world. Bringing clarity to the study of neurosemantic environments became more urgent than ever, for Korzybski regarded Nazism as a set of "wars *of* and *on* nerves" and "wars of *verbal distortion.*" In fascist and totalitarian environments, specific terms, through a process of "dumping on human nervous systems," became the basis for disordered reflexes and states. Although Korzybski did not refer to U.S. race hierarchy in his book, the general environmentalism and focus on language Wright discovered in the book may have encouraged his own efforts to supply "new knowledge and new orientations" about the relationship between racial categorization, environment, and psychological disorder on the American scene.

Like the psychotherapeutic thinkers to whom Wright was drawn, Korzybski advanced theoretical models that implicated everyday social maladjustments, psychoses and neuroses, and "common inferiority feelings."[90]

For Wright, segregation and race hierarchy had everything to do with "our emotionally conditioned past" and an existentialist psychoanalysis was vital for delving into that past and undoing its power.[91] Wright and other antiracist writers in the 1940s turned to psychological inquiry to undertake explorations that had not yet been attempted, and to look beyond the degraded sociality produced by racism and segregation. *Psychology* came to represent a set of resources and general critical idiom that promised as-yet-unavailable assessments of the racist social order. In an unpublished essay, "Towards the Conquest of Ourselves," Wright reflected on the wartime status of the Negro Problem and offered clues as to why psychotherapeutic and other models came to figure so prominently in his thinking. Eager to communicate the "inner feel of the tension" that defined much of African American life, Wright determined that his work would return to a key question: How are African Americans "bearing up under this strange burden of crossed-up feelings, of a yes and no life, of a dream-it-but-can't-have-it-existence, of a way of life that results in a state of continuous tension?" Wright wished to understand the contemporary moment in African American life "from within outward" and therefore set out to present stories about African American life heretofore unrecorded. "America has yet to know us," he wrote. The "conquest of ourselves," the realization of self-knowledge would be key to the achievement of social justice, and psychotherapeutic resources provided among the best available modern vehicles for self-knowledge. The vision Wright intimated had momentous national implications, but he did not see his interests in an antiracist and existentialist psychoanalysis as reducible to one nation-state. At the dawn of the era of decolonization, African American life held a "global meaning." "Our fight is nothing less than a fight for the recognition of our humanity," he wrote.[92]

CHAPTER THREE

Race and Minorities from Below

The Wartime Cultural Criticism of Chester Himes,
Horace Cayton, Ralph Ellison, and C. L. R. James

During World War II, Richard Wright did not relent in furthering a cultural politics that put segregation and race hierarchy firmly within national debates. In a period that seemed to require unanimity of thought and the suppression of dissent to harness collective effort, Wright continued to press the story of African American freedom struggles into public consciousness, as did many African American writers and journalists. The war placed racial ideology and colonialism on the international agenda in profound ways, bringing the plight of minorities and colonized populations to the fore. The African American press furnished evidence that black Americans seemed to arrive at internationalist perspectives on both the war and the rise of fascism more readily than many other Americans.[1] In African American journalism, racial ideologies were, even more pointedly than in the past, tied to capitalism and imperialism.[2] Wright both drew inspiration from and advanced the internationalist wartime exploration of race hierarchy in African American writing. Simone de Beauvoir considered Wright's wartime work among his greatest achievements. In *The Ethics of Ambiguity,* her treatise on freedom and existentialism, Beauvoir commends him for his refusal to set aside criticism of racial subjugation at a time when African American cultural and political leaders were asked to do so in the name of wartime consensus. Wright "thought that even at a time of war his cause had to be defended." In her book, Beauvoir invokes the figure of "sub-man," whose economic and social circumstances delimit his capacity to act in the world and who makes his "way across a world deprived of meaning toward a death which merely confirms his long negation of himself." For the individual operating within such constraints, "the world appears to him as given." Beauvoir regarded Wright's wartime work as a refutation to the political cultures that produced "sub-man" and therefore as a means of "surpassing the given."[3]

Wright's example and work ramified throughout the thinking of antiracist writers during the war, serving as the basis for a range of new interventions. Chester Himes, C. L. R. James, Ralph Ellison, and Horace Cayton were especially drawn to Wright's work and inspired to make psychological problems prominent features of their own investigations of race hierarchy. Throughout the 1940s, Cayton, Himes, Ellison, and James were among Wright's closest readers and most important interlocutors. In both published work and personal correspondence, each writer communicated the desire they shared with Wright to remake commentary on race thinking and racial antagonisms. The social scientific analysis of Cayton and the political writing of James, like the fiction and nonfiction of Himes and Ellison, provide a composite picture of a moment of intellectual renewal around the analysis of race hierarchy. In many ways, each writer represented a variant on Wright's existentialist psychoanalytic disposition. In this chapter I offer intellectual snapshots of each writer, emphasizing the ways psychological investigation served as a principle within a range of literary and critical endeavors.

It was during the war that Wright devised a prospectus for a new magazine, a project to which he devoted extensive time and one that promised a radical renewal of cultural commentary on race hierarchy. He envisioned "criticism toward the culture of the nation as a whole" devised through the prism of minority situations and wartime race problems. "American Pages: A Magazine Reflecting a Minority Mood and Point of View" would focus attention on the "psychological happenings in the minds of black and white populations," considering, among other things, the "emotional causes" that led many to follow the Klan or join Marcus Garvey's movement. It was to include "one crime story a month, analyzing the motives." Psychoanalytic and psychological inquiry would help shape the magazine's overall critical mission by bringing psychiatric concepts to bear on investigations of the attitudes of minorities. Tracking the appeal of psychoanalysis among different sectors of the American public, black and white, would also fall within the magazine's purview. The various aims ascribed to the magazine fed an overarching critical impetus: an "attack on the problem of race and minorities from below, at the root."[4]

Wright's hopes for the magazine went unrealized, but his plans for the publication reveal his major intellectual concerns in the early to mid-1940s. Wright envisioned a largely white, middle-class readership, for he believed that critical and original perspectives on racial ideology had to be articulated and translated to make them meaningful and urgent in the major public spheres of American life. Only in this way could Wright and his fellow writers convince others that the problems of minorities represented "phases of one over-all national cultural problem." The proposed project had everything to do with refuting conventional categorizations of race problems as

parochial concerns. The "magazine I have in mind would be a means of psycho-
analyzing the American middle class reader," rendering "him conscious of his false
illusions about race and 'subject peoples.' " Confident that the magazine could help
to revise "rigid tendencies in American thinking," Wright anticipated nothing less
than a "public cathartic agent," giving readers a "popular sense of the emotional cost,
among majorities and minorities alike, of living in America."[5]

In 1944, another project animated Wright's thinking and led to collaboration with
C. L. R. James, the Trinidadian Marxist thinker then living in the United States, the
sociologist E. Franklin Frazier, and others. Wright and his fellow writers envisioned
an anthology, "The Negro Speaks," based on the premise that African Americans
needed to struggle as African Americans, "as a preliminary step toward complete
integration into American life." This project had a somewhat different orientation,
as Wright meant for the anthology first and foremost to educate members of progressive and labor movements about dynamics and perspectives in African American life.
Alongside subjects such as "Class Consciousness vs. Race Consciousness," Wright
hoped to address themes including the contradictions that inhered in concepts such
as "racial writing." Like "American Pages," the anthology would proceed from a
"minority mood and point of view," yet it would urge "acceptance of the 'Negro'
point of view as a non-racial" one.[6] The insistence on a nonracial viewpoint indicated that Wright and his collaborators understood their work as a counterpoint not
only to race hierarchy, but to the pressures of racial categorization and ascription
generally.

Like "American Pages," "The Negro Speaks" never came to fruition. Yet if Wright's
projects failed to emerge as he envisioned them, they revealed themselves in other
ways, often in the work of friends and fellow writers similarly dedicated to psychological explorations of racial antagonisms. Although Wright lacked a single circle of
writers with whom he gathered, he nevertheless belonged to a network of like-
minded friends who pictured "American Pages" and "The Negro Speaks" transforming American cultural criticism and intellectual preoccupations. They shared an
abiding sense of the insufficiency of conventional formulations derived from political
economy for making sense of the volatile wartime moment. This led them to devote
more attention to the complex psychological ground of fascism and racial thinking.
During the war years, Himes, Cayton, Ellison, and James helped form Wright's
network, and their writings can be read in light of the aims and ambition of "American Pages" and "The Negro Speaks." Each was affected by Wright's work and explored problems of racial thinking in conversations with him. Like Wright, all four
refused to defer to parochial frameworks for the analysis of racial oppression.

Chester Himes and Wartime Race Thinking

"*Native Son* rocked the nation like a bomb, like the great revolutionary novel that it was," Chester Himes recalled. Wright had "opened the way" for a new generation of African American writers. The timing of this new period of creativity coincided with an important phase in Himes's biography. "Racism became a big problem for me in 1940, when I found that I was barred from most of the employment I could find. Segregation hadn't really affected me until then, but it became tangible."[7]

A short-story writer and novelist, Himes also wrote essays about race hierarchy in wartime America. His commentary, like much of his fiction, focused on the socially volcanic and personally debilitating power of racial sentiments and ideologies. Himes's wartime writings demonstrate that most of the psychological exploration of race hierarchy undertaken by writers did not take the form of an exclusive interest in the situations of African Americans. The range of racial meanings and practices that defined American life became his subject. Writing for periodicals such as *The Crisis, Common Ground,* and *The War Worker,* he described the predicaments faced by Mexican Americans, Japanese Americans, and African Americans and paused over the emotional power that accrued in whiteness as a cultural value. Significantly, he refused to characterize African American calls for justice in exclusively racial terms. He proclaimed in "Now Is the Time! Here Is the Place!" that African American freedom struggles were vital for the future of American democracy and thus "more than racial," for they had to do with an ideal that included a "form of government in which people will be bound together, neither by race, nor creed, nor descent, but by common objectives and aims for the benefit of all."[8]

Himes's essays urged readers to confront domestic racial ideologies and the psychological maladies they revealed. "Democracy Is for the Unafraid," which appeared in *Common Ground* in 1943, directed attention to the "psychoses of racial antagonisms." Rather than invoke the Negro Problem, he defined racial antagonism in terms of white supremacy, claiming that the fate of racist ideologies rested on how whites responded to the mounting sense, domestically and in many colonial situations, that minorities would no longer endure exploitation. He worried that the inevitable response would be driven by fear. The "growing weakness of the white race," evident in "its present fear-driven actions," suggested that "dictatorship may come to the United States before we know what true democracy is like."[9] Like Wright, Himes linked tendencies in American life to fascism in order to underscore the pervasive reliance on racial ideologies in everyday social life and to argue for remedies for the plights of minorities in advance of heightened racial antagonism.

Himes's observations about wartime anxieties followed from the premise that the affective and subjective power of racial ideologies had intrinsic importance, and he understood his work as expanding the domain of psychological explorations of race hierarchy beyond the Negro Problem and other frameworks that black writers increasingly discredited. "Certainly I would not attempt to offer a solution to the 'Negro Problem,'" Himes once wrote sardonically. His work moved away from the Negro Problem template, for it offered only "a tiny facet of the frustration inherent in the lives of present-day Americans, both black and white, and the compulsive behavior resulting therefrom." The concept of frustration had become an important social scientific category as a result of psychoanalytic sociologist John Dollard's arguments about the relationship of frustration to aggression. Himes's work appropriated the term to examine the subject of racial antagonism, including "racial-sexual conflict." For Himes, understanding race conflicts called for assessing the frustrations and emotional patterns that shaped personalities. This could mean that his writing elicited complaints for its lack of positive representations, a charge he answered when he wrote that as "long as this nation is what it is and its human products are what they are, then that is what I will write about, beautiful or not."[10] Himes elaborated on his approach to writing in "The Dilemma of the Negro Novelist in the United States," where he wrote that notions such as inferiority complexes, self-hate, and fear and hatred of oppressors were common to all exploited minorities. To the extent that the "sense of inferiority" and "fear and hate and self-hate" appeared in black experience, writers had an obligation to reflect upon and describe them. For him, African American writers, however varied their literary styles, had to confront the question, "How does the fear he feels as a Negro in white American society affect his [own] Negro personality?"[11]

In describing Lee Gordon, the protagonist of his 1948 novel *Lonely Crusade,* Himes wrote that he had created a figure governed by "many self-destructive forces—fear, insecurity, anti-Semitism, color psychosis," among other "psychological barriers."[12] Yet *Lonely Crusade* was not the first time Himes had treated self-destructive forces and the psychological conditions generated by oppression in his work. *If He Hollers Let Him Go* (1945) described the racial and gender codes faced by black workers in Los Angeles, focusing on the all-encompassing dread and fear that suffused the life of protagonist Robert Jones, both within and beyond his work in a wartime shipyard. The novel's powerful representation derives from a commitment to narrate both the sociological details of a wartime urban environment and the psychological pressures and affective dimensions of a setting thoroughly organized by race.[13]

If He Hollers Let Him Go contributed insights about national belonging and racial ideology by demonstrating the volatile wartime varieties of psychological disaffection and identification that Bob Jones alternately adopts and disavows in relation to

America. At the start of the novel, Jones claims that he is scarcely stirred by the passions surrounding the war, although this assertion is complicated by his own admission of wanting to "see the Japanese win."[14] Once inside the machinery of the war through his work at a plant, Jones feels included where he "had never felt included before." His identification expresses itself as a "wonderful feeling," a "feeling of my country." The first-person narration and careful tracking of Jones's mental fluctuations and fear-driven dreams make the freighted wartime setting the occasion for a meditation on the complex of emotions generated by the impulse toward national identification within a society organized by race. Jones's initial response to the war is to "never give a damn one way or another," which is to say, to minimize its significance so that it cannot have any bearing on his thoughts and emotions. But his position is already one of determined hostility, which gives way to a fantasy of American defeat through a romantic identification with an enemy that has morphed into an emblem of heroism. Himes delivers Jones's changing responses to the war in rapid succession, making it difficult to believe that any one of them is altogether banished. Each response indicates instead an orientation that may yet resurface. When Himes has Jones arriving at a "feeling of my country," he describes not fleeting or misguided sentiments but the very contradictory terrain of wartime life for African Americans. Jones's fluctuations provide ways of understanding both "the immensity of the production" and the personal mediations prompted by the war.

Through Himes's concern with identification and psychological dissonance in *If He Hollers Let Him Go,* the common sense of racial categorization becomes available for scrutiny. In select scenes, he brings wartime iterations of whiteness into relief, delivering a picture of whiteness as a psycho-historical process. When Jones gives a couple of teenage white sailors a lift in his car, he falls into an easygoing conversation about their shared sense of dislocation: the sailors are new to Los Angeles, and Jones himself hails from Ohio. The brief ride does not dissolve race hierarchy, but it does suspend racial antagonisms to the extent that Jones reflects on whiteness afterward: "I got a funny thought then; I began wondering when white people started getting white—or, rather, when they started losing it. And how it was you could take two white guys from the same place—one could carry his whiteness with him like a loaded stick, ready to bop everyone else in the head with it; and the other would just simply be white as if he didn't have anything to do with it and let it go at that. I liked those two white kids; they were white, but as my Aunt Fanny used to say they couldn't help that."[15]

Himes leavens with humor the novel's rendering of whiteness as something that entails activation, a process that involves contingencies personal and historical, producing real effects. The psychological character of the novel and its ability to bring the disturbing effects of wartime racism on Jones into sharp focus also allows Himes to describe whiteness in terms of emotional investments that unfold through uneven, yet potent, historical and social mechanisms. However, whiteness is not the only form of racial thinking Himes contemplates. In a memorable passage, Jones recalls Rike Oyana, a young Japanese American boy, "singing 'God Bless America' and going to Santa Anita with his parents the next day." The Japanese internment impresses on Jones the reach and complexity of the racial tensions of Los Angeles, another layer of fear, and a startling demonstration of how "taking a man up by the roots and locking him up without a chance" had become social practice. If the growing black-white antagonism within and beyond the shipyards is not enough to induce fear, the internment of Rike Oyana and his family "started me to getting scared." Jones has no doubt that " 'yeller-belied Jap' coulda meant me too."[16] Through a blend of literary expression and cultural interpretation, Himes firmly situates the Japanese internment within a narrative alert to the racial ideologies intensified by the war.[17]

For many critics, Wright included, *If He Hollers Let Him Go* represented a "sea of prose so blindingly intense that it all but hurts your eyes to read it."[18] According to Cayton the novel performed work similar to Wright's *Black Boy* in forthrightly presenting the "subjective reaction" of minorities to oppressive social conditions: "The courage of these two young writers to thus bare their inner landscape of fear and hate is something to be wondered at."[19] For Cayton, the novel "was in the nature of a psychic catharsis" because it brought forth the "enormity of the attack which the environment was making on the Negro personality." Cayton pointed to Wright and Himes, along with the sociological and psychoanalytic literatures he had encountered, as enabling him to "see America . . . with different eyes."[20] James Baldwin noted with approbation the "disturbing perception" Himes brought to his representations of racial conflicts and his ability to show the "enormous role which white guilt and tension play in what has been most accurately called the American dilemma."[21] The young Martinican psychiatrist Frantz Fanon introduced war plant worker Bob Jones, Himes's main character, to readers of his 1952 *Black Skin, White Masks* as a vivid illustration of the psychological patterns nurtured by racist social environments.[22]

After publishing *If He Hollers Let Him Go,* Himes applied for fellowships to travel to Europe. He believed the distance from America would benefit his craft and allow him to understand American life in more perceptive ways. "I want to go to Europe so that I may see America better," he wrote, citing the choices of none other than Wright: "In order to write clearly and convincingly of the South, the short story writer and novelist, Richard Wright, had first to live years in the North." Literary and cultural arbiter Carl Van Vechten supported Himes's proposed endeavors, commenting that if Himes was not "the greatest writer of fiction among contemporary American Negroes, at least there is none greater." Leonard Bloom, a sociology professor at the University of California at Los Angeles, called Himes "a serious student of human relations and a penetrating observer of the American scene." These words echoed those of novelist Jack Aistrop, who had written the introduction for the British edition of *If He Hollers Let Him Go,* and who compared Himes's capabilities as a writer to the " 'camera eye' and the 'recording brain' so necessary in the world today."[23] When *If He Hollers Let Him Go* was reprinted in the 1960s at the height of the black power movement, Himes commented that the novel "expressed feelings that black people had always known, things that were always kept quiet, but are today exploding into the American consciousness . . . But when it was written, even black people were shocked by what I wrote."[24]

Horace Cayton and the Search for Psychological Truths

"Something has happened to the world between the two wars and this has made the Negro not only a national problem but a global problem," wrote Horace Cayton.[25] A "lack of complete identification with the purposes and aims of the majority group" and an interrelated "tendency toward psychological identification with other non-white" peoples was the logical outcome of "deep-set emotional drives which have arisen out of the Negro's isolation."[26] Novels like *If He Hollers Let Him Go* brought the altered, wartime patterns of racial organization on the home front into representation, demonstrating the close spatial and social proximity of white and black workers prompted by the machinery of war in contradiction to traditional codes of race hierarchy. Even as the wartime movement of people and rapid transformation of industry carried with it racial tensions and violence, it also generated, in Cayton's words, a distinctive cultural-intellectual moment defined by an "upsurge in Negro thought." Cayton understood that moment not only as historically set apart but also as one with worldwide implications and connections. The international conflict brought colonized peoples onto the global stage, and African Americans linked their situations to those of nonwhite peoples throughout the world in ways Cayton considered unprecedented.[27]

In large measure through his readings of Richard Wright, Cayton gained confidence that black writers were venturing "a school of thought, a point of view, a philosophy," both "psychological and sociological," that could "penetrate the problem of race rather deeply." The complexities of "Negro" and "white" "wartime psychology" demanded approaches sensitive to mental conflicts and maladjustment. Cayton believed the timeliness of such interventions had to do not only with chang-

ing attitudes among minorities but also with contradictions and psychological dissonance among the majority of whites. The difficulty many had in "conceiv[ing] of the
same type of liberation for the American Negro that they are trying to obtain for the
European minorities" provided evidence of such dissonance. Some were determined
to keep African Americans in subordination while others took uncompromising
stands for an end to racist practices. The range of responses could be attributed to the
discordant collective mental state of thinking about race hierarchy.[28]

The son of a journalist, Cayton was born into a middle-class black family in
Seattle. Having studied sociology, he moved to Chicago in the early 1930s to participate in social scientific research conducted at the University of Chicago. It was there,
in sociologist Louis Wirth's office, that Cayton first met Wright. Not long afterward,
Cayton began research on the black political machine in Chicago's South Side and
eventually initiated a large-scale project with sociologist Lloyd Warner on the complex social world of the African American South Side. By 1939, Cayton's research was
so firmly rooted in the life of black Chicago that he was chosen to head a South Side
social and cultural center that later became the Parkway Community House.[29]

Throughout this period, Wright loomed large in Cayton's thinking. "About the
whole problem of psychoanalysis I would like to talk to you at length," Cayton wrote
to Wright, and indeed, conversations among the two revolved around racial ideologies, culture, and psychoanalysis.[30] For Cayton, Wright's great achievement had
to do with the legitimacy he gave to psychological exploration of race hierarchy and
racist social environments. Through imaginative skill and the "objectivity of the
social scientist," Wright had directed his talents toward topics and social spaces most
writers ignored.[31] Cayton had discovered in Wright a model of intellectual work he
deemed valid and urgent.

Cayton participated in the remaking of writing on race problems during the
1940s. His autobiographical reflections in "The Bitter Crop" (1948) underscore the
impact of psychoanalytic thinking on writers determined to develop new perspectives on the racist social order. "Psychoanalysis is probably the sharpest tool we have
for understanding people, for it gives insight not only to the cultural matrix in which
the personality is nurtured, but describes the emotional conflicts set up both by
personal and social problems," he wrote. Although he had first turned to the study of
human personality to "understand and better control my unruly emotions," psychoanalytic vocabularies soon began to furnish him with ways to revisit problems involving the psychological impact of the social codes and prohibitions of race hierarchy.[32]
Psychoanalysis and psychoanalytic inquiry provided Cayton the means of exploring
the interplay of culture and personality, moving interpretations of racial ideologies in
America beyond "mores, the folkways, [and] the patterns of segregation" to the realm

of "emotional conflicts." For Cayton, a "substratum of emotions covered by intellectual formulations" had to be exposed by writers willing to bring to the fore the psychological and ideological dynamics driving racial antagonisms and race hierarchy.[33]

In the mid-1940s, Cayton envisioned a collection of essays on the "folkways of race relations" and shared his thoughts on the project with Wright. What Cayton called a formidable "folklore of race relations" already embedded in American culture prevented the "careful, intellectual scrutiny" of racial thinking.[34] Cayton also envisioned writing an essay on Gunnar Myrdal's *An American Dilemma*. Like Wright, he had applauded the broad ramifications of Myrdal's focus on the conditions of African American life. Yet, because he found no real reckoning with the "psychological substructure" of African American life, especially African American leadership, Cayton believed Myrdal had produced a limited account of racial antagonism. Further analysis had to address areas the otherwise seminal work had explored inadequately.[35] Cayton attached practical implications to the reconfiguration of antiracist criticism along the lines of a "psychological substratum." A "deeper psychological understanding must be used, for we cannot . . . deal effectively with the problem if we refuse to allow ourselves to get insight into the fundamental conflict in human personalities which this social situation has produced," he claimed."[36] The literatures on racial hierarchy had yet to forthrightly attend to psychological questions; without definitive statements on the psychological factors shaping the racist social order, collective understandings of one of the central predicaments of American life could scarcely come into view.

Fear of the dominant society and resentment over the "terrorizing" nature of racial codes engendered what Cayton called a "fear-hate complex" in African Americans. Recognizing these patterns was a pivotal step in discovering "constructive channels through which they can be discharged."[37] The notion that the complexes brought to life by the racist social order could be discharged led Cayton to think, more and more, about the subject of mental health. Like Wright, he sought out experts who shared his view of the potentially transformative political implications of persuasive analyses of the emotional dynamics that helped propel race hierarchy. Psychiatrist Helen V. McLean, in "The Emotional Health of Negroes," presented emotional health as a category that helped demonstrate the malevolent effects of racism. McLean cited "self hate" resulting primarily from fear of the dominant society.[38] Cayton expanded on this concept to argue that "at the core of the Negro's mentality there is a fear-hate-fear complex." Although fear and anxiety were features of everyday experience in highly complex societies, in "the Negro the psychological problem is intensified," often taking the form of resentment and hatred toward members of the dominant social group, Cayton argued.[39]

Cayton came to know McLean well, acknowledging in his autobiography that he underwent psychotherapy with her during the 1940s.[40] McLean, a member of the Chicago Institute of Psychoanalysis, worked in the "field of racial conflict" and participated in the Race Relations Institutes organized by sociologist Charles S. Johnson at Fisk University. She believed her psychoanalytic background equipped her to provide social scientists with information and public guidance regarding the "unconscious irrational factors which can, in spite of the best laid rational schemes, upset any program for racial cooperation." She speculated that African Americans were by and large mentally healthy, but that much African American life involved widespread anxiety deriving from adaptations to fear, as well as from the process of erecting a "façade of passive acquiescence" in the face of discriminatory practices. McLean's assessments also looked beyond African American life, as when she declared that too "many white people working for better race relations have a latent belief in their own white superiority," which often created vacillation between an exaggerated evaluation of African Americans and a "disillusioned, contemptuous one." Perhaps the central assumption of McLean's work in racial conflict was the difficulty of freeing oneself from "socially acquired attitudes about race." But that difficulty did not lead her to conclude that such a process was impossible.[41]

Significantly, McLean did not see research in race relations, psychological or otherwise, as undoing racial conflict. She held that the facts of job and housing discrimination and other fundamental economic and social problems had to be altered before psychological insights could be used in meaningful and lasting ways.[42] Yet psychological research could play a pivotal role in challenging the popular beliefs that sustained racial discrimination. McLean regarded Wright's work as an encouraging sign of movement in this direction.[43] Indeed, her own thinking was marked by her familiarity with his work. Wright gave an informal talk at the Chicago Institute of Psychoanalysis, elaborating on themes of fear and reactive hostility he had developed in *Native Son*. From his commentary, McLean surmised in an essay titled "Racial Prejudice" that fear is "probably the predominating feeling of any persecuted minority toward the strong dominating group." Cayton had brought McLean's work to Wright's attention, and several of her essays can be found among Wright's papers, suggesting that he, too, drew from her ideas.

Entering psychiatric treatment gave Cayton an appreciation for the insights that could be acquired through psychological exploration. Cayton regarded his role as analysand as, on the one hand, personal in nature but, on the other hand, part of larger intellectual terrain that attracted antiracist writers of his time. Undergoing analysis was nothing like the representations one found of the experience "in the movies [or] the slick magazines," he remembered.[44] Cayton's work represented an effort to reinvent the study of the racist social order, making it sensitive to the emotional hazards and dynamics that marked the effects of race hierarchy. Like Wright, he considered institutional interactions with psychoanalysis highly relevant to the intellectual reconstitution of antiracism.

Although Cayton never completed the book he tentatively called "The Folklore of Race Relations," he did complete a component of the work, which later appeared in essay form as "The Psychological Approach to Race Relations." Stressing the aggression and psychological vulnerability of war, Cayton began with the premise of a "close analogy between Negroes living in America and a soldier under battle conditions." The analogy allowed Cayton to characterize race hierarchy as a crisis requiring national attention and large-scale measures, for the condition of the returning soldier had led to a range of studies of combat neuroses undertaken by psychological experts working within military and government agencies. Cayton made the case for adapting studies of the combat soldier for the specific purpose of interpreting "situations in civilian life where men exist under great stress, tension and fear." The "Negro has had to learn, like the war-hardened veteran, to adapt himself to fear in order to survive." What he sometimes called an "oppression psychosis" arose from African Americans' fear for themselves and their group in a racially stratified social order. Cayton insisted on the socially and environmentally produced character of this "psychosis," which involved "all those barbs, indignities, heartaches, and the thousand shocks that black flesh is heir to," while also emphasizing the individual psychological consequences of such patterns and effects.[45] Just as battle led to discernible conditions in soldiers, so did the everyday circumstances of segregation and race hierarchy entangle African Americans in psychological patterns that required skillful exploration and meaningful national consideration.

In Cayton's estimation, the study of the effects of race hierarchy on African Americans formed part of a complex and overarching topic: the "feeling in our culture about race." Exploring this larger topic meant thinking about the beliefs and behavior of both whites and blacks and, not least, the mechanisms both employed to "avoid arriving at any sort of emotional maturity." At times Cayton put forth arguments that focused on the compensatory effects of the racial codes for whites. "If our industrial American society has robbed white men of both their dignity and their economic, emotional and social security, some relief from this deprivation can be found in acting like Gods in attempting to control the fate of Negroes." Cayton presented frightened and emotionally distraught people, "casualties of our industrial civilization [who] turn to the Negro to find an object for their frustrated hate and love." Concentrating on psychological fissures in whites in relation to racial ideology could provide a means of identifying and making sense of the "feeling in our culture about race." Cayton referred to culture not as ethnic or racial particularity but more generally as a way of life. This definition of culture informed his view that the American "failure to achieve a mature culture in which Negroes and whites alike can accomplish some aspect of personality integration has within it the seeds of political fascism."[46]

Parsing ideological conceits regarding race in American life meant thinking about culture as a whole. The cultural underpinnings of the racial ordering of everyday life implicated everyone, and all people concerned with the "preservation of the human personality" bore a responsibility to become knowledgeable about race hierarchy's many dimensions. Such work amounted to a prerequisite for making "ourselves effective agents for social change." Cayton believed unambiguously that the psychological dimensions of racial ideology and racist practices encompassed the psychological defects exhibited by whites within a social order that insisted on racial hierarchy: "White people, too, are anxious in their dealings with colored people. They, too, are fear-ridden."[47] Prior to the *Brown v. Board of Education* decision, psychological patterns evident in the bearers of racist attitudes constituted an important part of the overall complex of race problems. After *Brown,* questions related to feelings of black inferiority arguably began to replace the wider range of subjects that had earlier represented valid areas of exploration in the study of race hierarchy.

If the concept of culture figured in Cayton's stated aim of making sense of the "feeling in our culture about race," it also signaled a move away from approaches dependent on static figures of racial victimization and racist behavior. Racial tensions and antagonisms belonged to the "psychological sub-strata of emotion and thought in white and Negro people alike which arise out of the contradictions in our culture and the frustration that confounds when we attempt to deal with the problem."[48] As the following section shows, Ralph Ellison's wartime writing paralleled that of Cayton in its commitment to the concept of culture.

Ellison and the Sea of Irrationality

Connected to the world of the Communist Party and familiar with psychological literatures, Ralph Ellison was perplexed by debates that raged around him in the late 1930s and early 1940s. In these debates either "Marx was raised up and Freud put down, or Freud raised up and Marx put down."[49] He recalled that in attempting to gain his intellectual bearings, he felt fortunate that he could "discuss such matters with Richard Wright." Ellison had commented publicly on *Native Son* in "Richard Wright and Recent Negro Fiction," arguing that the novel represented a break with previous literary work by African Americans and praising the book as fiction "more full of the stuff of America" than most literary ventures. Where African American writers had generally "avoided psychology" and thus circumvented the "deeper problems arising out of the relationship of the Negro group to the American whole," Wright's work refused any such evasion. Wright moved beyond what Ellison considered the narrowly racial and nationalistic orientations of much African American writing by presenting a literary practice that disclosed complex truths and rebuffed "political and cultural segregation."[50]

Wright encouraged Ellison's attempts at literary and cultural criticism. Indeed, Ellison's first published piece, a review of Walter Edward Turpin's novel, *These Low Grounds*, in 1937, came about through Wright's encouragement.[51] The review emphasized the "closer examination of consciousness" that novelists needed to make central to contemporary writing. In this insistence, Ellison's budding critical voice replicated Wright's conviction that the area of inquiry most in need of artistic development was the representation of consciousness. Ellison found Wright's literary and intellectual example indispensable in a world plagued by fascism and war: the difficulty of the times required that emotions "be observed in their nakedness."[52] Ellison appreciated that Wright, though a member of the Communist Party, had interests in cultural life and literary theory "not limited to areas prescribed by the party line." Becoming "very curious about how one could put Marx and Freud together," Ellison felt validated in his intellectual dispositions when discussing the subject with Wright.[53] Both Ellison and Wright put forth claims about race hierarchy designed to reinvent American cultural criticism. For Ellison, such reinvention had everything to do with creating a criticism informed by readings of literature and culture alert to the "irrationalities" bequeathed by history.

Like Wright and other antiracist writers, Ellison often placed the "Negro Problem" in scare quotes, casting suspicion on one of the dominant phrases of the period. From the vantage point of what Ellison called the "race problem in our culture," the discursive universe of the Negro Problem resembled a "sea of irrationality," something to be shunned in favor of superior understanding and valid analytical angles on race. Moving toward such understanding involved working with psychoanalytic concepts, often converting them into an idiom compatible with cultural commentary. A "nation of ethical schizophrenics," Ellison wrote, had produced an intellectual environment that made it impossible to broach race hierarchy and racial thinking with directness. The Negro Problem filled the vacuum where forthright discussion belonged, but in the end it was little more than a label for a "guilt problem charged with pain."[54] The war had brought about an intense period of "self-evaluation" for African Americans, Ellison stated in *Negro Quarterly* in 1943.[55] His work in this short-lived journal indicated the ways he hoped to both comment upon and direct antiracist writing.

Ellison believed African American writers had special responsibilities, perhaps most significantly to attend to the "psychological attitudes and incipient forms of action which the black masses reveal in their emotion-charged myths, symbols, and wartime folklore." The zoot suit, Lindy Hop, and other cultural forms, far from arbitrary styles of expression, revealed "complexities of the Negro situation," codes through which to access the workings of racial ideology and race hierarchy. Conceptual frames that weighed the meanings of cultural expression, broad social trends, and psychological attitudes promised information on the volatile and "racial" character of the wartime American scene, but such frames demanded much work and innovation. "When concepts, techniques and theories do not exist," African American writers had to "create them." More so than Cayton and Himes, Ellison stressed the importance of reading cultural forms to gain purchase on the psychological dimensions of the racist social order, yet he shared with Wright and the others a desire to dispense with intellectual habits that failed to provide avenues into the "race problem in our culture."[56]

Ellison began to develop his views on American culture at the time categories such as *schizophrenia* and words such as *irrational* increasingly entered popular social and intellectual life through the cultural authority ascribed to psychological, especially psychoanalytic, thought. The newly available vocabulary promised alternative lines of inquiry into race problems and simultaneously pointed to the inadequacy of established vocabularies and frameworks. Critical of African Americans who advocated participation in World War II while ignoring domestic discrimination, Ellison wrote that behind such an "attitude lies a fear and uncertainty that is almost psychopathic." In *Negro Quarterly,* he described the range of views on the war he gleaned within African American life, noting that they included both unqualified acceptance and unqualified rejection of African American participation, and employed psychoanalytic terms to parse the limitations of the different perspectives.[57] For all his criticism of African American entry into the war, Ellison also had problems with those completely opposed to African American involvement. The difficulty with such wholesale rejection was that it did not "recognize that Negroes *have their own stake in the defeat of fascism.*" "Unconsciously," such a categorical position was adopted by those who regarded "all acts of aggression against Negroes as inevitable, the forces behind those acts as invincible." The comparative thinking afforded by considering the history of fascism provided Ellison with ways to assess the specificities of U.S. race hierarchy. The total rejection of a war against fascism made little sense to Ellison in light of the history of fascists in Europe who had "made the manipulation of myth and symbol a vital part of their political technology." In turn, he connected that history to the ways in which the "Southern ruling class" had acquired skills in "psychology and ideological manipulation" for the maintenance of racial codes.[58]

In 1945, Wright's *Black Boy* inspired Ellison to write "Richard Wright's Blues," where he argued that the book drew on insights from Marx and Freud. If Wright's book was generally understood as a psychological exploration, Ellison's commentary interpreted the book in unmistakably cultural-psychological terms. He began by arguing that the South of Wright's childhood offered only three ways for African Americans to respond to the sociopolitical conditions they encountered. They could subscribe to the roles imposed by the dominant social order around them, perhaps assuaging the concomitant conflicts of such a decision through the "emotional catharsis of Negro religion." A middle way, the search for respectability, entailed repression of anger about Jim Crow. Finally, electing to "reject the situation, adopt a criminal attitude, and carry on an unceasing psychological scrimmage with the whites" carried penalties of violence or worse.[59] This mix of psychological and cultural interpretation came to define Ellison's growing body of criticism and the forms of analysis and description he considered vital to antiracist writing.

The psychoanalytic notion of the defense mechanism proved especially important in Ellison's thinking. In its classical Freudian formulation, the defense mechanism involves unconscious mental processes that protect the ego or conscious mind from conflict. In Ellison's hands the term became a way to reference social conflicts in general and racial antagonisms in particular, even as it continued to carry connotations of unconscious behavior. In his view, racism and racial structures gave rise to defense mechanisms in African Americans that provided protection from "those forces *within himself* which might urge him to reach out for the social and human equality which the white South says he cannot have." For an African American child who did not find ways to rebel against racist social arrangements, as Ellison claimed Wright had done, the result could be "masochistic submissiveness and the denial of the impulse toward Western culture when it stirred in him."[60] Psychological patterns that separated individuals from their own impulses only served to entrench feelings of hostility. For Ellison, confronting the racist social order required a vocabulary capable of clarifying the powerful psychological consequences of race hierarchy. He thus meant his own psychological descriptions to reveal in persuasive narrative terms the historical and social repercussions of "race."

Psychological inquiry and description in Ellison's writing served humanistic ends.

"Twentieth-Century Fiction and the Black Mask of Humanity," written in 1946 but published in 1953, includes some of his clearest statements on psychology, literature, and American culture and offers information about his aims as a writer in the 1940s. The essay explored American writing as a "struggle over the nature of reality"—a formulation Ellison attributed to Wright—undertaken by whites and blacks. Starting with the distance between whites and African Americans, a distance "not so much spatial as psychological," Ellison examined distorted forms of humanity in representations of African Americans in twentieth-century literature. In lieu of a quantitative examination of dehumanized images or a charting of the racial attitudes of white writers, Ellison organized the essay around the *quality* of the images, a sense of "what they truly represent, both in the literary work and in the inner world of the white American." In a blend of literary analysis and cultural history, Ellison held that the inability in American writing to conceive of black life in terms of the "full, complex ambiguity of the human" indicated a "projection of processes lying at the very root of American culture."[61] Such processes did not represent ancillary aspects of race hierarchy but instead provided the basis for the naturalization of racial thinking. Increasingly throughout the 1940s, Ellison regarded mental projections and psychological investments as basic to the emergence and workings of the racist social order. The "Negro stereotype is really an image of the unorganized, irrational forces of American life, forces through which, by projecting them in forms of images of an easily dominated minority, the white individual seeks to be at home in the vast unknown world of America," he argued.[62]

The model of criticism Ellison advocated involved examining the "processes molding the attitudes, the habits of mind, the cultural atmosphere," and the "artistic and intellectual traditions that condition[ed] men dedicated to democracy to practice, accept and, most crucial of all, often blind themselves to the essentially undemocratic treatment of their fellow citizens." Images of African American life in literature did not merely exist as sociological facts, for stereotypes worked in expressly psychological ways. For Ellison, adherence to racist ideologies and practices derived "from an internal psychological state; not from misinformation alone, but from an inner need to believe."[63]

Although the conditions of African Americans could scarcely be understood absent consideration of domination and the "stigma of color," Ellison speculated that the "object of the stereotype is not so much to crush the Negro as to console the white man." In "Twentieth-Century Fiction," Ellison finally suggests the possibility of an ethical route beyond the emotional needs of dehumanized imagery and the psychological distance mandated by racial thinking. Indeed, the idea of American writing as an experimental "ethical instrument" ran parallel to his understanding of the malleability of personalities and cultures—an orientation associated with mid-century psychological research and expertise. The path to American writing as an ethical instrument had everything to do with attentiveness to psychological dynamics, to "psychology and symbolic ritual."[64]

Perhaps Ellison's most significant wartime reflection on the antiracist turn to psychological inquiry came when he sat down to review Myrdal's *An American Dilemma* in 1944.[65] His evaluation captured a moment of transition in which the frame of the Negro Problem gave way to a broad rethinking of race problems. Amid the general approbation garnered by Myrdal, Ellison delivered a complex reading of the value and limits of the study. Ellison considered Myrdal's focus on contradictions between professed ideals and racist practices salutary, for the "inheritance of the American dilemma" stood as a barrier to democracy and affected all the political cultures in the nation, not least that of liberal and left organizations. Myrdal demonstrated decisively that the dilemma was part of the "very tissue of American thinking." Ellison believed that Myrdal's study carried special relevance for the Left because Marxist frameworks, for all their contributions, had mistakenly minimized the "moral problem centering upon the Negro." By insisting on a problem of national proportions that crossed political affiliations, Myrdal had told a story that revealed lacunae in the thinking of left-liberal groups. According to Ellison, he had "done the Left a service in pointing out that there is a psychological problem which, in this country, requires special attention." By drawing attention to "those points where economic and psychological pressures conflicted," Myrdal had identified an entire moral and political space where activists and intellectuals had not trained their energy and skills. For Ellison, the foremost virtue of *An American Dilemma* was that it showed that the "mechanism of prejudice operates to disguise the moral conflict in the minds of whites produced by the clash on the social level between the American Creed and anti-Negro practices."[66] Several of Ellison's essays carry formulations that mirror that central contention of *An American Dilemma,* as when he argues that "myths of racial superiority and inferiority" in American life set in motion "endless sacrificial rites and moral evasions." In the process of erecting these myths, "race became a major cause, form and symbol of the American hierarchical psychosis."[67]

The essay on *An American Dilemma* was striking not least because Ellison imagines cultural commentary on race hierarchy soon surpassing the form put forth by Myrdal. Although Ellison by and large accepted Myrdal's sociopsychological characterization of the dissonance caused in whites by racist ideology, he disagrees with Myrdal's unbending psychology of victimization in descriptions of African American life.[68] In Ellison's view, *An American Dilemma* marked a dramatic but flawed starting point for further investigation: it would "take a deeper science than Myrdal's to analyze what is happening among the masses of Negroes." Perhaps most interesting among the criticisms presented in the essay is Ellison's suggestion that Myrdal at times endowed the concept of race with undeserved explanatory power. Scholars and writers had for too long circumvented the difficult work of interpreting African American social and cultural life by "clinging, as does Myrdal, to the sterile concept of 'race.' "[69] In criticizing Myrdal's uses of race, Ellison pointed to an increasingly prominent feature of midcentury antiracist writing, namely the insistence on analyzing the mystifying nature of the race concept by examining the emotional needs met, and social relationships sustained, through the powerful and seemingly incontrovertible meanings it had acquired. Ellison advocated literary and intellectual work on the power of race thinking on American culture, but he argued that such efforts would only be valuable if not impeded by the tendency to give the concept of race an unexamined explanatory force.

If the concern with "race relations" evinced in Myrdal's study brought out Ellison's skepticism, so too did popular cultural forms that treated racial antagonism. He displayed this contrarian perspective when he wrote about a set of films released in 1949–50. The film cycle that included *Home of the Brave, Intruder in the Dust, Lost Boundaries, Pinky,* and *No Way Out* was the first explicitly produced to depict the effects of racism on African Americans and whites. In *Home of the Brave* an Army psychiatrist treats an African American soldier whose wartime trauma turns out to predate the war and originate in the inferiority complexes created in social environments of his youth and upbringing. In "The Shadow and the Act," published in *The Reporter* in 1949, Ellison delivered a subtle and complex rejoinder to the first four films (*No Way Out* had not appeared). He understood the cycle of "message movies" on "anti-Negro prejudice" as an important, if contradictory, development: "Despite the absurdities with which these films are laden, they are all worth seeing, and if seen, capable of involving us emotionally."[70] For Ellison, the films held an intrinsic interest because of their break with racist Hollywood representation and the broader changes in American life he believed they intimated.

Following literary and cultural theorist Kenneth Burke, Ellison considered films and other narratives as "forms" offering clues about the "psychology of the audience." Ellison was drawn to the complex meanings of the cycle, deciding finally that the films "all display a vitality which escapes their slickest devices" because of their capacity to address "deep centers of American emotion." He claimed that antiblack images in film, beginning with *The Birth of a Nation* (1915), "were (and are) acceptable because of the insistence throughout the United States of an audience obsessed with an inner psychological need to view Negroes as less than men." These dynamics provided many of the "justifications for all those acts, legal, emotional, economic and political, which we label Jim Crow." This film cycle represented something different, Ellison acknowledged, even as he noted facile narrative resolutions that limited the impact of the stories. In *Home of the Brave*, "repeating again that the Negro is like everybody else," the psychiatrist produces a cure, but only by directing the "audience's attention away from reality to focus it upon false issues." For all the psychological acuteness with which the filmmakers aimed to depict the effects of racism, *Home of the Brave* failed to pose "the question of whether Negroes can rightfully be expected to risk their lives in an army in which they are slandered and discriminated against."[71]

The long-term relationship of intellectual affinity between Ellison and Burke began with a meditation on psychology, fascism, and race thinking. In 1936, Ellison had attended a lecture titled "The Rhetoric of Hitler's 'Battle,'" in which Burke analyzed *Mein Kampf*.[72] The lecture impressed Ellison in large part because of the premium Burke placed on psychological analysis, for the very choice to read rather than simply denounce *Mein Kampf* reflected a critical temperament willing to cull valuable information about cultural and psychological patterns obtaining in Europe. Writers inflicting a "few symbolic wounds" on the book were "contributing more to our gratification than to our enlightenment," Burke argued. There were good reasons to reject such gratification and explore in greater depth Hitler's paths toward his ideas: understanding the "medicine" he created was a step toward knowing with more accuracy "exactly what to guard against, if we are to forestall the concocting of a similar medicine in America." Burke identified in Hitler's work a projection device wherein the "ability to hand over one's ills to a scapegoat" made possible a curative process that promised "purification by disassociation."[73] Coupled with the ideology of race superiority, the scapegoat created a complete worldview. The fissures in Hitler's writing were as important as the words he wrote, and Burke's effort involved exploring how the concept of race was invoked to smooth over analytical failures. The interpretation of economic ills led to an obsessive search for their "true" cause, a turn of attention which, in Hitler's scheme, relentlessly gave rise to assertions about "race."

In veering away from the economic and political frames of the Communist Party, Ellison may well have had Burke's psychological reading of *Mein Kampf* and Nazi Germany in mind. Burke's writing animated in Ellison a rethinking of Marxist social thought and aesthetics, as well as a tendency toward the exploration of questions of a psychological and cultural character.[74] Burke had speculated that Hitler's worldview met genuine needs: "Did not much of his lure derive, once more, from the bad filling of a good need?" Wright would later develop a similar line of argument in his introduction to *Black Metropolis,* where he compared the conditions and social aspirations of the masses in Nazi Germany to those of dispossessed blacks in urban America. Burke's analysis made possible more precise understandings of psychological and ideological patterns and, correspondingly, made historical dynamics and cultural problems available for more nuanced exploration. In much the same way that Burke proposed exploring "*case histories* of fascism," Wright, Ellison, and other antiracist writers devoted much of their energy to making the psychological dimensions of racial antagonism in America the basis for renewed cultural and historical investigation.[75]

Ellison and Burke both extended the notion of irrationality beyond the constellation of individual mental aberration, for the term implicated all manner of human endeavor.[76] Ellison explored the irrationalities of race in his cultural commentary and literary works. Much like *ambiguity, irrationality* was a key term for him as he established his credentials as a cultural critic. Through his criticism, Ellison brought the analytic utility of irrationality directly into the discussion of racial ideology, suggesting along the way that the work of human rescue or "salvation" that Burke had identified in Freudian thought had much to do with the challenge of racial ideology and race hierarchy and their attendant irrationalities. He therefore claimed, rather matter-of-factly, that the "problem of the irrational, that blind spot in our knowledge of society where Marx cries out for Freud and Freud for Marx, but where approaching, both grow wary and shout insults lest they actually meet, has taken the form of the Negro problem."[77] Burke's criticism combined socialist theory and a psychoanalytic approach to literary and cultural artifacts. The comprehensiveness of Freud's formulations meant that even a "man who had been wholly bewildered by the 'irrationality' of his conduct was given a scheme of motivations which promptly brought him back into the realm of 'logic.' "[78] Burke valued Freudian thought because, by way of "therapeutics of suggestion" and "perspective by incongruity," new questions could be brought to bear on longstanding patterns of thought and behavior. This rendering of psychoanalytic thought led Burke to conclude that Freud's investigations represented a secular reconstitution of the "matter of human rescue."[79] For Ellison, Burke's Freudianism brought human rescue and the investigation of forms of irrationality squarely within the purview of the cultural critic.

Ellison's 1945 "Working Notes for *Invisible Man*" offers a glimpse of his creative process and thinking. He wrote explicitly about the meanings he ascribed to invisibility, but the concept as his protagonist came to understand it derived from two sources: "the racial conditioning which often makes the white American interpret cultural, physical or psychological differences as signs of racial inferiority" and "the great formlessness of Negro life wherein all values are in flux." His working notes establish his starting point for the novel: the "tempo of development from the feudal-folk forms of the South to the industrial urban forms of the North is so rapid that it throws up personalities as fluid and changeable as molten metal rendered iridescent from the effect of cooling air."[80] Ellison conceived of psychological differences in the African American setting as the results of social and cultural formation. To identify and focus consistently on psychological differentiation provided a way to think beyond the logic of "racial inferiority" and reject prevailing forms of "racial conditioning." Because the dominant society regarded African Americans under the sign of racial inferiority, the challenge of presenting African American social worlds in terms of specific historical, cultural, and psychological patterns proved daunting, Ellison claimed. The vast investment in racist ideologies made much of African American life invisible and such basic racial conditioning served as the impetus for the major themes and plot lines of his novel.

The importance of questioning the Negro Problem as a framing mechanism, so much a part of Wright's thinking, figured in Ellison's notes as well, for at the center of his narrative was a protagonist surrounded by whites who seldom looked "past the abstraction 'Negro' to the specific 'man.'" His hero lives within the "tight framework" that the term *Negro* affords, and for much of the story he tragically "blinds himself to all those factors of reality which reveal the essential inadequacy of such a scheme for the full development of personality."[81] Ellison's notes designate the effects of race thinking on personality formation as his central thematic concern as he prepared an outline of the novel. Although these working notes were not published until the end of the twentieth century, they reveal, along with his other writings from the 1940s, the extent to which the reencounter with race hierarchy via psychological inquiry—irrationalities and ambiguities—featured in his cultural imagination. In this way, Ellison's novel bears the marks of a theoretical reorientation in the interpretation of racial antagonisms, one that animated and helped to define Ellison's relationship to Wright and Burke and that prepared the ground for his own literary achievement.

In the 1950s, when *Invisible Man* catapulted him to literary prominence, Ellison continued to stress how pivotal the effort to rethink race had been to his ambitions as a writer. Language, he argued, is "most alive when it is capable of dealing with the realities in which it operates," and when the writer sets out to triumph over the "domain of the unstated, the undefined" even in the everyday. As Ellison saw it, African Americans were inextricably part of the social and cultural patterns that defined all Americans. One important difference, however, was that they had "no reason to assume that race has a positive value" and thus rejected "race thinking wherever [they found] it." Read retrospectively, Ellison's observations indicate how thoroughly he participated in rethinking approaches to race hierarchy and racial ideology, and how much the investigation of the mystifying qualities of the concept of race figured in that rethinking. Ellison linked his own intellectual work and African American history to strategies that challenged what he called "those savageries which for centuries have been committed in the name of race."[82]

In his 1971 lecture "Remembering Richard Wright," Ellison described his intellectual debts to Wright. The two had met in New York in 1936. Wright's work accelerated Ellison's interest in modern writing and African American literary efforts in particular. Conversations with Wright and short writing assignments Wright asked Ellison to produce for *New Challenge,* a magazine Wright was then editing, led to the first stirrings of a life in writing. He recalled that the psychological and therapeutic concerns that became the "driving passion of Richard Wright" informed his insistence that "this country recognize the interconnections between its places and personalities, its act and its ideals." In "talking with Wright," Ellison added, "my plans and goals were altered—were, in fact, fatefully modified by Wright's."[83]

C. L. R. James and American Civilization's Race Question

A Trinidadian, the cultural critic, historian and essayist C. L. R. James lived in the United States from 1938 to 1953. Prior to his arrival in America he had been involved in demanding political activity in England and had already produced a large body of writing, including *The Black Jacobins* (1938), a history of Toussaint L'Ouverture and the Haitian revolution. Involved in intricate Marxist debates and internecine conflicts over the efficacy of different forms of socialist organizing, James also wrote about the America he encountered during his residence. His years in America would be among "the most important years in my life," even "the high water mark," he wrote.[84] Although largely unnoticed by readers during the 1940s, the publication in the late twentieth century of his reflections on American and African American subjects renewed interest in his corpus.[85] James's materialism never abated, but his writings on America anticipated forms of cultural studies that emerged in the second half of the twentieth century. Key to James's cultural studies avant la lettre was his attention to the psychological strains of modernity and the acute ways they emerged in the United States.

Of the books James encountered during his time in the United States, Wright's *Native Son* most clearly augured cultural and social transformation. In a 1940 pamphlet, "My Friends: A Fireside Chat on the War by Native Son," James parodied Franklin Delano Roosevelt's fireside chats, giving a Bigger Thomas–like protagonist, and, by implication, African America, the venerable task of commenting on the state of the union in lieu of the president. The title, "My Friends," references Roosevelt's habitual greeting, intended to put his listeners at ease, but the subtitle subverts the sense of calm, for the subject matter has been limited to the war. "Native Son" not only replaces executive authority but subjects that authority to his own questions: "My friends, why does the president want us to fight?" and later, "Tell me, Mr. President, what democracy do I defend by going to fight Hitler?" The claim to a fireside chat doubles as a claim on America as Native Son declares himself "as American as any white man in this country." An alternative to liberal views on racial conflict, James's fireside chat offered a rejoinder to political moves that would merely incorporate African Americans into the war effort. James's Native Son participated in the last war, was mistreated on his return, and was not willing to be "played again." Yet Native Son is not working solely on behalf of African Americans when he rejects entry into the Second World War, for African American suffering is part of a larger crisis that includes dispossessed whites, such as those depicted in John Ford's 1940 film adaptation of John Steinbeck's *The Grapes of Wrath*, who were "miserable and suffering almost as much as we Negroes suffer."[86]

In the early-to-mid 1940s, James and Wright met to discuss African American life, American culture, and the modern world more generally. James's confidence that his time in America was sharpening his ability to assess the cultural, social, and economic transformations of the modern world was buoyed when he met Wright. Indeed, he was effusive about their first meeting, in 1944, for he had "wanted to talk to him more than anyone else in America (political and literary) because from his books I felt that he understood the Negro question." Reading Wright confirmed for James that "neither white America *nor black America* had faced the Negro question for the deep fundamental things that it is in the life of *the nation as a whole*."[87] James shared with Wright the view that the Negro question required, in part, a psychological characterization. They agreed, too, that African Americans were a force in society "out of all proportion to their numbers," and that such potential derived from repression and frustration that "when socially motivated will become one of the most powerful social forces in the country." The "wonderful meeting" with Wright heightened James's feeling that "we are now on the eve, historically speaking, of a complete realisation of the purpose, meaning and potentialities of human existence." James believed Americans in the middle decades of the twentieth century faced a "terrible struggle for self-expression, self-realisation" that took place on a psychological plane: "in reality it is very intimate, affecting personal lives, sex relations of the most intimate kind, the development of personality; as Wright and I talked to-nite."[88] Wright's achievement involved an artistic exploration of this plane. For James, then, Wright brought race hierarchy to the fore of cultural representation and commentary but also addressed changes in the consciousness of Americans generally, offering up pictures of the personality formation and cultural negotiations that followed from the "struggle for self-expression [and] self-realisation."

James defended *Native Son* when critics charged that Bigger Thomas provided no entry point into typical African American life and that the novel put forth distorted pictures. James called Wright's book one of the most powerful novels of the last twenty-five years, distinct in its ability to make it clear that "it is the American social order that is on trial." James found the concern with typicality strangely inappropriate: "What is a 'typical' Negro? 'Typical' of what?" Wright's artistic vision transcended questions of typicality to convey, albeit in particularly intense and even gruesome forms, feelings and patterns that pervaded African American life. James went so far as to argue that the majority of African Americans felt as Bigger did in their hatred of the dominant society "but have learnt to suppress it." For him, the significance of the success of the novel could not be overestimated: *Native Son* carried immense political meaning by bringing a "nationally oppressed minority to the notice of the oppressing majority."[89]

For James, the 1940s had seen a "tremendous battle for the minds of the Negro people and for the minds of the population of the US as a whole over the Negro question." The struggle of African Americans "had a vitality and validity of its own" that had to do with its "deep historic roots in the past of America and in present struggles." The significance of the decade was exemplified in writings by Wright, Lillian Smith, Chester Himes, and others who decisively demonstrated that the "Negro question" could no longer be construed as "merely a class question," even as the story of African Americans in the twentieth century could not be dissociated from the general "decay of capitalism on a world scale."[90] The themes in Wright's work expressed the need to probe not only the independent validity of African American life but also the specificity of race hierarchy and racial ideologies.

James read Wright and Himes as commentators on all of American life. To be sure, he believed that after reading Wright and Himes, the proverbial Negro problem could no longer be construed exclusively in terms of legal and physical limitations, for all African American "intellectual and emotional life" had been placed on the cultural agenda. But if Wright and Himes had played especially important roles in transforming understandings of African American life, their observations finally provided ways of reenvisioning American culture. They presented the "intolerable psychological burdens" of race hierarchy as a fundamental part of the "intolerable strains and stresses to which the whole nation is subjected amidst contradictions within the social totality." Whereas many were prepared to read Wright and Himes only in terms of African American life, James found in their books fresh angles on

American cultural formation as such. The "twisted bitterness of the Negro people is an index of the suppressed angers which permeate the vast majority of the nation," he wrote.[91] James arrived at the conclusion that the race question in America had to be approached from two main perspectives: physical facts and psychological character. That conclusion informs the interpretations he put forth in *American Civilization,* his monumental, posthumously published, study of American history. Written hurriedly in 1949–1950, just prior to James's deportation, this book envisions renovations toward a renewed Marxist politics alive to the social and the subjective.[92]

Like Wright, Ellison, and Cayton, James considered psychoanalysis one of the great scientific discoveries of the century, "an integral part of modern man." He believed psychoanalytic thinking had plural functions, one of which was greater understanding of behavior toward an "integration of the human personality," a process that made possible the "mastery of the mind." Psychoanalytic exploration enabled an individual to move toward "the stage where he *must* live a truly human existence," and James therefore applauded forms of psychological inquiry and psychoanalytic readings of everyday life that intimated individual and collective transformations of the modern world. Unfortunately, psychoanalytic thought in the modern world was typically far from liberatory, for most of its uses amounted to a "refuge from social ills." James found the "football that American intellectuals had made of it" disturbing. Those who failed to link the insights of psychoanalysis to social and cultural transformation abstracted personality from its social environment and misguidedly placed it "at the door of psychoanalysis." James's socialist politics and knowledge of Marxist theory did not make him an opponent of Freudian thought, for his writing conveys appreciation for the return to the intricacies of the human personality afforded by psychoanalysis. His reservations had to do with the way dominant forms of psychoanalytic thinking facilitated an evasion of social and cultural renewal.[93]

Much like the Trinidadian-American Marxist sociologist Oliver Cox, who ascribed considerable analytical importance to the psychological study of racial antagonisms, James understood his observations on the "socio-psychological pressure of color prejudice" as part of a materialist and historical approach to race hierarchy. Cox described the "collapsing effect upon the individual's self-respect" of racism and racist ideologies, and he even argued that the sociopsychological force of "color prejudice" worked to reduce the individual to a "condition of no social consequence." In the environment created by American race hierarchy, not all racial minorities were "tortured by racial prejudice," Cox claimed, but many minorities to varying degrees had accepted the social definitions imposed by dominant racial codes. For Cox and James alike, modern racial conflict—"the lurid psychological complex called race prejudice"—required the bridging of material and psychological approaches.[94]

Cox believed that as "mass psychological instruments," racial ideologies carried determinate social and political effects, and race hierarchy and racial ideology therefore required psychological avenues of investigation.[95] It was the central idea running throughout Wright's work, and one that James considered pivotal to the cultural power both Wright and midcentury antiracism more generally had acquired.

That power was increasingly on display in the work of female authors in the 1940s. In 1946, Ann Petry, an African American writer, published *The Street,* a novel sharing the thematic territory of *Native Son.* Petry, like Wright, was born in 1908, and her prose style recalled *Native Son* in its intense exploration of urban disorder. Her narrative about racially charged urban life involved Lutie Johnson, a black woman in Harlem, who battles social forces and antagonists as she tries to improve circumstances for herself and her young son. According to one critic, what "*Native Son* did in profiling the life and times of a slum-shocked Negro youth on Chicago's Southside, Petry's novel does with virtually the same devastating, appalling effects in her story of a Harlem tenement." Petry, like several of her male African American literary and intellectual counterparts, developed forms of antiracist cultural work during World War II, influenced by, yet not reducible to, the Communist-led Popular Front.[96] Critics described *The Street* as an example of naturalism in the vein of Wright's *Native Son,* although that literary descriptor, with its connotations of passivity in relation to social environment, has always obscured more than it reveals.[97] Petry demonstrated the "penetration of a psychiatrist," as one critic put it, in presenting her protagonist and the social pressures of her environment, creating along the way a "vivid symbol of all that is wrong with race hate."[98]

Another writer, white Southern novelist and cultural commentator Lillian Smith, gained national recognition in the 1940s and urged intellectual and cultural reckoning with the psychological dimensions of racial ideology, especially as it impinged on the value vested in whiteness. Smith displeased liberals, especially in the South, because her vocal antiracism did not comport with traditional liberal pronouncements about the Negro Problem. After reading Smith's *Killers of the Dream,* Horace Cayton dashed off letters to friends indicating his enthusiasm for the book; he even proposed to Langston Hughes that he devote one of his syndicated columns to Smith's work. Cayton wrote to Wright, "Lillian Smith is absolutely sound politically, psychologically and morally. I think she deserves our complete support."[99] As the next chapter demonstrates, the attraction of Smith's work for a range of writers and readers had to do with her ability to merge cultural and psychological interpretation.

CHAPTER FOUR

Strange Fruit
Lillian Smith and the Making of Whiteness

In 1945, an interviewer asked Richard Wright about "white writers crusading for the Negro." White writers "should combat white chauvinism while Negro writers combat Negro nationalism," Wright responded. Moreover, in the place of "special pleas to the Negro to increase his militancy," white writers needed to do more to "grapple with the deep-seated racial notions of white Americans."[1] In his estimation, Lillian Smith provided writers with a model of such critical work.

Smith began her career as an observer of the political, social and cultural scenes of the American South in the 1930s and by the mid-1940s had attained a national profile in American letters. Fusing her antisegregationist politics into her fiction and nonfiction, she became a controversial voice in a turbulent period, particularly in the South, where she refused to follow the well-worn paths of liberals who long avoided criticizing the codes of segregated social life. An intellectual activist in the years leading to modern civil rights politics, Smith was among the first American writers not only to give concerted attention to the intersections of racial and gender ideologies but also to make her criticism a site for the investigation of "whiteness" as a cultural force. As a writer and public figure Smith helped to engender conditions for the emergence of alternative forms of antiracism.

Greeting civil rights workers and the organizers of the Institute on Non-Violence and Social Change on December 5, 1956, the first anniversary of the Montgomery bus boycott, Smith delivered a speech—"The Right Way Is Not a Moderate Way"—centered on the concept of moderation. *Moderation,* Smith argued, was an ambiguous word that suffused mass culture, often with "hypnotic" effects. Any comprehensive exploration of the pervasiveness of moderation in the culture and politics of the mid-twentieth-century United States required an appreciation of the very "history of the psychology of our times."[2] Smith's views influenced Martin Luther King Jr., who acknowledged in writing his close readings of Smith's arguments and kept a copy of her speech among his papers.[3] Both Smith and King sought practices and languages that would serve as alternatives to the lure of moderation. Intended as a response to social and political backlash and retrenchment in the midst of growing civil rights activism, Smith's speech was also in keeping with concerns that had long been central to her intellectual biography. Smith's corpus can be interpreted as various efforts to describe and understand the "history of the psychology of our times."

Smith described patterns of social life and the effects of racial ideologies by drawing from her readings in psychological literatures. Her critical commentary, defined by an open and mobile psychological idiom, posited the mutability of cultural patterns. Smith conceived of the psychological idiom of her criticism not as inventive content but as a practice that encouraged readers to examine the racial ordering of their social environments. The psychological questions Smith posed led her to develop innovative interpretations of the languages of race and made possible a concerted exploration of "whiteness" as a locus of cultural power and social coercion. Anticipating by several decades the "whiteness studies" that would become an active area of research and critical commentary on racial ideology among American academics, Smith took the psychoanalytic focus on conformity and personality formation as the basis of her investigation of the ideological power of whiteness.

During the war Smith's writings often pivoted on the idea of the "white man's conscience," which she described as psychologically divided. For Smith, the social and political manifestations of segregation were deeply bound up in the refusal among whites to confront racial conflict. The Negro Problem framework represented a diversion, a singular means of ignoring the relationship between social patterns and the everyday beliefs of individuals. If whites constructed the Negro Problem to avoid examining their own implication in racial conflicts, such evasion seemed to Smith instrumental in the making and reproduction of the color line. As with Wright, much of Smith's writing involved deliberate movement away from established explanatory models for understanding race thinking and racial antagonisms. By the time of *Killers of the Dream,* her work of autobiographical cultural criticism and psychological exploration, she writes less of "white conscience" and more about "whiteness." The book concentrated on the conformity produced by the South's dominant social arrangements, which were organized through pervasive and continual appeals to whiteness as a vehicle of social control.

Paula Snelling, Smith's life partner and intellectual co-worker, noted that Smith had described how a generation of Southern whites had been "taught to act, feel, and become White."[4] Smith and Snelling became catalysts for one another, expanding each other's interests and analytic concerns, not least those involving psychological theory. Snelling had earned a master's degree in psychology from Columbia University and would publish essays on Freud with the specific aim of presenting his "hypotheses, experiments, conclusions, in a brief comprehensible [and] readable but not too dilute form, for the intelligently interested layman." In a joint application to the Julius Rosenwald Foundation to fund a project on southern literature and culture, Smith and Snelling defined their goal as a "philosophical and psychological comprehension of the South's problems." The exploration of the South's literary output would proceed from the assumption that narratives could be read as symptoms, and, in the case of the South, symptoms were inescapably part of a particular "societal-racial-psychological context." They hoped their book would draw on social scientific studies because social scientists had compiled a fund of material that had become part of the "body of southern literature itself" and that benefited anyone who could make use of its insights. The availability of social scientific facts made the development of critical perspectives—"sharpened perceptions which psychoanalysis can give"—both a viable and pressing task. While many disciplines might inform the kind of analysis that Smith and Snelling brought to bear on their study of the South, they suggested throughout their application materials that psychoanalysis would organize their thinking generally.[5]

Although the book, tentatively titled "Southland," was not completed, the themes and perspectives developed in the joint application found their way into *Killers of the Dream* and other works. The collaboration Snelling and Smith forged inspired confidence from many quarters that the two had important new things to say about the American South. Supporters of their work stressed a "new standard of literary criticism and of political thought in the South" Smith and Snelling had begun to provide in essays and occasional writings. Many focused on the specific intellectual abilities Smith and Snelling brought to their writings. "Trained as they are in the arts, in sociology and in psychology, they are able to bring to bear a broader and more just criticism than most of the literary lights are able to do," wrote one recommender, while another emphasized the studies each undertook on the complex "factors entering into human relationships."[6] Intellectual allies believed that the interdisciplinary ambition exhibited by Smith and Snelling, together with their social scientific and psychoanalytic literacy, promised fresh and synthetic understandings of the cultural patterns and psychological dynamics of the American South.

Reflecting on her work in the 1960s, Smith claimed to have undertaken "various analytical studies of race concepts."[7] Her book delved into the "edgy blackness and whiteness of things," interpreting "metaphors we created and watched ourselves turned into," the "breathing symbols we have made of the blackness and the whiteness."[8] In *Killers of the Dream,* Smith pointed to "whiteness" and "white culture" (136) in an effort to disavow the routine naturalization of these ideas by bringing them into representation as a "strange, mad obsession" (17). In Smith's criticism, racial ideologies represent symptoms of social and psychological maladies that could not, in tautological fashion, be explained by "race." Smith concurred in large measure with the culture and personality scholar Ruth Benedict, who had argued that to understand "race conflict, one has to understand conflict, and not race."[9] The psychological dynamics that gave life to racial thinking and racial hierarchies were never merely a set of beliefs: "race" brought socioeconomic practices and neuroses, politics and fantasy, into a complex, volatile mix.

The Promise of Psychoanalysis

In their intellectual collaborations, Smith and Snelling stressed the value of psychoanalytic investigation for understanding a range of cultural patterns and social predicaments. In one co-written essay, they pressed upon readers the relevance of psychological research for the most urgent crises of modern life. So "long as we do not act constructively on it," they predicted, the "submerged, unflattering psychic motivations which propel us to war, . . . the scope and needlessness of human misery, . . . the inadequacy and insanity of mass murder as a solution to social ills" explored by psychological thinkers would only be compounded. Yet if the research of psychologists and social scientists was not discarded, it "could transform the world."[10] Just as for an individual, the society that hoped to surmount its emotional defects had a duty to think through the implications of psychoanalysis. This assumption shaped Smith's writings on racial thinking and racial practices. Indeed, her explorations of racial ideologies were shaped by her confidence in the value of psychological inquiry generally. Because racial meanings and racial conflict in much of her writings constituted symptoms, Smith wanted to understand the psychological dynamics underlying these symptoms. Smith anticipated fuller comprehension of the cultural persistence of racial thinking and concomitant strategies for combating its pernicious effects. Rather than merely direct readers to psychoanalysis as a body of knowledge, Smith integrated psychoanalytic insights into a distinctive idiom of cultural criticism about the meanings of racial divisions in the American South and in the nation at large. She envisioned expansive cultural recognition of the value of psychoanalytic inquiry for making sense of racialized social conditions through such intellectual labors.

One of the psychoanalytic thinkers whose work most influenced Smith was Karl Menninger. Writing in the 1920s and 1930s, Menninger had insisted that the social value of psychoanalysis extended far beyond caring for the mentally ill. In the late 1920s he published several articles in *Household Magazine* on the mental health of children. The articles were collected in a volume, *The Healthy-Minded Child* (1930), edited by Menninger and Nelson Antrim Crawford, that stressed the value of scientific insights in the rearing of children. The book fit well with Menninger's aim of bringing psychoanalytic thinking to bear on everyday social life, for his goal was to reach "average parents, with average education, average opportunity, and the average number of problems in bringing up their children." For Menninger, everyone bore responsibility for detecting mental problems since mental health encompassed "betterment of both personality and environment." Much as Smith would in her writings, he looked to the culture at large for moments when "personalities first show evidences of instability."[11] In "The Formation of Habits," one of the pieces included in *The Healthy-Minded Child,* child specialist Lawson G. Lowrey presented a theme that would recur in Smith's work, namely the emergence of feelings of inferiority and superiority. Lowrey cautioned that parents "frequently suggest inferiority feelings and superiority feelings in their children," and even when this was not the case, it was incumbent on parents to determine "exactly what the child is satisfying with a given bit of behavior."[12] Lowrey was certainly not the first to use these concepts, but his essay gave lay readers a point of entry for such ideas.

Although *The Healthy-Minded Child* did not relate environmentalism, inferiority, and superiority to racial ideologies, research on race prejudice became increasingly important to both academic psychologists and psychoanalytic thinkers in the 1930s and 1940s. By the mid-1940s, the anthropologist Hortense Powdermaker spoke for many liberal social scientists and commentators when she wrote that "young children consciously and unconsciously absorb prejudices from their social environment." Such environmentalism became a standard part of much liberal social science, which posited that "prejudices lie in the realm of emotions and feelings and that these have a way of functioning independent of reasoning."[13]

Menninger's general disposition on matters of social interpretation served as a model for Smith, who was highly sympathetic to his view that meaningful social analysis required a consideration of emotional factors and conditions. Smith gravitated toward psychoanalysis with a passion, and Menninger's writings on psychoanalysis were as interesting to her as his assertions about child psychology were directly relevant to her work. Her examinations of the social and political customs of the South were informed by a recurrent expectation that the sensitive exploration of psychological maladies represented the necessary starting point for any subsequent attainment of mental health. Smith linked psychological investigation to the possibility of mental health and thereby figured the emotional health of individuals as a measure of democracy. Menninger, who became one of the popularizers of psychiatry in the United States, was part of a "generation of dynamic psychiatrists" that attempted to move beyond the prevailing concern with classification that marked psychiatric practice in the early twentieth century.[14] Books written by this group of American psychoanalytic thinkers imparted the potential of psychiatric knowledge to improve individual lives and social life generally. In 1930, in *The Human Mind*, Menninger set out to shape the course of psychoanalytic training in the United States and to convey the significance of Freudian principles to the general public. "No mind is ever shut up in a laboratory," Menninger wrote, in making a case for exploring the practical implications and possibilities of psychoanalytic research. The defining value of psychoanalysis had to do with the concerted focus on emotions that it enabled and the concomitant assumption that "mental health is attainable."[15]

Smith's work brought together many of Menninger's arguments—including the view that modern psychology deserved a more purposeful role in American public life. She held that the frustrations and aggressions woven into dominant social patterns of segregation and race thinking in the South could not be analyzed adequately without addressing the large areas of investigation that modern psychology had recognized. Menninger posited the fundamental principle that the "capacity for love and hatred is developed in childhood as a result of parental attitudes and behavior." Since "most of the injuries to the child occur while the parent is unconscious of the fact that he is inflicting them," and because children repress those injuries into their own unconscious, modern psychology considered this area of investigation a "terra incognita." For Menninger, entering this territory was crucial because discovering the origins of aggression was the "most important step in correcting it, and thus enabling us to replace it with love."[16] Smith wrote that as a "physician, as a psychoanalyst, Dr. Menninger is to this reader very fine," in part because his writings exhibited the mind of "both the scientist and the artist," a balancing act that Smith sought to emulate.[17]

Just as Smith and Snelling looked to Menninger as a leading psychological expert, he regarded them as important modern cultural critics who offered interpretations that advanced psychological knowledge. For *Love against Hate* (1942), a book about the frustrations of women and children, Menninger borrowed liberally from the formulations on women, psychology, and culture that Smith and Snelling had developed in an essay titled "Man Born of Woman." He was not the only psychologist to draw on Smith's work. Psychologist Gordon W. Allport's *The Nature of Prejudice* (1954), which summarized a vast amount of midcentury psychological research for both scholars and lay readers, also included several references to ideas about culture and conformity presented in Smith's fiction and nonfiction.[18]

A "Little Magazine" from the South

In 1927–28, Smith had enrolled in psychology, education, and history courses through Columbia University's Teacher's College, and at the same time she taught music part time in a public school in Harlem.[19] In autobiographical notes, Smith wrote that she had spent a winter semester at Columbia for the express purpose of acquiring "help for my new job" and that while in New York she read in the fields of child guidance, psychiatry, and psychoanalysis. A ten-year period of reading and study began that came to include "Freud, Jung, Adler, Ferenczi, Rank, et cetera; gestalt psychology; the behaviorists; then Gesell and others who were studying childhood, then Anna Freud, Melanie Klein, Karl Menninger, Lawrence Kubie," among others.[20]

Calvin Warren Smith, Lillian's father, decided to open a summer camp for girls after a business setback in 1920. The camp, called Laurel Falls and situated in the foothills of the Blue Ridge Mountains outside Clayton, Georgia, became popular with many white families. At first, Smith was not especially interested in becoming part of the operation of the camp. In fact, she spent much of the first few years of the camp away in Huzhou, China, where she taught music through a Christian mission. But Smith did return to manage the camp in 1925 as her father had wanted, starting what would be a challenging period of her life and one that was critical to her career as a writer and intellectual. Smith eventually decided that the camp could be the impetus for deepening her intellectual interests and a way to leave a lasting mark on the world. She reshaped the camp based on her readings in child development literature and psychological theory. Smith adopted an individualized approach to camp life that emphasized the psychological health of each child. With the help of camp counselors, emotional experiences and changes in children became the organizing principle of summer camp life. Smith's reorientation of the camp also involved offering candid discussions of sexuality. Part of Smith's attraction to the work of psychoanalysts was their collective willingness to open—rather than recoil from—the subject of human sexuality. Talks given by Smith would often be "about the body, sex and babies," offered up in the form of facts but also engendering discussions of specific attitudes and feelings about relationships. Smith used creative methods to dramatize concepts such as guilt, and she organized plays in which girls could explore different socially and psychologically complex topics. "Summer after summer," Smith wrote, "we talked about scapegoats, about arrogance, about war and peace, racial problems, poverty, class snobbery, conformity, acceptance of differences."[21] Laurel Falls served as a space for the development of Smith's ideas about psychology, child care and the complexities of the social world.

Smith's work as head of the Laurel Falls summer camp led directly to her emergence as a public intellectual. The writing she did for camp brochures and correspondence persuaded her that her skills as a writer could attract readers. "The bitter and inescapable fact is that our children in America, white and colored, are growing distorted, twisted personalities within the frame of this segregation which our fears and frustrations have imposed on them," Smith told a group in 1943. "We know a child's personality cannot grow without feelings of emotional security."[22] Though personality development in children would remain a theme in Smith's writing in the 1940s, her work moved toward the impact of segregation and racism on the psychological development of individuals on each side of the color line.

Working out of their home at Laurel Falls in the mid-1930s, Smith and Snelling created and edited a "little magazine" that became a major venue for writing on literature and social life in the South. Even as the publication attributed exploitative racial practices in the South to powerful economic and political interests, much of its focus was on the "rest of us," by which Smith and Snelling meant whites who needed to "face and acknowledge our unconscious desires, our indirect gains from these more ruthless activities of the 'powers,' and our identification with white supremacy."[23] *South Today* (and its earlier incarnations as *Pseudopodia* and the *North Georgia Review*) became one of the few publications where writers could broach the subject of a desegregated South. Smith's psychological idiom offered a way to dramatize the difficulty of both personal and social change and to show that all white Southerners were implicated in the racial hierarchies and habits of their surroundings. For Smith and Snelling, economic, political and psychological factors worked in powerful combination to create and sustain segregated social relations. The two writers wanted their publication to "gather up the economic, cultural, political, psychological strands that tie the South into its present hard knot."[24] Smith wrote to W. E. B. Du Bois to share her enthusiasm for a magazine prepared to reflect on race problems in economic, social, political, and psychological terms. "I can follow with deep understanding your desires for the *North Georgia Review*," Du Bois replied, comparing Smith and Snelling's efforts to the work he had done to found the *Crisis* in the early twentieth century under the auspices of the National Association for the Advancement of Colored People.[25] The dedication and learning that they brought to their publication paid off. *South Today* attracted many subscribers and became widely recognized as the leading source of liberal-left commentary in the South. In Washington, D.C., *South Today* "is catching on like Wildfire," the African American writer Pauli Murray reported to Smith.[26]

From the start, Smith and Snelling promoted psychoanalysis. In 1936 Smith wrote that the "findings of Freud and his followers have not only made for us enormous extensions of knowledge in the realms of the spirit but by their very nature are

changing the intrinsic quality of that spirit." Her willingness to consider psychoanalysis in the context of a language of "spirit" fits with her general reluctance to bury
her voice as a writer beneath psychological theory. Freud had offered perspectives that
writers would be remiss to ignore, and his ways of considering human experience
represented "very simply a sine qua non."[27] From her earliest expressions of admiration for Freud, Smith viewed psychoanalysis less as a set of proclamations that needed
to be reiterated and more as a resource for different intellectual and cultural projects.
Snelling articulated this view in "Sigmund Freud: An Attempt at Appraisal." Snelling
held that it was "incumbent on novelists, critics and others who select human nature
as their province to acquaint themselves with Freud's hypotheses." She was careful to
note that she did not mean that "artists should discard their own vision and intuitions
and devote themselves to penning imaginary case-histories in support of Freud's
theories."[28] An understanding of Freudian thought could enhance the visions created
by different artists and writers without eclipsing their unique insights. Snelling, along
with Smith, emphasized the value of Freudian thought as a mode of cultural analysis.

Book reviews solicited for the magazine often centered on works based in psychoanalytic criticism. In "Southern Trauma," Du Bois praised the "brilliant psycho-
analytical interpretation" he found in John Dollard's *Caste and Class in a Southern
Town*. Although he thought the book could have benefited from more sociological
and economic background, Du Bois nonetheless considered Dollard's study of caste
as a "psychic phenomenon" to be the "most frank and penetrating analysis of southern mentality that I have ever read." Dollard's book represented a "distinct advance
in the study of the Southern scene." In addition to describing the caste status of
African Americans in Indianola, Mississippi, Dollard had presented "white aggression upon Negroes [as] at bottom a defense of income, of ownership of women and
inflated ego" and thus a means of preserving "white integrity." Dollard's approach
seemed to provide informative accounts of the circulation and power of social ideologies—such as that of the inferiority of Negroes—"whose significance is not that they
are true but that they are frantically stated and believed."[29] Dollard's psychoanalytic
framework brought into view the reactions, accommodations, and attitudes of blacks
and whites in one town, while also shedding light on larger regional patterns and
buttressing Du Bois's own work on the economic, social, and political conditions of
African Americans.

Religious values were not absent from the pages of *South Today*. In an essay titled
"There Are Things to Do," Smith listed religious belief as one possible impetus for
working toward social change. "Whatever our reasons for wanting to act: whether we
are stirred by love for our South or love for democracy; by our shame at being a party
to injustice, our desire to win the war, or our belief in the teachings of Jesus Christ;

whether by vision of a new world in which all men of all races will have an equal chance for food and freedom, or fear of a race riot in our own home town;—whatever our reason for wanting to ease race tension, there are things we can do NOW."[30] Interweaving religious themes into her writing, Smith shared her own beliefs and opened possibilities for greater identification with her criticisms of race hierarchy among her readers. A public letter Smith wrote to the members of a 1944 conference on social conditions in the South further illuminates her thinking on religious values. "The memory of our discussions at the Blue Ridge conference haunts me," Smith wrote. The conference members, southerners like Smith, were wrestling with many of the same problems that had shaped her: "You and I grew from the same cultural roots; we lived, breathed, experienced, so much that has created a common ground of memories." Describing her own experience of confronting racist ideologies, Smith listed the influential role of religious beliefs, though not of religious institutions. She distanced herself from "what the 'church' taught me or what I learned in Sunday School." (In noting the divergent trajectories of religious values and religious institutions, she introduced a theme that would return in *Killers of the Dream*.) Smith attributed her rejection of the race thinking of her upbringing in part to the "actual teachings of Jesus (and other great religious leaders), which I learned to take seriously as a child and which will always have a deep meaning for me."[31]

If religious teachings helped Smith reject the "arrogant and superstitious belief that being white is important," readings in psychoanalysis provided another kind of sustenance. Reading more and more in psychoanalytic literatures, Smith came to the conclusion that "science supports the fundamental teachings of Jesus about brotherhood and love." As she entered the world of public intellectual life, psychology and psychiatry "helped greatly," offering concepts and questions that would transform her thinking.[32]

The Cultural Vocabulary of Psychoanalysis

If Smith was not alone in turning to the analytic potential of psychological inquiry, neither was she alone in her increasing use of the concept of culture. *Culture* in Smith's formulations did not supply the background for a set of political arrangements. Rather, culture and political arrangements constituted a whole. Her psychological idiom encouraged readers to consider their own processes of identity formation in the context of the complex workings of culture. Smith's writings modeled an analysis of the individual in society, of the personal and the political, that she put forth as an urgent form of cultural criticism. Self-inquiry became a vital component of any bid to rethink cultural patterns and social values.

The distinctiveness of Smith's critical voice benefited from the energetic theorization of culture at midcentury. Among Smith's admirers was Caroline Ware, who had edited *The Cultural Approach to History* (1940). Ware's volume argued for interpretive possibilities based on the "assumption that every society has a structure of institutions, of values, of ideologies." In *The Cultural Approach to History* these different parts constituted a "cultural whole," to which many historians were increasingly sensitive even as they investigated specific areas of research. Pressing for the extensive use of the concept of culture, Ware argued that historians who took up the analytic challenges the concept posed discovered "interrelationships among social functions not ordinarily considered akin." Ware considered the making of the "culturally acceptable personality" an intrinsically important subject of historical analysis and regarded the concept of culture as a tool for making sense of the formation of "nondominant as well as dominant groups."[33]

Ware organized the opening essays of her book under the heading "Techniques of Cultural Analysis" and supplied reflections by Geoffrey Gorer, Goodwin Watson, and Franz Alexander, an anthropologist, social psychologist, and psychoanalyst, respectively. For the three contributors, the techniques of cultural analysis were bound up with the insights provided by the psychological sciences, especially psychoanalysis. Ware and her contributors posited the urgency of the concept of culture given that the "acceptability of democracy depends upon the extent to which the culture has developed independence in children and youth."[34] For a growing number of historians, as for writers like Smith, the concept of culture held the promise of clarifying the relationship between disparate and sometimes contradictory components of societies. Within its analytic reach, culture included patterns of social organization and the individual's complicated relationship to those patterns.

Smith's work overlapped analytically with, and drew inspiration from, culture-and-personality studies, which brought together the perspectives of anthropologists, social psychologists, and psychoanalysts. Culture-and-personality studies had begun to take recognizable shape in the 1930s, receiving the attention of intellectuals within and beyond these fields. In a column from the early 1940s, Smith spoke favorably of the studies of sexuality and culture undertaken by Margaret Mead, a leading figure associated with the culture-and-personality approach. "No one can read Margaret Mead or Franz Alexander [the émigré psychoanalytic thinker] without having a lot of windows opened in his imagination. Sometimes, one wishes a few of our southern liberals who recently have been moaning so pitifully about the South's 'peculiar' and unchangeable way of life, would take time off from their lamentations and read a few books on social anthropology and psychoanalysis."[35] Smith's writings shared the assumption of many American anthropologists, especially those who worked in the area of culture-and-personality studies, for whom separating cultural and psychological investigation was neither analytically desirable nor practically possible. Culture "regulates our lives at every turn," wrote the anthropologist Clyde Kluckhohn, and thus no person could be "emotionally indifferent to his culture." These were among the reasons that culture mattered and a concerted focus on its workings was necessary. Avoiding idealized or overly negative understandings of the concept, Kluckhohn held that "cultures create problems as well as solve them." All "individuals in a culture tend to share common interpretations of the external world and man's place in it." Basic to Kluckhohn's arguments was the idea that culture involved personality formation and that the malleability of personality in turn rendered culture an ever-changing process: "There is a continuous and dynamic interrelationship between the patterns of a culture and the personalities of its individual members."[36]

In Smith's writings, the concepts of culture and personality were imbued with that same sense of process communicated by Kluckhohn. Indeed, Smith's cultural commentary emerged as an analogue of sorts to the interdisciplinary social science of her day. In 1949, Kluckhohn wrote:

> The unstated assumption has been that human behavior took place in a series of watertight compartments. Hence the economist must study "economic man," the political scientist "political man," the sociologist "social man," etc. . . . Scholars in other fields have also become increasingly dissatisfied with carrying their investigations only so far as the conventional boundaries and abandoning them upon an intellectual dumping ground. As to what students of man actually do, the tight distinctions are disappearing. Already there are scientists for whom it is arbitrary to say "he is a social psychologist" rather than "he is a sociologist" or "he is an anthropologist" . . . A few psychiatrists can well be called anthropologists.[37]

Smith also believed traditional divisions in humanistic and social scientific thought were unduly constricting. In her writings on racial segregation, she stressed that the political, economic, and psychological dimensions of its practice were interrelated, thus making necessary a form of commentary that could make their mutually informing dynamic clear. Studies emphasizing the economic or political dimensions of racial division at the expense of analyses of personality reduced a "complex, subtle, tragically profound problem," Smith wrote.[38] As she told Richard Wright in a letter, Smith took race to be one of many large problems in society, and thus as one that needed to be understood in the fullness of its relation to "other aspects of culture and personality."[39]

The psychoanalyst Lawrence K. Frank wrote about "cultural environments" and "cultural worlds," espousing much the same view of culture as a whole way of life that

Smith presented in her work. The two shared a dynamic understanding of culture as "patterned, selective transactions with the environment" and as a "man-made creation."[40] The focus on culture within much midcentury psychoanalytic thought offered Smith a model of critical analysis that was very broad yet capable of bringing within its purview the specific word or symbol. Smith's analysis of the Negro Problem echoed the concern in Frank's work with how language directed behavior. Smith identified the isolation of the Negro Problem, a prime example of the naming of the "other" as the problem, as a constituent part of the pattern that worked to maintain dominant social relations. Smith insisted that this naming was a choice, an act that revealed the interconnected status of cultural worlds and social patterns that regulated behavior in order to maintain rules and conventions. Like Wright, Smith bristled at the analytic and political constraints imposed by the dominance of the Negro Problem paradigm. "I have never written about the Negro problem because I don't think there is one," Smith once wrote.[41]

Smith's views of culture and cultural problems carried the same sense of emotional toll that literary critic Lionel Trilling elaborated in his interpretations of psychoanalysis. In *Strange Fruit* and *Killers of the Dream* Smith offered stories about cultural belonging that are full of danger, loss, and emotional pain. Reading segregation, the deification of white womanhood, and the ideological contradictions of religious practices as the stuff of culture, Smith emphasized that culture exacts costs. Trilling and literary intellectuals, like their peers in the social sciences, identified the turn to the concept of culture as a development enabled by psychoanalytic perspectives on the modern world. Trilling asserted that culture exerted a greater influence on people's everyday lives in modern society. The "growing power of culture to control us by seduction or coercion," Trilling believed, made Freud's insights especially significant, for it was Freud who demonstrated how "deeply implicated in culture we all are." Among midcentury literary humanistic thinkers, Trilling was perhaps the most explicit in connecting psychoanalytic thought to cultural analysis. He claimed that by focusing on the effects of family life, Freud's studies had "made plain how the culture suffuses the remotest part of the individual mind," showing that his approach to psychic life involved "culture in its very essence." Implicit in psychoanalytic thought was the idea that the "development of the individual mind recapitulates the development of culture." "In the dissemination of the idea of culture," Trilling added, "Freud has no doubt had a chief part."[42] Trilling understood culture in terms of its hazards. Freud informed this view because he had affirmed the "right of society and culture to make great demands upon the individual" but "looked with grieving eyes upon the pain which had to be endured in satisfying these demands."[43]

Whereas Smith did not personally know most of the midcentury psychoanalytic thinkers whose works she read, there was one significant exception. Smith maintained a correspondence with the American psychoanalyst Lawrence Kubie. Not coincidentally, Kubie took a stand against segregation in the armed forces during the Second World War.[44] Explicit in his endorsement of psychoanalysis and its possibilities, Kubie linked his area of expertise to cultural change. For him, psychoanalysis centrally involved the broader "task of culture and religion to learn enough about man and his nature to be able to bring his unconscious primitive struggles into closer harmony with his conscious ethical aspirations."[45] Kubie's willingness to see the insights of psychoanalysis as related to religious traditions and ethics may have been what most attracted Smith. In Kubie's view, religion and psychoanalysis shared many things, among them the charges often directed toward them. Both stood accused of adjusting people to all the "inequalities and abuses of life," even as "many deeply religious people have been revolutionary in their attitude toward economic, social, and political wrongs, proving that a passive and uncomplaining acceptance of evil is certainly not an essential part of religion." The accusation leveled at religion was "equally invalid" when it came to the "essential goal and purpose of psychoanalysis," which Kubie understood as fundamentally oriented toward personal and cultural transformation.[46]

In Kubie's writings, psychoanalysis becomes a technique designed to "free the patient (or analysand) from enslavement to the obligatory repetitiveness which is at the heart of the neurotic process" and thus to "recapture for the patient the freedom for continuing and evolving change." Psychoanalysis was not meant to be a tool for normalizing dominant social and political patterns, and when the profession served such ends it negated its originary impulse to question social mores, cultural patterns, and psychological habits. Psychoanalysis was patently not a "philosophy of passive submission to the status quo" because the ideal of adjustment involved giving a patient the ability to admit suffering, empathize with others, and, ultimately, find "courage and clarity in his efforts to correct those defects of society that exist all around us."[47]

Smith's view of psychoanalytic inquiry as an indispensable development in modern thought relied on psychology's potential for social transformation, which aligned her with Kubie's values. Kubie favored a simplification of psychoanalytic languages and frequently reflected on the "impact of psychoanalysis on the cultural scene." As a "cultural instrument," psychoanalysis held out the possibility of the "maturation of human culture" through the resolution of "cultural problems."[48] For both Smith and Kubie, to interpret cultural problems was to consider the psychological components of personality formation. Similarly, to think in terms of the value of the psychological sciences in the broadest terms was to think about the remaking of culture. Smith relied on such precepts in her investigations of the culture of racial domination. Investigating the circulation of racial ideologies and their effects on personality formation, Smith set her analytic lights on what Kubie called the repetitiveness that marked neurotic processes. For Smith, repeated and systemic patterns of racial antagonism represented neurotic symptoms, among the tragic possibilities of culture. But insofar as patterns of racial domination developed as forms of psychological illness, efforts to better understand the psychology of racism and racial categorization served as a response to dominant sociocultural arrangements.

Strange Fruit and Racist Culture

The conceptual richness that Smith saw in the concept of culture and psychoanalytic questioning led her to delve into the myriad worlds of racial thinking with fresh intellectual energy. The sheer power of racial ideology to shape lives required more sustained exploration than was typically summoned in either fiction or nonfiction. This belief led Smith to write the novel, *Strange Fruit,* which told a controversial story of love across the color line and advanced a meditation on racial categorization. The novel decisively altered Smith's life: *Strange Fruit* sold three million copies, making Smith a recognizable quantity on the cultural and literary landscape and at the same time bringing financial security.[49]

The publishers of *Strange Fruit* anticipated debate, if not controversy, and made plans for a literary event through ads in the *New York Times Book Review* and other publications. One 1944 announcement proclaimed an important novel by a writer whose career included work as a teacher, editor, and child psychologist. Smith's long-standing interest in psychology, the courses she took at Columbia University, and her work as the head of a summer camp for children were no doubt part of the reason behind the child psychologist label. Yet the rationale behind calling *Strange Fruit* the novel of a child psychologist probably had less to do with descriptive accuracy and more with the literary and intellectual connotations of midcentury psychological thought. Reynolds and Hitchcock, the publishers of *Strange Fruit,* were no doubt aware that a background in psychology suggested specific ideas and dispositions. Psychological inquiry implied greater openness in discussions of sexuality, an ability to explore the emotional conditions that nurtured social prejudices, and a general inclination to challenge conventional interpretations of the modern world. Reynolds and Hitchcock wanted to promote—and Smith likely wished to project—a southern writer who was also an intellectual, one well-versed in psychological theory and capable of bringing it to bear on her representations of American life. It also made sense to unite the categories of teacher, editor, and psychologist in Smith's case, for these roles were profoundly interconnected in her biography. Indeed, these roles were significantly blended for Smith, a public intellectual whose career was organized around the political and pedagogical value of psychological insight.

Strange Fruit presented a love story involving a young white Southern man named Tracy and a young black woman named Nonnie. Smith's writing explored relationships in Maxwell, a fictional town in Georgia near the Florida border, so as to develop a deeper understanding—for herself as much as her readers—of the seductive and mercurial aspects of racial thinking as both a physical organizer of space in the South and a locus of historically resonant emotions and feelings. Smith was familiar with the Billie Holiday song when she suggested the title "Strange Fruit" to her publishers. But whereas Holiday sang about the scourge of lynching, and even though a lynching takes place in the novel, for Smith "Strange Fruit" referred primarily to the personalities that resulted from "racist culture." "We, the people, white and colored, are the Strange Fruit which our culture has produced," she wrote.[50] Smith regarded the novel as "primarily about segregation—about all it does to the mind and heart and spirit as well as the economy of the South." The culture of segregation did "strange things" to whites and blacks, as "*any* pattern as destructive psychologically as segregation" would.[51] Her words suggest a key line from Wright's introduction to *Black Metropolis:* the book showed "how *any* human beings can become mangled, how any personalities can become distorted when men are caught in the psychological trap of being emotionally committed to the living of a life of freedom which is denied them."[52] Both writers wanted to better understand and depict the complex imbrications of social-material arrangements and the formation of personalities.

Tracy cannot reconcile his love for Nonnie with the expectations and feelings stipulated by Maxwell's color line. Tracy "knew what the facts were": "The anthropologists had proved there was no superior race. Sure, he knew that. Guys in the Army said the South was wasting half its money and energy and time keeping the Negro in his place; if they'd stop doing it, things might not be so bad down here. He knew that too. Books were written showing this, telling it, proving it even."[53] These lines situate Smith's novel in a contemporaneous intellectual context as the omniscient narrator references modern anthropology's discrediting of scientific racism, making skepticism toward longstanding beliefs about race a feature of the narrative. Yet the facts of social scientists are no match for the force of race thinking in Maxwell. Smith concentrates on the mental dissonance that racial thinking brings and explores the cultural and psychological dimensions of Maxwell's prevailing common sense, while also stressing the violence and material conditions sanctioned by that shared logic. A lynching at the end of the novel underscores the fact that the deadly results of race and the rigid geographical demarcations of the color line are presented not as a self-evident landscape but rather as the result of ideas and behaviors. At his mother's insistence, a wayward Tracy consults with a preacher who is aware of his affair with Nonnie. The affair is excusable so long as Tracy ultimately cedes to the codes of racial difference. "You see, Deen, you have to keep pushing them back across that nigger line," the preacher says.[54] Meanwhile, Nonnie's own family is baffled by her behavior. Though she completes college, she cannot conceive of a social world she would like to occupy beyond that of Maxwell. Though Nonnie remains a mysterious, dreamy figure whose love for Tracy trumps even her own sense of well-being, her meditations on the vagaries of race are central to the narrative. Though she feels powerless to change them, Nonnie questions the putative certainties of race thinking. "Race is something—made up, to me," she tells Tracy.[55]

Smith balked at the tendency among critics to label *Strange Fruit* a problem novel, a designation often applied to works that treated controversial social themes. The ready-made marketing category did not suit Smith, who complained that critics had reduced her story to an effort to improve "race relations," whereas she understood her narrative as carrying broader cultural ramifications as a story about the modern world. Smith published "A Personal History of *Strange Fruit:* A Statement of Purposes and Intentions" in part to address the limiting nature of the "problem novel" label and as a direct response to several southern newspapers that charged Smith with advocating the "mongrelizing [of] the white race." Smith's readings in psychoanalysis were on display in her response to her critics. The Negro Problem, first and foremost, signaled a struggle within whites for which the "Negro was a handy thing on which to project it." The evasive nature of the Negro Problem framework signaled larger problems of culture, including the "over-esteem of one's skin color, whether in individuals or in masses of men." The valorization of skin color, in Smith's view, emerged from a regressive narcissism and represented but one symptom of a deep-seated "psychosexual maladjustment." In tying the South's racial codes to sexual beliefs, Smith previewed the line of argument that would recur in *Killers of the Dream.*[56]

Despite her irritation over the problem novel label, Smith was very much aware that her story had great contemporary relevance. She hoped that publishers would see her novel "as a thing to be promoted and promoted now when race is a real challenge to our country."[57] And this is in fact how many reviewers interpreted *Strange Fruit.* W. E. B. Du Bois praised the novel, calling it "one of the fundamental studies of the present day South" and an "immortal picture" that represented a counterpoint to other representations of the region, notably the "cheap melodrama of 'Gone With the Wind.' "[58] Du Bois's views of Smith's novel demonstrate the complementary nature of their perspectives on race. In the 1940s, when Smith entered public intellectual life and denounced dominant racial ideologies, Du Bois reiterated what had long been his critical perspectives on "the constant lesion of race thinking." Both writers examined the power of racial ideologies in shaping modern life, rejecting the "race fiction" presented "in schools, in newspapers, and in novels." Smith's work in editing *South Today*, as in her books, was predicated on the urgency of what Du Bois called "deliberate and organized action on the front of race fiction," which was routinely used to justify economic deprivation and injustice in the world.[59] Du Bois found that Smith excelled in her treatment of the love affair between Tracy and Nonnie, who took on "reality from their weakness, their fumbling after an impossible ideal, their collapse in the face of an iron convention." Smith told a story about the American South "with the severity of a Greek dramatist," as when she followed lynchers and onlookers home after a "catharsis of hate," wrote Du Bois. Her potent novel deserved wide reading "on both sides of the Mason-Dixon line."[60]

The psychological dimensions of the novel attracted notice. In the *New York Times*, John Chamberlain wrote that *Strange Fruit* excelled as a "study of white psychology trying to reconcile appetite and convention."[61] "*Strange Fruit* is an un-coated story of frustration," wrote another reviewer, evoking John Dollard's *Frustration and Aggression*, a well-known work in the study of prejudice. Smith's ability to represent the effects of fear and ignorance on whites and blacks resulted in the "most significant novel that has come out of the South." Several commentators seemed to agree that no "novel by a Southern white author has probed so deeply and revealed so frankly the emptiness of life and the utter decadence of a large part of the Southern scene."[62] In the pages of the *Chicago Defender* Ben Burns wrote that *Strange Fruit* derived its power by "astounding many unknowing white readers with the facts of life on Dixie's front porches and back alleys," thus evoking the race problem in "more dramatic ways than any street corner demonstration or March On Washington."[63] Another reviewer characterized the book as one that worked on behalf of African Americans in a "world made conscious of a concept of global democracy," noting how the "influence of sex" hung portentously over the characters, allowing Smith to develop the novel in part as a "Freudian treatment" that was "an outstanding characteristic of the book."[64]

Richard Wright expressed enthusiasm about *Strange Fruit* in an interview he gave in 1945. "Lillian Smith is very good when she is dealing with the mentality of the upper class Southern whites," Wright said.[65] For Wright, Smith's particular strength as a writer lay in her exploration of the complex terrain of beliefs and motivations of different classes of whites in the South. She was a modern writer who eschewed caricature in presenting stories about racial antagonism, enabling the representation of the emotions and psychological dynamics nurtured by the color line. Her novel addressed whites in terms of their implication in the entire complex of relations governed by prevailing race codes. The book rebutted the conceptual tenets of the Negro Problem, opening up several lines of inquiry into the racial formation of the American South. Thus while casting her gaze at the history and social specificity of one locale, Smith's artistic venture paralleled Wright's efforts to break out of the analytic hold of available narratives and categories in order to conceive of literary and cultural work in relation to problems of race in different ways. Smith had not set out to write a problem novel, yet she did have many things to say about race thinking. The theme of her novel finally concerned the "effect upon not only lives but minds and emotions which the concept of race in the South has," as she wrote in a letter.[66] Many of the themes in *Strange Fruit* would recur in *Killers of the Dream,* Smith's 1949 meditation on the interwoven effects of racial, sexual and religious belief in Southern history and culture. Upon the publication of *Killers of the Dream,* Smith sent Wright an inscribed copy.[67]

African American scholars and writers followed Smith's work closely, lauding *Strange Fruit* as a realistically drawn picture of race relationships in the South. African American critics remarked on Smith's focus on the emotional predicaments that emerged from conditions of segregation. According to a critic writing for the *Journal of Negro Education,* Smith belonged "to that pitifully small minority of white Americans who sees the bitter personality conflicts and the cultural losses resulting from the social isolations and deprivations forced upon Negroes by the fascist ideologies of the majority of the Southern whites." Smith was among the few writers confronting the effects of the South's dominant social patterns on the "destinies of so many white and colored Americans."[68]

The Cultural Worlds of *Killers of the Dream*

"Even its children knew that the South was in trouble." The first line of Smith's *Killers of the Dream* did not self-evidently reveal a psychological approach. Yet in making the figure of the child her point of entry and giving the opening chapter the title "When I Was a Child," Smith suggested a psychoanalytic conception of children as the bearers of social turmoil, as figures who could intuit a problem "so big that people turned away from its size" (25). Unlike adults, children could not self-consciously distance themselves from the social pressures that marked the world around them. Those manifold pressures were bound up with the "bleak rituals of keeping Negroes in their 'place'" (27). Both the pressures and the rituals created a "haunted childhood" shared by the generation born at the turn of the century (25).

Killers of the Dream belonged to a broad set of reflections on society and culture produced by writers influenced to varying degrees by psychoanalytic thought. In the essay "The Historian as Therapist" (1944), Lawrence K. Frank suggested that historical insights were basic to midcentury psychocultural studies since every "cultural group, like the individual patient, is governed by its interpretation of the past, which exercises a compelling direction upon all its present activities, its fear, expectations, and aspirations."[69] Whether or not Smith would have used the term *psychocultural* to describe her own work is unclear, but the historical dimension of *Killers of the Dream* took recognizable form through the book's geographical specificity, focus on particular social and political traditions, and central concern with the "generation born around 1900." According to Frank, the work of historian-therapists held out the promise that societies might "free man from the coercion of his traditions, from those versions of the past as he now sees and feels and understands it."[70] Smith's objectives as a writer often involved the interpretations of traditions. In seeking to convey the historical weight of tradition, she did not claim either the title of historian or therapist. Yet the central assumption of *Killers of the Dream* was that an accounting of destructive traditions was a necessary starting point for any cultural or socially therapeutic process.

If Frank's notion of the historian-therapist offers insights into how Smith may have conceived of her aims in writing *Killers of the Dream,* so too do the writings of Hanns Sachs provide further clues. Smith was familiar with Sachs's *The Creative Unconscious: Studies in the Psychoanalysis of Art* (1942), which considered Freud's notion of the unconscious in relation to the work of artists. Sachs considered psychoanalysis a "historical science" that was not "confined to the bounds" of the historical.[71] As an account of the past and the present that reflected long-standing social traditions, Smith's *Killers of the Dream* was based in an analysis of history but actively abandoned the traditional boundaries of historical interpretation by venturing arguments about the symptom and the dream and by generally concerning itself with "psychic reactions," a phrase that appears in both Sachs's and Smith's writings. The ambiguity of form in *Killers of the Dream* in particular may have drawn on Sachs's contention that the "line dividing" poetry and prose was "uncertain" since both forms involved striving for a sense of unity through different techniques. Creative expression for Sachs was predicated on the artist who stores up a "host of assorted memories, impressions, and sensations, elements of form and style, all without coherence and fixed relation to each other."[72] In the vignettes, anecdotes, references, historical asides, and investigations of personality that made up *Killers of the Dream,* Smith presented readers with selected examples of the raw material that was the basis of creative work according to Sachs. Smith appears to have embraced something akin to Sachs's belief that creative inspiration had to do with a "power" that impels the artist to choose from mental "trifles, which are all over the place, just what it needs for the work, brings distant parts together and welds them into the organic entity of a harmonious composition."[73] Erich Kahler, another psychoanalytic thinker on Smith's reading list, emphasized that "no presentation of facts without interpretation" could occur in humanistic thought because "the choice of facts in itself constitutes an interpretation, whether it is determined consciously or unconsciously."[74]

Killers of the Dream could not be identified with one genre of writing because Smith herself never worked with one generic form. For *South Today,* she was editor, columnist, essayist, and fiction writer. *Killers of the Dream* introduced a more pronounced autobiographical voice, yet the book did not fit adequately into the category of memoir. The historical context rendered her book an alternative history of the South, an effort to present readers with a multidimensional, historical account of the present. Smith did not present her chapters as a comprehensive narrative about the South, yet her stories, observations, and analyses of different aspects of life in the South did follow from a specific temporal scheme. The story she wished to tell was one that "most white southerners born at the turn of the century share with each other." The generation born around 1900, the social institutions they inherited, and especially the racial ideologies they used to shape the world around them were the central subjects of the book. Although she would devote several sections of the book to black life in the South, Smith was concerned foremost with the generation of white southerners to which she belonged. Born in 1897, Smith had a story to tell about a social and historical world marked by traditions that were in crisis in the mid-twentieth century. Smith did not seem to believe that a comprehensive, objective account of the subjects she wanted to explore was possible. "As I try to weigh the forces that pressed down on these children of my generation I know I am assuming an impossible task" (114). Nevertheless, Smith concluded the she could lend some partial narrative order to her story. The resulting work combined autobiographical reflection, readings of different southern texts, parables, commentaries on significant intellectual movements, ethnographic perspectives on "customs," and other generic forms. For Smith, the complicated subjects and arguments brought within the pages of her book made a range of different modes of analysis critically important.

The proposition—striking for its time—brought into public life by *Killers of the Dream* was the idea that southerners, while shaped by geography and other material realities, were even more profoundly shaped by received wisdom about race and sex. Millions of white Southerners who would always remain anonymous to each other were bound by the effects of a discrete set of beliefs. The most important thing about the South, Smith averred, was not geographical boundaries but the dominant social patterns, psychological needs, and silences that suffused everyday life. Writing about her aims in the book, Smith said that she wanted to explore segregation as "an idea so hypnotic that it bound together a whole people, good, bad, strong, weak, ignorant and learned . . . making them one as only a common worship or a deeply shared fear can do."[75] For Smith, the subjects of sex, race thinking, and culture in the South exhausted the analytic possibilities of any single genre and, indeed, of any combination of genres. The goal therefore was not a comprehensive account of southern life but a dynamic mix of generic forms that approximated the complexity of the subjects at hand.

Writing often dealt with facts but also involved "feelings and symbols, and memories that are never quite 'facts' but sometimes closer to the 'truth' than is any fact," according to Smith (13). Smith's opening chapter details one incident whose symbolic weight would convey something significant about Smith's childhood while also introducing one of the prevailing themes of the work: the vagaries of race thinking and its power to shape lives.

A little white girl was found in the black section of our town, living with a Negro family in a broken-down shack. This family had moved in a few weeks before and little was known of them. One of the ladies in my mother's club, while driving over to her washerwoman's, saw the child swinging on a gate . . . "They must have kidnapped her," she told her friends. Genuinely shocked, the clubwomen busied themselves in an attempt to do something, for the child was very white indeed. The strange Negroes were subjected to a grueling questioning and finally grew evasive and refused to talk at all. This only increased the suspicion of the white group. The next day the clubwomen, escorted by the town marshal, took the child from her adopted family despite their tears. (34–35)

Janie would come to live in Smith's large home while authorities investigated how she came to be with a black family. In the interim, she stayed in Smith's room and a "deeply felt bond grew between" the girls as Janie was slowly schooled in the comforts of her newfound home. The investigation completed, Smith learned that Janie would be returning to "Colored Town" for authorities had determined that Janie was indeed black and had recently been adopted from a Negro orphanage. "Why is she leaving?" Smith asked. "She likes us and she hardly knows them. She told me that she had been with them only a month." The incident represents a key point in the book that links Smith's own childhood to the larger "drama of the South"—the transmission of racial codes and ideologies—that the book explores through a range of themes. To Lillian's insistent questioning about Janie's departure, her mother supplies stern responses: "You have always known that white and colored people do not live together." In what amounts to an illustration of the absorption of race thinking among members of her generation and that of her parents, Lillian's exchange with her mother is replicated in the final encounter between Lillian and Janie. When Janie asks Lillian about her claim that white and black children cannot live together, "because they can't" is all that Lillian can muster. But the resolute nature of her response cannot purge Lillian's prevailing sense that "something was wrong" (37). Smith writes herself directly into a narrative of a South that even children knew "was in trouble" (25).

The story of Janie opens a window on Smith's home life. Although her parents adhered to progressive principles, they readily accept the dominant racial codes that surround them. The incident is all the more tragic for Lillian because she knows her "parents betrayed something which they held dear" (37). Yet the incident finally illuminates more than Smith's childhood and family circle by offering up an evocative picture of the organizing power of racial thinking. Determinations of racial difference alter the course of Janie's life as her temporary racialization as a white girl brings her material comfort and the advent of future opportunity. Just as surely, her re-racialization as a black girl spells conditions of material deprivation and physical isolation. The incident integrates biographical, generational, and critical elements. The story of Janie is the opening salvo in a critical set of reflections on categories of racial difference, racial thinking as such, and the pressures to "conform to [their] slide-rule measurements" (29). Through stories such as the one about Janie, *Killers of the Dream* distinguished itself from other work of the period on "race relations," for Smith did not simply want to convey the value of an antisegregationist political stance or improved "race relations." She wanted to scrutinize the mercurial power of racial thinking and its myriad effects.

Smith rejected received wisdom about how a writer could discuss race and in so doing made racial categorization itself a subject of her critical analysis. Recounting the historical legacies that her own generation and her parents' generation inherited through a brief, synthetic account of events before and after the Civil War, Smith argues that justifications for slavery involved "making the black man 'different,' setting him outside God's law, reducing him to less than human" (61). Though Smith's assertion that slavery dehumanized was hardly revelatory, her decision to emphasize the ideological process whereby people were made "different," coupled with the undermining scare quotes she placed around the word, indicated that ideas about racial difference were best understood as analytical problems, not taken-for-granted facts. Just as the story of Janie perforce raised questions about the arbitrary logic of racial difference, so too did the language of Smith's book urge a reorientation in which racial thinking itself became part of the overall problematic that any analysis of the race problem had to address. If psychoanalytic psychiatry turned fantasies into the stuff of rigorous clinical concern, Smith advocated a more general but not altogether dissimilar approach to race in which the work of fantasy became available for critical scrutiny. The processes that made the "black man 'different' " had developed in tandem with "lies about white superiority," which had in turn become a "maze of fantasy and falsehood" in which truth was ever more difficult to discern (61).

If the racial difference long ascribed to African Americans did not belong to the realm of self-evident fact in Smith's analysis, the same was true for the dominant racial category of American social history par excellence: whiteness. In Smith's estimation, the meanings inscribed on bodies by racial ideologies led to a paradoxical overvaluation of whiteness within a belief system that conflated the body and humiliation. Simulating the arguments used to validate white dominance to better expose their internal logic, Smith writes: "Now, on the other hand, though your body is a thing of shame and mystery, and curiosity about it is not good, your skin is your glory and the source of your strength and pride. It is white. And, as you've heard, whiteness is a symbol of purity and excellence" (89). As in other parts of her chapter on "The Lessons," Smith conveyed her views on the interlocking relationships that connected "sin, sex, and segregation." The body's putative sinfulness and the attendant refusal to speak about sex were related to the political inviolability ascribed to segregation. The presence of an intermittent psychoanalytic vocabulary in Smith's elaboration on the lessons suggests the significant role psychoanalytic thinking played in Smith's examination of the "triangulated" relationship between sin, sex, and segregation (94). The signs placed over doors served to naturalize segregation just as other kinds of signs had "been put over forbidden parts of our bodies," Smith wrote, contending that the prohibitions on people and sexuality reinforced a habit, instilled since childhood, of prohibiting one's wishes, "which we learned to send to the Dark-town of our unconscious" (90). The South's dominant ideologies exacted psychological costs that affected the unconscious of individuals, Smith suggested. In such a situation, whiteness played an important compensatory role, for as the various repressions generated by society decreased one's sense of worth, the value that inhered in skin color became ever more important: "There, in the Land of Epidermis, every one of us was a little king" (90).

Although she did not present a systematic psychoanalytic perspective on the value assigned to whiteness, Smith did argue that the power of whiteness and racial ideologies generally derived from the psychological needs they met, and from the powerful ways in which they suffused one's mental life, conscious and unconscious. A continuum existed between the physical dividing lines created by segregation and the mental fissures in the unconscious of whites, in Smith's estimation. Approaches that ignored the psychological dimensions of the race problem could scarcely begin to address the actual power of racial ideology, which profoundly affected the unconscious as surely as it organized the social spaces of the segregated South. Smith's use of "whiteness" provided a way to address the psychological dimensions of prevailing racial ideologies and thus offered a means of isolating for analytic purposes the ideological content of racial thinking itself. Smith wanted to explore the assumptions and multilayered meanings that were bound up in signs over doors reading "white," declining to treat racial categories as self-evident facts. The identification of an alternative subject—whiteness—brought Smith closer to the critical standpoint she desired, for in creating analytic distance from everyday racial categories, she could begin to itemize the different ideological components and processes through which racial ideologies attained their thoroughgoing power. Smith's frustration with the Negro Problem paradigm had to do with the evasion of whiteness that it enabled. Because the race problem and the Negro were conflated in so much public commentary, questions related to the power and effects of whiteness escaped criticism. Smith regarded her psychoanalytic orientation and concern with ideology as means of eluding this habit of thought.

The South's words were deeply important to Smith. The terms and texts of the South offered a way to understand the power of racial ideology and its relationship to longstanding beliefs about sin and sex. Thus, in moving farther along in her investigation of racial ideologies, Smith supplied nearly two full pages of excerpted texts, one passage after the other, from significant figures in the literary and political cultures of the South. Placing these texts within the space of her own narrative, she implicitly argued that they offered up a picture, like her book as a whole, of the culture of the South. Smith presented the words of writers such as William Alexander Percy, David L. Cohn, and Hodding Carter; statements by several southern politicians; and a sentence from a September 26, 1948, *Atlanta Constitution* editorial: "Only a fool would say that the Southern pattern of separation of the races can, or should be overthrown" (78). All of the excerpts were variations on the editorial's segregationist theme, and a few raised the specter of "amalgamation" as the central rationale for maintaining the status quo. In placing the disparate yet ideologically consistent words of different figures together, Smith presented a powerful composite text that indicated the many different interests that jointly upheld the social order. But Smith did not see strength in the consistency of the positions expressed. She detected "deep anxiety in men's hearts" in the excerpts, which led her to ask, "Why has the word [segregation] taken on the terrors of taboo and the sanctity of religion?" (78). The system of white supremacy that Smith opposed could not be disentangled in her mind from its languages, including the racial categories that the system brought to political life.

The word *segregation,* Smith insisted, had entered the lives of individuals in ways that analyses focused on politics and social life alone could not satisfactorily grasp. Segregation "had acquired inflated values that extend far beyond the rational concerns of economics and government, or the obvious profits and losses accruing from the white supremacy system, into childhood memories long repressed" (80). Smith gave her readers a sampling of segregationist texts less to convey the uniformity of thought that existed on the issue but more to impart a sense of the psychological patterns that might be discerned in the vocabulary of white supremacy. Smith interpreted steadfastness about the need for segregated social relations as a form of anxiety, or as what she refers to as the "mask of white supremacy" (76). Smith accomplishes her larger aim of bringing about a rethinking of segregation by asking what lay underneath the commitment to segregationist positions. She did not suggest that she could answer such a question comprehensively, or even by herself, but in her descriptions of the psychological dimensions of segregation, she encouraged her readers to enlarge their understanding of the race problem to include the emotional power that defined concepts and words. Her assemblage of segregation's texts indicated complex emotional investments and disquiet that demanded further questions.

An ethnographic approach also shaped Smith's writing at times. As in the work of the culture-and-personality scholars, Smith's ethnographic impulse involved close attention to the psychological aspects of cultural patterns. She analyzed southern religious practices largely by focusing on the social and cultural significance of the revivalist tradition, arguing that the churchgoing practices of the region "shaped and gave content to the conscience of the southerners, rich and poor" (103). Evangelist preachers "won allegiance by bruising and then healing a deep fear within men's minds," Smith wrote, because "they were shrewd in the use of mass psychology" (105). Alluding to the mass psychology of fascism, Smith presented a portrait of revivalism that combined wonder and danger. The tradition of revivalism represented one mechanism of cultural transmission by which sex, sin, and segregation became ideologically entangled. She wanted to use cultural analysis as a wedge in an area of southern life where it was off limits. Revivalist preachers expressed visions of sin that "stubbornly refused to assent to the possibility that culture had had any role in its creation" (105). Just as Smith brought "sin" within the purview of cultural analysis, so too did revivalism, which helped to disseminate the region's notions of sin, demand concerted interpretation.

Smith's point is not merely that revivalism buttressed segregation, giving ideological cover to dominant social arrangements. She regards the revival as a social institution capable of providing information about cultural and psychological patterns in the South through the specific analysis of revivalist preachers and the audiences whose allegiance they secured. The revivals mattered because culture mattered, and it was in and through culture that the effects of the revivals could be felt long after the tents were gone. Smith's own feelings toward the revivals come close to the aversion to religion expressed in Richard Wright's *Black Boy*. Smith writes, "[It] was after the preacher had sent the town home vibrating with guilt and fear, after the grown folks were asleep and so remote from us who lay terribly awake; it was then we remembered the threats. Then, in the darkness, hell reached out bright long red fingers and seared the edge of our beds. Sometimes we would doggedly whisper to ourselves, 'We are saved too,' but even as we said it, we believed ourselves liars. I remember how impossible it was for me to feel 'saved.' Though I went up to the altar and stayed until the revivalist pried me off my knees, I was never convinced that my kneeling had effected a change in either my present or future life" (110). Yet childhood ambivalence about the revivals, which Smith implies extended beyond her own doubts about salvation, is no match for an adult world that had come to rely on the revivals to renew and disavow feelings of guilt. Because guilt was "the biggest crop raised in Dixie" (103) traveling revivalists and "southern personality" needed one another, Smith suggests (101).

Smith brought an ethnographic eye to her psychological investigation of white women, painting a haunting picture of a society that had so saturated white womanhood with political and cultural significance that the personality formation of white women became an impossible burden. Nearly fifteen years before the publication of Betty Friedan's *The Feminine Mystique* (1963), Smith offered a portrait of southern white women both stark and grave in its implications.[76] The conditions endured by southern white women, she suggested, had a severity all their own, and that had everything to do with the contradictions of the racial formation of the South. She believed that many white children grew up developing strong bonds with their black nurses, transferring maternal feelings to these nurses and away from their biological mothers, although these feelings would later have to be disavowed in order to conform to prevailing racial codes. This social arrangement left many white women in psychological distress as they became symbols of sacredness even as their maternal instincts were thwarted. Like Friedan's suburban mothers, Smith's southern white women suffered from anguish "that could not be acknowledged" (139) even as they "made for themselves and their families what they called a 'normal' life" (141). Though they were imperiled psychologically by the cultural visions of "southern tradition," white women all too often became its most "vigilant guardians," according to Smith (151), as they acceded to the architecture of beliefs that shaped "Sacred Womanhood," including the long-standing "menace of Negro men" (145). Smith's account of white women, one of the more disturbing parts of her reliably disquieting book, also displayed sympathy. As if responding directly to the midcentury tendency in American intellectual culture of blaming mothers for all manner of social problems, as in writer-provocateur Philip Wylie's rebuke of what he called "Momism," Smith wrote, "Sometimes we blame Mom too much for all that is wrong with her sons and daughters. After all, we might ask, who started the grim mess? Who long ago made Mom and her sex 'inferior' and stripped her of her economic and political and sexual rights?"[77] Smith also included a counterpoint to the picture of white women as guardians of the dominant social order in the emergence of the Association of Southern Women for the Prevention of Lynching in 1930. Though they may not have confronted the full complexity of the "sex-race-religion-economics tangle," Smith credited the white women who formed the association for their courageous political stance (128).

Killers of the Dream developed variations on the theme of the "ideology of white supremacy" as a "constellation of skin-color-purity concepts that fixed and supported it and kept the mind of the people from questioning its 'truth'" (203). Smith's ethnographic renderings and psychological portraits performed that critical work, as did the use of a parable she called "Two Men and a Bargain." The parable involved Mr. Rich White and Mr. Poor White and the bargain they struck in order to maintain the segregated social order. Smith distills the bargain by having Mr. Rich White say to Mr. Poor White: "You boss the nigger, and I'll boss the money. How about it?" (176). Her story about the agreement forged between representatives of would-be antagonistic classes of whites to deprive blacks of economic and political power is straightforward enough. Indeed, the simple nature of the parable is finally meant to convey the freighted ideological and cultural work that has to take place for the bargain to come off. Thus, the parable becomes a way to convey the complex interaction of racial ideologies and economic interests. Though her two main figures stay the same, their encounters bring many different subjects to the fore, among them the pacifying effects of churchgoing on poor whites and the decisions that kept blacks out of unions. Mr. Rich White's opening monologue sets the terms of the bargain, emphasizing that part of what he proposes is the compensatory power of whiteness: "If you ever get restless when you don't have a job . . . remember that you're a sight better than the black man" (177). The parable of two men from different classes and the accord they reach on Jim Crow is the part of the book that most stresses the economic component of the "sex-race-religion-economics tangle." Smith's parable comments on the power of racial ideologies to shape relationships among and across classes, and it indicates the entwined power of the economic and the psychological in the South.

Responses to *Killers of the Dream*

Smith had written a book that stood as a challenge to all Americans. Yet what kind of book was it? How did reviewers and readers understand its meanings and implications? Because Smith's narrative choices in *Killers of the Dream* were complex, some reviewers crafted innovative terms to describe the book. A writer for the *Journal of Religion* called it a "psychohistorical study of segregation in the South." Never before had the "South been subjected to an analysis whose basic psychiatric insights have done so little violence to historical facts." Before an actual field of scholarly investigation called "psychohistory" emerged, Smith's work was given that attribution because of its widely acknowledged ability to present psychological perspectives on the past that, for many, deepened historical understanding. Through her poetic imagination, Smith "transmuted voluminous historical data into a memorable picture of an awful tradition," displaying a "subtle comprehension of man's spiritual infirmities and a profound compassion for their eternal victims."[78] The use of the term *psychohistorical* was, above all, an effort to make sense of the hybrid quality of Smith's narrative and to account for the interplay between historical contextualization and psychological interpretation that characterized her approach.

Many African American writers responded to *Killers of the Dream* with enthusiasm. Horace Cayton in particular was highly impressed with the book, which he called a "fearless discussion" of the problems of racism and segregation. He endorsed the view expressed in the book that held whites to be the central obstacles to the possibility of changing social life for whites and blacks alike. Cayton expanded on the psychoanalytic vocabulary Smith employed to render the thoughts and actions of many southern whites, citing the exemplary analysis of the "narcissistic preoccupation" of whites with skin color. Cayton also made use of a language of "emotional maturity" and "emotional growth," both of which he associated with psychological health. Whites who worked to maintain the racist social order did so out of a "hysterical resistance to emotional growth." But whites were scarcely alone in deflecting the emotional pressures that suffused race problems in the South. According to Cayton, "the presence and the inferior position of the Negro in the South have provided to men of both races a convenient mechanism by which to avoid arriving at emotional maturity." In Smith's work, Cayton located both perceptive observations on psychological aspects of race thinking and a therapeutic understanding of what constituted emotional health. In describing much of southern society as marked by a "cultural malaise" that threatened personalities across the color line, Smith provided a formulation that could further investigations of race and racism generally. Cayton regarded her analysis as "applicable also, in greater or lesser degree, to the North." Smith examined an "archaic system" based in "a neurotic need to suppress weaker people," bringing to light a feature of racisms in general and contributing to a body of writing that challenged the centrality of the Negro Problem paradigm.[79]

Alain Locke wrote that *Killers of the Dream* represented a "sound parable of race prejudice and its killing effects upon both black and white," one that made "effective use of the principles of psychoanalytics," giving the "ordinary layman insight into the roots and results of prejudice."[80] The *Journal of Negro History* identified the "dream" of Smith's title as "human dignity and the sacredness of personality," praising the book as one that "psychoanalyzes slavery, the brutal greed of its origin, and the hate-complexes which have resulted from the blood and carnage exacted in the Civil War and continue to rage in America today."[81] Striking a similar note, the white film director Joshua Logan, a native of Louisiana, conveyed a strong emotional response to Smith's book, finding "truth in every line." In the filmmaker's view, Smith's writing suggested that she "had a private window somewhere under my shoulder blade where you could look inside me." On reading *Killers of the Dream*, Logan, who would direct films with antiprejudice themes in the 1950s such as *South Pacific* and *Sayonara*, was "on fire with the excitement and illumination" of Smith's work, and went so far as to predict that it would "do more for the South and Southerners and therefore for our country than anything that has been written in our American history."[82]

Within the pages of the *Psychoanalytic Quarterly*, Smith's book was regarded as a "psychological study in the best sense" and one that displayed facility with "dynamic psychology."[83] Smith had written a book "of importance to psychoanalysts." *Killers of the Dream* came to the attention of psychoanalytic thinkers in part through the endorsement of Lawrence Kubie, who claimed that Smith "has found her way through a maze of technical complexities with great clarity, fusing the relationships of individual developmental forces and of social forces in conscious and unconscious levels of human development with an insight I have rarely seen duplicated even in technical writings on this problem."[84] Kubie's identification of Smith's criticism with "militant liberalism" suggested that he understood her writings on individuals and social forces, on culture and personality, as effectively exceeding the boundaries of available liberal thought, and therefore as work that could move liberalism in politically vital directions. Smith's analyses of race thinking and its pervasive meanings represented the kind of radical intervention that could invigorate intellectual life and even remake American political culture. Karl Menninger's comments on the book also offered an implicit political understanding of Smith's achievement. "You have written something so keen and earnest and insistent and inescapable," Menninger wrote to Smith about *Killers of the Dream*. "This is a social diagnosis by a keen physician who knows the disease from personal experience, and having cured herself, is pointing a way for others to follow, if they have the guts."[85]

Some significant parallels between Smith's work and midcentury psychoanalytic thinking escaped the attention of reviewers whose knowledge of psychoanalysis derived from its general dissemination in intellectual life and less from readings in psychological theory. Familiar with the work of Franz Alexander, Smith may well have had his *Fundamentals of Psychoanalysis* (1948) in mind as she composed *Killers of the Dream*, given many striking resonances. For Alexander, neurosis referred to the relationship between a personality and its social setting. Alexander considered the mid-twentieth century a time of especially rapid social change, which in turn posed severe challenges to people who could no longer rely on the "comfort of living according to well-tested traditions." Accelerated social change demanded personalities that were flexible and an individual adept at "knowing himself, his desires, impulses, motives, and needs." The imperative for the formation of different personalities had to do with the need to resist a "conspicuous tendency to conformity." Without a more introspective and self-reliant mode of personality formation, individuals could "become the prey of power-seeking minorities who will induce him to believe that his security lies in doing what he is told."[86] These are the terms in which Smith casts her narrative of white domination in the South, as the story of a white minority capable of bringing a white majority into agreement with policies of racial segregation. Indeed, *Killers of the Dream* expressed many of Alexander's views on the pressures exerted on social tradition, the dangers of conformity, and the environmentalist underpinnings of neurotic personality formation. The active and critical personality formation Alexander posited as a vital resource in times of dramatic social transformation underwrites Smith's narrative.

Reading Race, Engendering Therapy

Smith's characterization of race conflict as a symptom became a defining feature of her writing, one enabled in large part by her immersion in psychological, especially psychoanalytic, thought. Beginning in the late 1930s, Smith argued that race was a part of the "myth-making" of "the scientific age." Where the demonologies of devils and ghosts from earlier epochs once stood, the race thinking of the scientific age had arisen, but the underlying reasons for the creation of demonologies were unchanged:

"As long as we have unconscious personal conflicts, as long as we have deep-laid environmental frustrations, we shall have hate—and demonologies, false and real." Psychoanalysts, among others, Smith said, had done a "fascinating job of telling this story of primitive man's battles with himself." Her interest in the psychological dimensions of race conflict represented a strategy of furthering critical rereadings of race as myth and cultural symptom.[87]

Yet, more sophisticated interpretations of race thinking did not represent the only objective of Smith's cultural politics. An irreducible component of her analysis of race concepts had to do with the therapeutic value of undoing corrosive social categorization. An understanding of the midcentury psychological idiom that Smith developed requires an appreciation of the language of therapeutic transformation that was inextricably tied to the analysis of racial ideologies in her thinking. For Smith, the value and effectiveness of social change could be measured by the mental health that resulted. In her work, a therapeutic language of health-mindedness reflected the belief that people were governed by both thoughts and reflexes and that any social process that moved society in the direction of desegregation and antiracism would set in motion a beneficial "reconditioning of reflexes." Personality stood at the center of the discourse of health-mindedness that Smith presented in her work. "We are making a good bargain in swapping our old segregated culture, our segregated southern culture, our segregated personality, for love and wholeness and dignity in men's relationships with each other and with themselves," Smith said during a commencement address at Kentucky State College, in 1951.[88]

Smith's dedication for a reprinted version of *Killers of the Dream* invokes the memory of her parents, who had "valiantly tried to keep their nine children in touch with wholeness though reared in a segregated culture." Although Smith's parents come under criticism in the book for their capitulation to social codes, especially in the episode involving Janie, Smith conveys their progressive tendencies as well. She shared Lawrence Frank's view that "wholesome personalities who have self-confidence" were vital to the "tremendous tasks of renewing our disintegrating culture." Her abiding idea in *Killers of the Dream* echoed in Frank's work when he said that to "improve the social order, the human personalities that made up that social order must be ready and willing to change."[89] The subject of wholesome personalities provided Smith with a recurring set of questions that in her estimation belonged at the center of modern social thought.

The difficulty of changes and the psychological trials of social transformations figured prominently among Smith's themes. "Our people are afraid to give up their cherished symbols. The reality changes will be so small; they will affect the white man's external life so little: then why does he fight so desperately for the old way of segregation? Because, of course, it is changing his dream life; his symbolic experiences, all his psychic defenses are challenged."[90] In the mid-1950s, Smith also commented on the impact decolonization movements had begun to have on writing: "Subject matter is changing; esthetics are changing; technics must, therefore, change." By *technics* Smith referred to the overall set of strategies and technical possibilities writers bring to bear on their work.[91] The psychological idiom Smith advanced had centrally defined her own "technics," for it led to cultural readings of the southern scene different from those that had previously obtained. As the civil rights movement emerged, the psychological themes of her cultural commentary remained central to Smith's thinking, and international and domestic reconfigurations seemed to call for yet further ways of conceptualizing the history of the South.

In the foreword to the 1961 edition of *Killers of the Dream,* Smith placed greater emphasis on the internationalist dimensions of her thinking by making assertions present in the original version more explicit. Writing against the historical backdrop of the decolonization movements in Asia and Africa, Smith continued to attack "colonialism's twin brother, segregation," which "not only lives but wields power." Her foreword, like the book, continued to explore the specificity of the racial ideologies that shaped American social life, drawing further attention to the "strange and mad obsession" with whiteness that "segregationists, South and North," advanced and nurtured. Looking back on her career in the mid-1960s, she wrote, "My talent was for writing and speaking; and my job as I saw it was to make a direct attack on the philosophy and system of segregation itself; to show its spiritual and psychological evils, how it was both symptom and symbol."[92]

Smith died in 1966 after a long battle with cancer. Commenting on Smith's intellectual contribution, Snelling observed that *Strange Fruit* had told a "Romeo-Juliet story, in Deep South setting, with such compassionate clarity that the dead-endedness of skin worship, for adherents anywhere, would now be evident to readers everywhere."[93] Smith had participated in what she herself had called the "semantic journey from 'the Negro problem' to 'the human family,' " even as the conundrums of "race" continued to swirl at the time of her death.[94]

If Smith's career as a writer encompassed studies in culture and personality, the same can be said of James Baldwin, whose own assessments of the meanings of race in American life derived from direct and indirect exposure to the psychological inquiries of Wright, Smith, and others. Commenting on Smith, Baldwin would say that she was "very great" and "heroic," a figure willing to endure a great deal in order to do what she thought was right.[95] In the immediate postwar decade, Baldwin expanded in his own style on major aspects of her work, not least the concern with the mutability of culture, the psychological complexities of personality, and the workings of whiteness. Like much of Smith's work, Baldwin's essays were based in a psychological conception of culture and presented psychological interiority as a principal site for the making of cultural meanings. Baldwin's modernist cultural and literary enterprise in the late 1940s and early 1950s, the subject of the next chapter, diverged in many respects from the work of Smith and Wright. Yet the ground for the antiracism that runs through his modernist experimentalism had been prepared by Wright's existential psychoanalysis and the larger work of yoking antiracism and psychological inquiry that predated his entrance into the literary world.

CHAPTER FIVE

Notes of a Native Son
James Baldwin in Postwar America

In "Alas, Poor Richard," written not long after Richard Wright's death in 1960, James Baldwin addresses Wright directly, invoking the "argument which you began in me."[1] Baldwin first met Wright, sixteen years his senior and the most famous black writer in America, in 1944. In the intervening years, Baldwin would also become an internationally known writer. The enduring sense of intellectual indebtedness imparted by the "argument you began in me" had much to do with the commitment to psychological inquiry Wright had modeled in his fiction and cultural commentary. Building on Wright's fiction and criticism, Baldwin made the "basic and profound dislocation of the Negro" the major subject of his work. The result was a distinctive form of cultural criticism that fused a modernist idiom with an unblinking exploration of the effects of racial divisions and racial thinking. Baldwin investigated what he called the "basic error, that Negroes, or any other group or race is 'different' " as a profound cultural problem that "threatens all of us and must therefore be challenged on as many levels as lie within our power."[2]

Wright's intellectual labors, his insistence on reframing race thinking and racial antagonisms as central features of American social life, supplied a practical starting point for Baldwin. Yet the two writers unquestionably emerged from distinct moments in cultural and intellectual history. Wright entered the national and international literary scene in the early 1940s; Baldwin attracted notice later that decade, around the time of the onset of the Cold War. Veering away from the modes of literary expression associated with Wright, Baldwin played no small role in stressing the differences between Wright's artistic imagination and his own. The differences were real enough. Whereas Wright at one time searched social scientific and psychoanalytic sources to gather insights about a social world organized by race and saturated with racial antagonisms, Baldwin followed a different course, preferring to nurture psychological inquiry through a form of literary and cultural criticism that rebuffed clinical data and looked askance at the strictures of social science. In a portentous move, Baldwin called himself an "observer" and turned away from any inclination toward writing that resembled a diatribe against the nation.[3] Yet Baldwin's tactical strategies as a writer were complex, for at the same time that he rejected what he took to be prevailing mistakes that marred writing on race in America, he placed race thinking and the dislocation of African America at the forefront of his literary ambitions.

If Wright was critical to Baldwin's trajectory, so too was the intellectual environment created by the writers who came to be known as "the New York intellectuals." The centrality of modernist aesthetics and psychoanalytic thought in the work of the midcentury critics who made up the New York intellectuals influenced Baldwin, who would contribute in turn to the concern with subjectivity that marked much of postwar cultural and literary criticism. Baldwin early on dedicated himself to a life of writing and formed his critical acumen in concert with modernist themes of interiority and psychological observation, attaching the label "observer" to himself when describing the kind of writing he produced.[4] The New York intellectuals, arguably the preeminent American literary intellectuals of the mid-twentieth century, adopted a questioning and antagonistic position in relation to dominant social forces. Yet, as their political radicalism abated by the 1950s, and as their connections to radical social movements grew tenuous, the role of the literary intellectual as a cultural observer free of political entanglements took on an increasingly important symbolic role. The ability of the literary critic to stand apart from radical politics became a prerequisite for inhabiting esteemed quarters of postwar intellectual life. For the New York intellectuals and Baldwin alike, writers held a special social responsibility. Developing his profile as a young writer in New York in the postwar period, Baldwin adopted a literary-critical style marked by skepticism of radical politics. Echoing the response of many writers to Baldwin's prose, the novelist and critic Mary McCarthy praised "quick, Olympian recognitions that were free of prejudice."[5]

Yet if the anticommunism that coincided with Baldwin's rise to prominence informed his literary and critical work, he was not merely a product of postwar reconfigurations of intellectual life. The challenges to race thinking and race hierarchy brought to the fore during the 1930s and war years under the auspices of antifascism also figure in Baldwin's emergence as a cultural critic. Antifascism had helped to give the problem of racial ideology national and international inflections during the war, and examination of the psychological characteristics of fascism carried over into the postwar period even as its immediate political rationale diminished. The concerted focus on psychology, fascism, and prejudice that became part of public debate before and during the war entered postwar literary and cultural criticism in many ways, not least through Baldwin's persistent return to problems of racial ideology. Although Baldwin departed stylistically from Wright and other antiracist writers, he in many ways resumed the investigation of the psychological under-currents of race hierarchy and race thinking that they had begun to pursue in earnest in the early 1940s.

Asserting that the meanings of race for American life were more profound than had yet been shown, Baldwin presented his readings of American culture as a means of grasping the psychic economy of racial thinking that had structured American history. Working in concert with the broadly modernist and psychoanalytic orienta-tion of the New York intellectuals, Baldwin sought unsentimental interpretations of race thinking and racist practices. Through his fluency with literary critical perspec-tives informed by modernism and psychoanalysis, Baldwin translated problems of race into the privileged vocabulary of psychological interiority, thereby putting them on the postwar intellectual landscape in forms both unanticipated and acclaimed. In so doing, Baldwin introduced a unique element into the world of the literary cognoscenti and into American letters more generally. His midcentury writing, par-ticularly the essays, acquired a complex character as emblems of postwar intellectual gravitas that communicated misgivings about radical political visions while simulta-neously carrying forceful, even searing, accounts of racial discord and social aliena-tion. For all of the distinctiveness of his path into literary-intellectual life, Baldwin returned repeatedly to the terrain of racial ideology and segregated life through the very terms—culture and psyche—that Wright had proposed.

Baldwin, Wright, and Psychological Inquiry

If Wright's major themes involved the psychological dynamics of racial antagonisms within American urban life, these themes were also, inevitably, questions. Through his essays from the late 1940s and early 1950s, Baldwin would offer his own responses to these questions. In his earliest literary efforts, he drew from Wright's corpus even as he attempted to diverge from the representational terrain Wright had staked. In his first published story, "Previous Condition" (1948), Baldwin creates a "paranoiac" main character, whose "hatred had corrupted me like a cancer in the bone." The protagonist is a young African American actor named Peter who scrapes together a living by taking small parts in different shows, but the story does not revolve around Peter's work on the stage. Instead, Baldwin primarily develops the theme of Peter's paranoiac sensibility in the face of the unpredictable dangers and slights of urban, racialized social relations. Peter feels as if the pressures he faces as a racialized subject will overtake him and bring about an explosion of violence. When a friend counsels Peter to relax, he admits that he probably comes off as a paranoiac, but he knows of no other way to convey his feelings. At one point he declares, "I've been fighting so goddam long I'm not a person anymore. I want to emancipate myself. If this goes on much longer, they'll send me to Bellevue, I'll blow my top, I'll break somebody's head . . . I'm worried about what's happening to me, *to me,* inside."[6] Readers undoubtedly picked up on the similarities between Peter and Bigger Thomas, but the differences were also apparent. The details that Baldwin introduces give his protagonist an artistic persona, and he is even more insistent than Wright about the specific psychological affliction—paranoia—that leads his protagonist to project his personal conflicts and attribute them to the alleged hostility of others.

If the connections of Baldwin's story to Wright were not evident enough, the latter soon figures in the narrative more conspicuously. Originally from an "old shack town in New Jersey," Peter finds himself in New York but does not necessarily feel most at home in Harlem. When, at the end of the story, he goes to Harlem after a series of insults, he thinks to himself: "A white outsider coming in would have seen a young Negro drinking in a Negro bar, perfectly in his element, in his place, as the saying goes. But the people here know differently, as I did. I didn't seem to have a place."[7] When Peter is offered the part of Bigger Thomas in a stage version of *Native Son,* he rejects it as an example of "type casting," lamenting the lack of decent parts available to him. Already in his first published short story, then, Baldwin was distancing himself from the social protest fiction tradition that he identified with Wright. Yet, through the figure of Peter, Baldwin ventured a character driven in large part by ruminations and fears that derived from the social and psychological worlds engendered by race hierarchy and race thinking. The story therefore shares the thematic zone Wright had made central to African American letters and, at the same time, demonstrates Baldwin's determination to present investigations of "race" that exceeded those of Wright in their psychological discernment.

In the well-known essays "Everybody's Protest Novel" (1949) and "Many Thousands Gone" (1951), Baldwin rejected the realist literary traditions with which he identified Wright. If Wright moved his work in the direction of psychological concerns, Baldwin's essays proposed that Wright had ultimately failed to present the actual psychological complexities of the racist social order. Although he may have aimed for such complexity, Wright had offered a defective product in *Native Son,* making the best-seller everybody's and nobody's protest novel at the same time, Baldwin claimed. These essays on the protest novel tradition were acts through which Baldwin secured a place within American cultural criticism, and they played a decisive role in shaping his intellectual profile. The essays examine protest literature as a mode of writing that insufficiently or inadequately addresses psychological dynamics in social and cultural life. They focus on the protest novel tradition in order to reflect on the limitations and possible directions of contemporary literature, pressing the point that literary culture had an obligation to move toward greater psychological acuteness.

Baldwin's essays have long invited readings that convert Wright into the younger author's literary father in an Oedipal drama. However, the inflated significance attached to such readings has meant that a more complicated and interesting history involving the two writers often goes unrecognized. Indeed, the wide salience accorded the stories of personal acrimony between Wright and Baldwin and the idea of inviolable literary camps endorsed by many accounts have obscured thematic and literary continuities in the works of the two writers. It can become difficult to recall that Wright encouraged Baldwin's first literary endeavors and all too easy to ignore the obvious fact that Wright provided Baldwin with the prototype of a successful literary career. Wright's work was crucial in preparing the discursive terrain for Baldwin's reflections, or "notes," on culture, race, and interiority. Working within the parameters of prized forms of midcentury literary and cultural criticism, Baldwin addressed the very psychological effects of racist social environments that had been central to Wright's work. Although Baldwin expanded the search for the meanings of race thinking within an intellectual landscape very different from the one that Wright found, he pursued such meanings nonetheless. The distinct but comparable approaches to race thinking that Wright and Baldwin created stand as continuities that extend across their bodies of writing.

Baldwin's criticisms of the protest novel tradition and Wright in particular were not sui generis. In his first published piece of criticism, "Maxim Gorki as Artist," Baldwin had already begun to indicate his preferred varieties of literary styles and present views that would recur in his essays. Baldwin evaluated a new collection of the Russian author's short stories and found the work superior to most other realist writing by virtue of its "tender, ironic, and observant" sensibility. Gorky succeeded in bringing readers "unpredictability and the occasional and amazing splendor of the human being." Despite his signature social realism, Baldwin wrote, Gorky frequently delivered psychologically meaningful and lively narratives. Yet, too often, "psychological acuteness" was missing from the short stories. Baldwin complained that Gorky's tales frequently indulged sentimentalism, as when characters were presented in "relation to oppression, but not in relation to ourselves." Through his appraisal of Gorky, Baldwin delivered some of his earliest published thoughts on the role of the writer. Expressing a view of literature as a privileged form, Baldwin suggested that all writers bore a responsibility to prevent literature from dropping "completely to the intellectual and moral level of the daily papers." To retain literary creativity as an endeavor that could not be confused with everyday forms of social expression, Baldwin urged that writers aim toward insight into the human heart and mind, into "human needs, desperations and desires."[8] In "Everybody's Protest Novel," Baldwin situated Harriet Beecher Stowe and Wright in a protest novel tradition that stretched across the nineteenth and twentieth centuries, and charged both writers with privileging categorization over complexity. He argued that protest fiction severed connections to a vital "web of ambiguity, paradox . . . hunger, danger, darkness, [where] we can find at once ourselves and the power that will free us from ourselves."[9]

While Baldwin refers to Wright's *Native Son* in "Everybody's Protest Novel," it is only in "Many Thousands Gone" that he offers an extended critique of Wright's work. Baldwin sees a novel "trapped by the American image of Negro life" and a "representation of [Bigger Thomas's] psychology" that falls short of conveying "any sense of Negro life as a continuing and complex group reality." "Many Thousands Gone" assigns *Native Son* to the 1930s, for the book came out only a few years after "bread lines and soup kitchens and bloody industrial battles" and soon after the "dissolution of the Works Progress Administration and the end of the New Deal." Baldwin contends that Wright's book leaves such themes as the "dehumanization of the Negro" firmly within the social arena and thus beyond the reach of more exacting and meaningful reckoning. But while the novel is faulted for shortcomings in this regard, Baldwin is finally more disturbed by how easily Wright's story might be domesticated and made to fit the panoply of conventional American narratives. The thrust of Baldwin's critique throughout much of "Many Thousands Gone" has to do with the reception and cultural praise *Native Son* received. The essay laments the novel's putative representation of racial antagonisms as a resolutely "social arena," for Wright's work activates a deeper anxiety for Baldwin, namely that Americans had developed a "remarkable ability to alchemize all bitter truths into an innocuous confection" and look at terrible facts "full in the face without flinching," to the point of transforming moral contradictions into a "proud decoration."[10] Baldwin's stated concern with the "dehumanization of the Negro" motivated his critique of Wright, but a larger apprehension having to do with American readers domesticating and finessing literary works addressing freighted historical problems seemed to trouble Baldwin most. Wright's work provided an occasion for Baldwin to bring this broader problem into view. The essay thus discloses Baldwin's unease about reception and readerships as an emerging literary artist intent on treating the "dehumanization of the Negro."

The limitations of Wright's novel for Baldwin can be summed up in the depiction of Bigger Thomas, who is characterized as a being so apart from the social worlds he inhabits that a sense of his personality evaporates. "What is missing in his situation and in the representation of his psychology," Baldwin writes, "is any revelatory apprehension of Bigger as one of the Negro's realities." Baldwin finds that Wright's story is caught within the parameters of the "American image of Negro life." While the novel rightly explores the myths that pervade conventional accounts of African American life, the "implications" of these narrative explorations are not pursued. By "implications," Baldwin indicates narrative impulses in the book that he finds forceful and important. He states plainly that "no American Negro exists who does not have his private Bigger Thomas living in his skull." But he suggests that his own pursuit of the implications of anger, frustration, and social estrangement would follow alternative paths of psychological representation. In particular, Baldwin is interested in the "paradoxical adjustment that is perpetually made" as African Americans find ways to "accept the fact that this dark and dangerous and unloved stranger is part of himself forever."[11] *Native Son* did not tell the story of such adjustment in Baldwin's estimation and therefore limited from the outset its ability to bring African American life into psychological representation. The essays maintain that Wright confined to a "social arena" what Baldwin wanted to bring into an exacting space of critical and psychological reinterpretation. Baldwin would not forgo the social dimensions of race, but he would not be "trapped" by them, as he claimed that Wright had been. The implications of Bigger Thomas's anger are marginalized, according to Baldwin, who wishes to bring greater psychological subtlety to the investigation of that anger, on the one hand, and analyze cultural evasions symptomatically for the meanings they disclosed, on the other.

In their own inimitable way, Baldwin's postwar essays both affirmed and criticized *Native Son.* According to Baldwin, the novel proceeds from a convincing premise: "that Americans, who evade, so far as possible, all genuine experience, have therefore no way of assessing the experience of others and no way of establishing themselves in relation to any way of life which is not their own."[12] The referencing of Wright's novel in the title essay of *Notes of a Native Son* was only the most obvious way in which Baldwin returned to that premise. By the mid-1950s, Baldwin's own intellectual and literary contribution was itself commonly interpreted as the exploration of American evasions, and his use of the word further discloses guiding assumptions he shared with Wright.[13] Although a contemporaneous critic held that Baldwin's writing in the immediate postwar decade had moved "above the breast-beatings of his racial forbears on the literary scene," Baldwin in fact proved adept at carrying themes and problems in Wright's work into the postwar American culture.[14]

In 1960, Baldwin recalled that despite the differences between the two writers, Wright's works from the 1940s "expressed, for the first time in my life, the rage, and the murderous bitterness which was eating me up and eating up the lives of those around me," making "Richard's work an immense liberation and revelation."[15] Baldwin told an interviewer that Wright had "described the life I lived," for he had represented the tenements and degrading conditions that defined his own biographical circumstances. "I knew that rat in 'Native Son,'" Baldwin declared. Moreover, Wright provided ways for Baldwin to connect with the fiction and poetry of Jean Toomer and Langston Hughes, writers he had previously regarded as removed from his experience.[16]

Baldwin's access to significant literary and cultural venues afforded opportunities to further open American writing to critical investigations of race thinking. Through an explicitly nontechnical brand of psychological inquiry, Baldwin emerged as a cultural critic who made questions of race and nation among his foremost intellectual priorities. During a period of increasing intellectual conformity, Baldwin translated questions of "race" into the idiom of high literary culture, and in so doing enlarged the contours of intellectual debate about race thinking and race hierarchy.

The New York Intellectuals and Psychoanalytic Thought

Like the New York intellectuals who gave him his start as a writer, Baldwin was interested in psychological insights, not in the social scientific procedure of much psychological investigation. Especially in the essays that were collected in *Notes of a Native Son,* Baldwin revealed affinities with the New York intellectuals, writers who prized the exploration of interiority and subjective experience. His relationship to the New York intellectuals and their circles in the late 1940s and early 1950s brings his work squarely within the political and cultural reconfigurations spurred by the onset of the Cold War. Yet, as we will see, Baldwin departed at times from the preoccupations of the New York intellectuals, traversing the boundaries of Cold War–era discourses.

In the words of one historian, the New York intellectuals "moved from a distinct variety of communism in the 1930s to a distinct variety of liberalism by the 1950s," a process that involved the attenuation of critical views about American political institutions and economic arrangements.[17] The New York intellectuals were some of the most influential writers to come out of the proletarian social movement that began in the 1930s, when many searched for ways to bring together radical politics and avant-garde literature—an intellectual project within which Marxism figured centrally. Philip Rahv, editor of *Partisan Review,* a publication intimately connected to the New York intellectuals, wrote that the "literary left-wing movement" in the United States was "native to New York" and found in Marxism its "underlying philosophy."[18] But a shift from Marxism to liberal anticommunism in the 1940s led to an ambiguous relationship to radical social thought and political movements as such. Although the intellectual as a figure of radical politics and alternative cultural values continued to play an important role, an ardent political anticommunism and an antagonistic relationship to left-liberal social movements came to define the world of the New York intellectuals in the postwar period.

The world of cultural commentary that Baldwin encountered as he began to envision life as a writer elevated the intellectual as a social type and validated anti-communism as a political horizon. The editors and writers for the quarterlies that Baldwin appeared in throughout the late 1940s and early 1950s were the New York in-tellectuals who had helped to bring about that altered critical environment, one largely closed to the forms of radicalism that had emerged in the 1930s. The changes in *Partisan Review* were emblematic. *Partisan Review* "found itself creating a counter-language to articulate anti-Stalinism and redefine radicalism in a non-Communist context."[19] The energy devoted by intellectuals in developing an effective and persua-sive anti-Stalinist discourse would expand in the late 1940s, joining a broader, cultural anticommunism that more and more exerted dominance in American thought.[20] That anticommunism went together with a heightened appreciation for American political culture that contrasted with an earlier intellectual antagonism. *Partisan Review* editor William Phillips expressed a view common among the New York intellectuals when he wrote that "American artists and intellectuals have acquired a new sense of belonging in their native land and have generally come to feel that their own fate is tied to the fate of their country."[21]

Key to this recalibration were editors and writers for the New York quarterlies— *Partisan Review, Commentary,* and the *New Leader*—who were often involved in organizations that emerged to channel the anticommunist activities of intellectuals and artists, including the Congress for Cultural Freedom. Many believed that the onset of the Cold War heightened the importance of defending principles of freedom and intellectual liberty—a challenge that could be met by the vigorous creation of anticommunist discourses "with the weapons of the intellect."[22] For the New York intellectuals, as for many others, the stakes in the Cold War conflict were high indeed. In a 1948 *Partisan Review* article, Robert Gorham Davis noted that intellec-tual life increasingly involved a "fight for Western Europe," nothing less than the "survival of a western culture."[23]

The trajectory traveled by the New York intellectuals from socialism to anti-Stalinist and, later, anticommunist political affiliation involved an accelerated re-thinking of literature and aesthetics that measured the value of modernist approaches in terms of their psychological complexity and, more importantly, their deviation from naturalist and social realist representation. Baldwin's early career developed in the midst of this elevation of modernist prose—a process in which psychoanalytic thought loomed large. Literary scholar Frederick J. Hoffman wrote that psychoanalysis had succeeded in "making the unconscious a living thing, available to him who wishes to go beneath the surface of his mind."[24] For many, the avenues opened by Freudian theory were superior to those on offer through existing intellectual models and promised penetrating interpretations of self and other in the modern world. Midcentury accounts of the contributions of psychoanalysis complement Baldwin's view of writers as figures distinguished by an ability to "examine attitudes, to go beneath the surface, to tap the source."[25] Hoffman's conviction that "our psychic peculiarities are in the end only available to the sober testimony of systematic investigation" parallels Baldwin's understanding of the role of the writer.[26] Baldwin's descriptions of the writing process indicated a Freudian disposition to both analyze comprehensively and concentrate on phenomena that did not present themselves in a transparent manner.

In the late 1940s, many of Freud's more accessible essays, some of which had long been out of print or unavailable in English, were compiled in volumes such as *Freud: On War, Sex and Neurosis* (1947) and came to figure prominently in intellectual and literary culture. A pivotal figure whose work emerged within the interface of medical expertise and a "revolutionary critique of our ethical and civil hypocrisy and timidity," Freud was the cultural critic most worthy of emulation in the view of many postwar intellectuals. The essays collected in *Freud: On War, Sex, and Neurosis* spoke "for themselves," writer Paul Goodman observed, "but a literary man cannot refrain from observing that just as belles-lettres some of them are masterpieces" that exhibited "swiftness, clarity, and adequacy of exposition."[27] If the authoritativeness of Freud's writing appealed to many postwar intellectuals, so too did his "strain of philosophical grief" seem useful as a resource in a period of political recalibration and uncertainty.[28] According to Lionel Trilling, Freud's method and formulations conveyed a "sense of human mystery, of tragedy truly conceived in the great terms of free will, necessity, and hope."[29]

Among the New York intellectuals, the waning of Marxism was accompanied by a heightened focus on the social and cultural implications of Freudian thought.[30] Freudian concepts and a general appreciation for the philosophy of psychoanalysis informed the writing of many critics in their efforts to shape a distinctive literary and cultural criticism. Even beyond the venues of the New York intellectuals, psychoanalysis was seen as an invaluable tool for the study of literature and culture. Among scholars in the humanities, including American Studies, psychoanalysis was increasingly taken to be a "necessary division of the modern intellectual's knowledge."[31] Freudian thought fit well with the New York intellectuals' modernist impulse toward interiority and subjectivity and, by the late 1940s, many writers who published regularly in the New York intellectual quarterlies were closely associated with psychoanalysis. Freud categorically belonged to the world of literary and cultural analysis, wrote Trilling, who went so far as to assert that Freud was the "chief proponent of the whole culture concept."[32] As one *Partisan Review* writer observed, it was psychoanalysis as a "cultural discipline" that attracted postwar writers and literary intellectuals.[33]

Postwar intellectuals largely accepted the Freudian view that characteristics of primitive societies, though modified by civilization, remained an irreducible part of the unconscious and hence persisted in modern cultural life. This claim, and Freud's further explorations of human neuroses, supplied a "psychological description of the history of culture" that could not easily be dismissed.[34] For many literary intellectuals, the inseparability of psychoanalytic thought and the history of culture obligated artists and humanistic thinkers alike to consider the inescapable determinants of the unconscious and the psychological dynamics that shaped human culture generally. In Baldwin's work, direct acknowledgement of these mainstays of mid-century intellectual life was scarce. Nonetheless, the Freudian conception of culture as a site of strife informed Baldwin's writing, showing up in the neurotic personalities and social maladjustments he presented and in his broader interest in unconscious patterns and social conflict. Baldwin's efforts to interpret the meanings of personal episodes and the unrecognized emotional patterns that pervaded American culture had much in common with the emphasis placed on historical and psychological processes in the Freudian understanding of the emergence of cultures.

The sociologist Ernest van den Haag argued in the mid-1950s that art could serve as a counterpoint to the dreamwork Freud did so much to theorize. If dreams worked in large part to obscure emotions, dissimulating one's fears and wishes and preventing their penetration into consciousness, art could work in an opposite direction. "Art discovers and attempts to reawaken the sleeper," van den Haag wrote, "intensifying experience and perception of the world and of the self." For many postwar writers, the psychological insights of the cultural critic could achieve a comparable result; artistic and critical labors based in acute psychological observation became the stuff of intellectual achievement. "Art transcends immediate reality to encompass wider views, penetrate into deeper experience and lead to a fuller confrontation of man's predicament," van den Haag continued.[35] Following from the Freudian thinking that defined much of postwar literary and cultural criticism, Baldwin brought an artistic eye to his essays in an effort to distill and describe aspects of American culture that often remained occluded. Indeed, the prose style in Baldwin's essays delivered interpretations predicated on the supposition that an individual's motivations, fears, wishes, and cultural beliefs were shrouded and constantly concealed.

Many influential literary and cultural critics who were drawn to the conceptual universe of psychoanalysis simultaneously set themselves apart from, and at times developed a dismissive posture toward, psychotherapeutic and academic expertise. Baldwin would adopt a similar position. The relationship between psychological expertise and the literary intellectuals became an increasingly freighted one as the New York intellectuals acquired a more assured status as cultural arbiters in the immediate postwar decade. For many intellectuals, psychological inquiry in literary and cultural criticism did not require any connection to formal institutions of psychological thought. Trilling's thinking on this subject was emblematic of the New York intellectuals: "Psychology is a science to which literary intellectuals feel affinity. But who knows just what is happening in psychology? Dr. Fromm and Dr. Horney and the late Dr. Sullivan, and their disciples, have great influence upon many members of the elite. What actually do they say? What is the worth of what they say? . . . Departments of psychology in the universities are detaching themselves from the faculties of philosophy in order to enter the faculties of pure science, on the ground that their science is wholly experimental. What is the value of the considerable vested interests of this academic psychology?"[36]

For all their authority, Trilling was not convinced that formal modes of psychological research contributed as much as they promised, and he was unambiguous about where his own intellectual allegiances resided: "The literary mind, more precisely the historical-literary mind, seems to be the best kind of critical and constructive mind that we have, better than the philosophic, better that the theological, better than the scientific and the social scientific."[37] The importance of psychological inquiry would expand in the postwar endeavors of the New York intellectuals but mostly as a mode of critical activity removed from the burgeoning arenas of the psychological sciences and clinical research. The New York intellectuals prized psychological complexity in literary and cultural criticism; they did not for the most part feel that they had to follow the dictates of any current or particular psychological school of thought, let alone any research agenda. Baldwin was influenced by this approach to psychological thought—an approach that differed from that of Wright. Whereas Wright sought out psychological research and expertise, Baldwin harnessed modernist artistic sensibilities to create an idiom of cultural analysis based in sharp psychological description. He valued psychological inquiry as a critical disposition, while likely sharing much of Trilling's condescension toward psychology's institutionalized forms.

Postwar Cultural Criticism and Anticommunism

By 1952, *Partisan Review* editor Philip Rahv observed, many of the New York intellectuals continued to "denounce the evils of Communism with deadly sameness and in apparent obliviousness of the fact" that anticommunism "has virtually become the official creed of our entire society."[38] If Baldwin drew from the anticommunism of the postwar period to mark his artistic preferences and writing style, he also circumvented the stasis Rahv noted. Though it served as a starting point for Baldwin, the anticommunism of postwar literary culture, for all the ways it buttressed his rejection of certain literary traditions, did not amount for him to an intellectual destination, as it had arguably become for some of the New York intellectuals. Many of Baldwin's essays from the postwar decade contain no overt references to communism or anticommunism, and where rhetorical examples of anticommunism do emerge, they take the form of space-clearing gestures, affording Baldwin ways of reenvisioning critical commentary on race thinking.

Important in themselves and deserving of exploration, such space-clearing gestures provided the vehicles through which Baldwin both extended and transformed antiracist commentary predicated on the psychological undercurrents of race hierarchy. Within the writings of the New York intellectuals, *mature* connoted anticommunism and signaled a literary culture possessing moral seriousness and capable of addressing psychological complexity. The premium placed on maturity served anti-Stalinist left-liberal writers who wished to discard any association with the socialist politics of the 1930s, which they now often coded as juvenile and infantile. The ability to distinguish between maturity and immaturity served as the basis for disavowals of communist and socialist affiliation, a stance of putative critical independence. In distancing their views from such earlier affiliations, many midcentury writers could claim an intellectual maturity made resonant and relevant in the midst of the Cold War.[39]

As a mediating concept, maturity informed the work of the New York intellectuals and Baldwin alike. Indeed, in his early critical essays, Baldwin revealed his connection to the rhetoric of political and artistic maturity that emerged from anti-Stalinist left-liberal and anticommunist discourse.[40] Baldwin worked with modernist tropes of irony, complexity, and ambiguity that in the postwar period became part of the New York intellectuals' contribution to literary culture. In the intellectual spaces within which Baldwin moved, these tropes could not be easily disassociated from the prevalent notion of "maturity" and the general disaffiliation from radical social movements that the notion implied.[41] In Baldwin's essays, the concepts of irony and maturity shaped his criticism and underpinned his claim that many American writers failed to address subjective life in effective ways because of commitments to naturalism and forms such as the protest novel. The high status accorded to psychological complexity in his thinking generally made Baldwin's essays a complement to the forms of commentary that emerged from the New York intellectuals and thus underscored the value of political and aesthetic maturity.[42] His identification with the politics of intellectual maturity could also be detected in the tendency he shared with the New York intellectuals of dismissing abstractions like "the common man" and the sentimentalism of mass cultural forms.

Like the critics he admired, Baldwin balked at the sentimentalism of popular culture. Artistic achievement and valuable criticism, he believed, had to proceed from an adamant rejection of established conventions and from alertness to the psychological dynamics at work in social and cultural life. Sentimentalism short-circuited literary creativity and hampered the recognition of psychological dynamics. That view conformed to Baldwin's general conviction that psychological inquiry had yet to be fully brought to bear upon writing about race thinking and racial antagonisms. His advocacy of unsentimental readings of race encouraged his aversion to works that offered simplistic depictions of racialized environments and the hardships they generated. Favoring unsentimental writing, Baldwin took exception to many postwar literary portrayals of oppressed characters. "I am not one of the people who believe that oppression imbues a people with wisdom or insight or sweet charity," he wrote in *Notes of Native Son.*[43]

Maturity had everything to do with installing a new intellectual dispensation in which psychological interpretation played a pivotal part. As early as 1941, the literary critic and founder of *Partisan Review* William Phillips had argued against what he called a "nationalist revival" and "militant provincialism" he observed among certain writers and in favor of the "complex and ambiguous symbolization of modern writing." In submitting to a "natural inclination to merge with the popular mind," Phillips held that many American writers threatened to "thwart the production of a mature and sustained literature."[44] Philips indicated the extent to which the intellectual circles that attracted Baldwin advocated a vision of psychological complexity in literature for the express purpose of bringing greater respectability to American intellectual life. Of course, Baldwin's work also garnered the praise of many New York intellectual writers. Trilling considered "Everybody's Protest Novel" a "remarkable document" because Baldwin imparted with eloquence the view that only a "mode of art which was subtle and complex and untrammeled by social theory could truly propose the idea of freedom by exhibiting the true nature of man."[45]

Trilling chose Baldwin's essay for a special issue of *Perspectives USA* in 1953. He also selected "Notes on the Decline of Naturalism," an essay by Philip Rahv, a literary critic and founder of *Partisan Review.* Rahv's essay noted the influence of modern psychological thought and attributed what he called the decline of naturalism to advances in psychological theory, even if literature constituted a province removed from psychology per se. The "influence of psychology," Rahv wrote, allowed literature to recover its "inwardness, devising such forms as the interior monologue, which combines the naturalistic in its minute description of the mental process with the antinaturalistic in its disclosure of the subjective and the irrational."[46] *Perspectives USA,* a journal published by Intercultural Publications, was made available throughout Europe as part of the Cold War–era effort to present the United States in a favorable light.[47] Intended largely for a noncommunist-left readership, the journal reached disparate audiences through French, German, and Italian editions. Bound up in the realist political sensibilities that shaped midcentury political thought, *Perspectives USA* eschewed anything resembling propaganda, but the publication served nevertheless to intervene in the politics of the postwar period. "No propaganda for the American way should be included" in the magazine, wrote the intellectual historian Perry Miller, because "that omission will, in itself, become the most important element of propaganda, in the best sense."[48] Direct recourse to polemic was largely unnecessary within the arenas of literary and cultural criticism that Trilling, Miller, and others inhabited. In projecting an image of American intellectual and cultural life to European countries, Trilling compiled writing that reinforced links between literary culture, psychological complexity, and moral seriousness that were coded as nonideological.

Rahv's and Baldwin's pieces were not meant to represent "American literary culture as a whole," according to Trilling, but a "special and particular part of that culture" that had figured considerably in the "moral and intellectual life of the country." The embrace of modernist tropes of interiority and the affirmation of the close connection between literature and psychological inquiry in the essays were lent gravitas by Trilling's editorial introduction. "I have exemplified a part of American culture which, although it is by no means unimportant, is special and particular, in the expectation that it will imply the complexity of the general life in which it has its existence," Trilling wrote. The exceptional intellectual group he had assembled, Baldwin and Rahv among them, would communicate American complexities and pierce "monolithic and impregnable" understandings of American life.[49]

How did Baldwin understand his own work in relation to available interpretations of modern American life? His connection to the literary culture of the New York intellectuals afforded a platform from which Baldwin attempted a far-reaching rereading of American culture in terms of race thinking. His deployment of modernist tropes and furthering of the politics of maturity were shot through with narrative tension, for his aims both coincided with and diverged from those of his critical counterparts. Baldwin argued for psychological analysis and a concerted focus on subjectivity as ways to transcend the incomplete and flawed frameworks he associated with existing discussions of racial antagonisms. His essays in particular would turn on the exploration of worlds of "race" as individual and national neuroses.

"The Harlem Ghetto" and the Essays

A 1946 essay by psychologist Kenneth Clark that appeared in *Commentary* and addressed "Negro-Jewish relations" shared a great deal with Baldwin's "The Harlem Ghetto: Winter 1948," which appeared in the magazine two years later. Indeed, Clark's "Candor about Negro-Jewish Relations" anticipates in a social-scientific language several of the claims put forth in "The Harlem Ghetto: Winter 1948."[50] The very presence of an essay by a social psychologist in *Commentary* indicates the central role accorded to psychological thought among the New York intellectuals, despite the prevalent skepticism about psychology's institutionalized forms. Clark held that it was necessary to see social tensions categorized as "Negro-Jewish relations" in terms of broad national patterns since the forms of race prejudice that shaped "Negro-Jewish relations" had to do with "pathologies of the dominant society" that "infect all groups and individuals within that society." Dominant forms of antiblack prejudice amounted to a "virus-like affliction" with myriad effects throughout American life, Clark argued.[51]

Clark situated his arguments about race hierarchy in the context of the "political, economic, and psychological function in the over-all pattern of American society," much as Baldwin would in his literary and cultural criticism. Endorsing a "framework of objectivity and realism," Clark expressed dissatisfaction with "sentimental, primarily moralistic" readings of the racist social order and leveled a critique much like the one Baldwin directed within literary culture.[52] Clark would later credit Baldwin for his demonstrated "sensitivity to some of the subtle forces which are significant in our complex social structure."[53] His affirmation of Baldwin as a likeminded analyst of the psychological dimensions of race thinking demonstrated the extent to which Baldwin became known for his insights into psychology and culture. "The Harlem Ghetto: Winter 1948" reappeared as "The Harlem Ghetto" in *Notes of a Native Son* (1955), a collection that brought his work to a larger readership. The book—modernist, terse, sharp—introduced a novel idiom to the analysis of race. Drawing on both the authoritative status and discursive elasticity of midcentury psychological inquiry, Baldwin's essays emerged as among the most significant contributions to postwar cultural commentary.

"The Harlem Ghetto" begins with a description of Harlem that evokes the photo-graphs of African American urban life in Wright's *Twelve Million Black Voices:* "All of Harlem is pervaded by a sense of congestion, rather like the insistent, maddening, claustrophobic pounding in the skull that comes from trying to breathe in a very small room with all of the windows shut." The essay demonstrates how central a psychological vocabulary had become to writing about prejudice. Much like Clark, who argued that "Negro-Jewish" relations formed part of the larger history of racial oppression, Baldwin writes: "Just as a mountain of sociological investigations, com-mittee reports, and plans for recreational centers have failed to change the face of Harlem or prevent Negro boys and girls from growing up and facing, individually and alone, the unendurable frustration of always being, everywhere, inferior—until finally the cancer attacks the mind and warps it—so there seems no hope for better Negro-Jewish relations without a change in the American pattern."[54] A condemna-tion of ideologies of inferiority, the essay locates such ideologies in history, in what Baldwin calls "the American pattern." As elsewhere, race prejudice is a disease—a "cancer" that "warps" the mind—that breeds further social antagonisms.

For Baldwin, descriptions of a marred mental life provided the most acute and direct discursive means of describing social worlds created by race. The reminder that children were even more vulnerable to such destructive processes became impor-tant to invocations of the prejudice discourse, helping to prepare the ground for social scientific arguments in civil rights legal challenges. As Baldwin writes, "I can conceive of no Negro native to this country who has not, by the age of puberty, been irreparably scarred by the conditions of his life. All over Harlem, Negro boys and girls are growing into stunted maturity, trying desperately to find a place to stand."[55] Among his first explorations of race thinking and social environment, "The Harlem Ghetto" borrowed keywords of the prejudice discourse and placed them in a literary-historical context.

The *Commentary* subheading for the original published version of the essay referred to Baldwin's theme as "The Vicious Circle of Frustration and Prejudice." Although the discourse of prejudice was a logical way of introducing an essay that explored anti-Semitism in Harlem, the essay did not simply reproduce the social scientific paradigm of prejudice. In fact, Baldwin was critical of the reliance on "education" common among social scientific studies of racial and religious preju-dices. In the essay "Journey to Atlanta," he disparages the emphasis on education as a panacea for social ills, for education had become a "vast, all-purpose, term, conjuring up visions of sun-lit housing projects, stacks of copy-books and a race of well-soaped, dark-skinned people who never slur their R's."[56] He believed that writing on preju-dice was hobbled by all manner of social agendas, which only served to make the meanings and effects of discriminatory practices opaque. Baldwin did not want to reproduce standard accounts of race thinking and racial antagonism; instead, he entered from his own distinctive vantage point the broad discussion that took place under the heading of "prejudice." Baldwin's essay was part of the prejudice literature of the 1940s, but he would soon further distinguish his arguments by placing them on a larger historical canvas.

Scapegoat, a term that appears in "The Harlem Ghetto," became a keyword in both social scientific and popular writing on prejudice in the 1940s. A term with a Biblical derivation, *scapegoat* became shorthand for blame that was wrongly attached to individuals or groups for social ills, and was routinely invoked to describe situations where individuals or groups became objects of irrational hostility. Baldwin argued that Jews were scapegoats among many blacks in Harlem. Like the processes that made antiblack prejudice socially pervasive, Jews became scapegoats because of a national pattern. In order to describe the relationship of blacks in Harlem to the nation at large, Baldwin also applied the concept of "self-hate," which psychiatrists had long employed to make sense of ideologies of inferiority. "When the Negro hates the Jew *as a Jew* he does so partly because the nation does and in much the same painful fashion that he hates himself. It is an aspect of his humiliation whittled down to a manageable size and then transferred." Of a piece with this sociopsychological phenomenon, Baldwin continues, the "Jew has been taught—and, too often, accepts—the legend of Negro inferiority." The confining physical spaces of Harlem, and the resulting sense of containment, serve as metaphors in Baldwin's essay for relations between African Americans and Jews. "The structure of the American commonwealth has trapped both of these minorities into attitudes of perpetual hostility," Baldwin writes.[57]

Situating race thinking in culture and history, Baldwin pressed Wright's claim that patterns of dissimulation among African Americans were related to frustrations related to racist social conditions. "It is part of the price the Negro plays in this society that, as Richard Wright points out, he is almost always acting," Baldwin wrote.[58] Working in intellectual concert with themes Wright had brought into American intellectual life, "The Harlem Ghetto" also demonstrates affinities with the work of Ralph Ellison. In the "Autobiographical Notes" that preface *Notes of a Native Son,* Baldwin applauds Ellison's ability to convey "the ambiguity and irony of Negro life."[59] Notably, Ellison also wrote about Harlem in 1948. Written for the *Magazine of the Year* but not published until 1964, Ellison's "Harlem Is Nowhere" shares a great deal of the critical sensibility on display in Baldwin's essay. Ellison similarly writes about the physical spaces of Harlem: "To live in Harlem is to dwell in the very bowels of the city; it is to pass a labyrinthine existence among streets that explode monotonously skyward with the spires and crosses of churches and clutter under foot with garbage and decay." Ellison's essay also devotes attention to the Lafargue Clinic (see chapter 2) and describes a democratic institution that did not allow segregation to impede the delivery of psychiatric care in Harlem. The essay describes a "world in which the major energy of the imagination goes not into creating works of art, but to overcome the frustrations of social discrimination." Ellison drew on the common psychological usage of the term *personality* to argue that the "blasting of this dream [of full democracy] is as damaging to Negro personality as the slum scenes of filth, disorder and crumbling masonry in which it flies apart."[60] Ellison, in language that recalls Baldwin's essays, suggests that American society can be interpreted as a psychological economy in which blacks were deprived of the "therapy" on offer to white Americans through patriotic rituals and identification with wealth and power. The two essays, written in the same year, identify Harlem as both a physical location and a space where particular psychological dynamics abound and hostilities circulate. Ellison borrows a phrase from Fredric Wertham—"free-floating hostility"—to describe Harlem's psychic economy, whereas Baldwin presents a comparable picture of such forces by appropriating the popular languages of the psychology of prejudice and fitting them within his chosen literary-critical idiom.

"The Harlem Ghetto" demonstrated Baldwin's willingness to examine challenging and pressing social phenomena, as well as his ability to describe them in lucid prose. Both first-person and third-person observations are used to present social conflicts, but the disorderliness and density of those conflicts do not disrupt the clarity of the writing. The essay enjoins readers to consider racial antagonisms as historical situations sustained by psychological dynamics active within the culture. Baldwin borrows freely from the available vocabulary of prejudice, though that word *prejudice* itself already seems too banal for the nuance he is after, and is notably absent. Instead, *inferiority, outlets, frustration, rage,* and *hate* help Baldwin to define specific social antagonisms in a particular location. A kind of pessimism is on display in the penultimate line of "The Harlem Ghetto": "But just as a society must have a scapegoat, so hatred must have a symbol." Yet Baldwin's pessimism is also a form of clear-eyed, clinical diagnosis. His ability to distill complicated social phenomena into a set of psychological relationships is one of the defining qualities of "The Harlem Ghetto," an essay that is finally about both its titular geographical locale and the nation at large.

In "The Harlem Ghetto," Baldwin distances himself from Paul Robeson and, by extension, from Communist affiliation of any kind when he writes, "It is personally painful to realize that so gifted and forceful a man as Robeson should have been tricked by his own bitterness and his total inability to understand the nature of political power in general, or Communist aims in particular."[61] Although Baldwin is referring specifically to a column written by Robeson on the anticommunist reprisals in Hollywood, he finds the content of the column less exasperating than Robeson's association with communism, which he portrays as a sign of gullibility and a failure of judgment. Baldwin sharply contrasts the realist logic associated with anticommunism and the naïveté and tragedy of communist politics. Yet even as Baldwin reinforces the cultural authority of anticommunism, "The Harlem Ghetto" redirects the logic of psychological realism, making it amenable to the exploration of race thinking.

Book reviews and other small pieces of writing Baldwin composed in the 1940s anticipate his efforts to press psychological inquiry further into the terrain of racialized social life. In "The Image of the Negro," for instance, Baldwin disparaged what he considered insufficiently complex psychological artistry, blending his criticism with the postwar discourse of maturity. Reviewing several novels that took the Negro Problem as their subject, including Sinclair Lewis's *Kingsblood Royal* (1947), Baldwin is unsparing in his evaluation of their literary quality. "Is the 'great work' these works are presumably doing in the world quite worth the torture they are to read?" he asks. Yet Baldwin concedes that the social conflicts and crises narrated in the books are compelling. He is disappointed by the ways the books address race problems, for the books are finally "exceedingly timorous studies of transgression." In *Kingsblood Royal,* after the unassailably "white" Neil Kingsblood discovers "black" ancestry, he transgresses prevailing social boundaries by embracing his newfound race. If part of Sinclair's aim involved scrutinizing the power of racial ideologies, Baldwin nevertheless considers the novel a story that fails to reckon adequately with the pervasiveness and power of race thinking. Despite Lewis's intentions, his book fails to approach a "reality that is more sinister, more treacherous, and more profound" and "above all, more personal." In the conclusion to "The Image of the Negro," Baldwin writes, "Beneath [the] fantastic subplots on which these books rely . . . are the centuries of fear and desire and hatred and shame that are peculiarly the province of the Puritan Anglo-Saxon, and which have made the oppression of black by white a more complicated reality than these novels indicate. The exploration of this reality may yet produce a very powerful literature; we are, in the meantime, confronted with a phenomenon not even remotely literary, which is only one more aspect of an enduring inability to tell the truth."[62] Baldwin's review discloses aspirations for his own writing, prefiguring some of the artistic concerns that will make their way into the essays in *Notes of Native Son.*

In his explorations of race as history, Baldwin put forth an understanding of culture much like the one presented by Trilling in *The Opposing Self* (1950). For Trilling, *culture* had ceased to refer exclusively to works of the imagination. Partly as a result of the advent of Freudian thought, culture came properly to encompass "assumptions and unformulated valuations," for the stuff of culture had to do with habits, manners, and even superstitions. Trilling believed that modern writers with sufficient skill could turn directly to the "unconscious portion of culture," making it "accessible to conscious thought."[63] For Baldwin, race hierarchy in the United States also comprised an unconscious portion of culture and required analysis alert to "history, traditions, customs, the moral assumptions and preoccupations of the country; in short, the general social fabric." Baldwin held that "the past is all that makes the present coherent, and further, that the past will remain horrible for exactly as long as we refuse to assess it honestly."[64] *Notes of a Native Son* defined honest criticism as the interweaving of history and psychology. Moreover, like Lillian Smith's *Killers of the Dream,* Baldwin's approach to nonfiction produced a synthetic relationship between biographical reflection and larger cultural readings. As in Wright's fictional and biographical writings, the prevalence of fear created by the segregation and race hierarchy emerges as a central theme for Baldwin, as when he describes fear of whites as a condition that the "American Negro has had to hide from himself as the price of his public progress."[65] Without a doubt, Baldwin's essays present his own sense of rage in the face of repeated instances of racial subjugation, producing stories of anger that encompass both the personal and the collective.[66]

History, Rage, Innocence

Some of the best known of Baldwin's essays united his affinity for modernist writing, his fluency with the discourse of maturity, and his determination to rethink the Negro Problem by way of psychological inquiry. In "Everybody's Protest Novel," he wrote that by "overlooking, denying, evading [the Negro's] complexity—which is nothing more that the disquieting complexity of ourselves—we are diminished and we perish." Yet modernist sensibilities and concern with psychological interiority offered paths beyond such a condition of impoverishment. Baldwin held that "only within this web of ambiguity, paradox, this hunger, danger, darkness, can we find at once ourselves and the power that will free us from ourselves." He presented a picture of a stagnant literary culture in which creativity was stymied by stereotype and an inability to bring psychological complexity into representation. It was just this "power of revelation which is the business of the novelist, this journey toward a more vast reality."[67] Crucially, Baldwin placed the history of racial subjugation squarely within the purview of psychology by using the vocabulary of interiority. Thus, even as Baldwin was shaped by the forms of psychological inquiry prized by the New York intellectuals, he effected a remaking of that inquiry, giving it particular relevance and traction in relation to historical predicaments of race.

This was perhaps nowhere truer than in the book's title essay, in which Baldwin tells of his relationship with his father and his experiences as a laborer in New Jersey. First appearing in *Harper's Magazine* in 1955, "Notes of a Native Son" recounts Baldwin's father's funeral, which coincided with a period of race riots in Detroit and Harlem. The essay brings together the personal and the political, as the riots provide another occasion for Baldwin to revisit questions about Harlem and the "white world" as interrelated conditions of individual pain and collective turmoil. The distant personality of the father and his regular, abusive "rages" are implicitly connected to the racialized social relations that shaped his entire life as a member of the first generation of free men. Baldwin paints a portrait of a figure "eaten up by paranoia" and a "disease of the mind" that, together with his tuberculosis, weaken his body.[68]

Baldwin goes back in time in "Notes of a Native Son" to the year before his father's death. In that year, Baldwin worked at a defense plant in New Jersey and learned, more acutely than he had previously, about the workings of racist social environments. While at the plant, Baldwin was "never looked at" but nevertheless felt "at the mercy of the reflexes the color of one's skin caused in other people." Baldwin narrates his own intense emotional responses to his new setting. In language reminiscent of "Previous Condition," Baldwin writes: "That year in New Jersey lives in my mind as though it were the year during which, having an unsuspected predilection for it, I first contracted some dread, chronic disease, the unfailing symptom of which is a kind of blind fever, a pounding in the skull." As in the short story, the disease is linked to a broader social condition. "There is no Negro alive who does not have this rage in his blood," Baldwin continues. After relating a moment of explosive anger in which he throws a mug at a waitress in a diner after being refused service, Baldwin describes the parallel but historically larger "rage" of the "ghetto's chronic need" to "smash something."[69]

"Stranger in the Village," the final essay in Baldwin's collection, recounts his experiences in a small Swiss village where he is the first black man ever to set foot within the town's limits. In an essay that develops into a consideration of American identity as part of European history and consciousness, Baldwin tells a story that is highly reminiscent of the psychiatrist Frantz Fanon's personal account of racial encounter in metropolitan France.[70] As he walks in the village, Baldwin is met with shouts of "Neger!" "The children who shout *Neger!* have no way of knowing the echoes this sound raises in me," Baldwin writes. More so than in other essays,

Baldwin explores the theme of rage in "Stranger in the Village." "The rage of the disesteemed is personally fruitless, but it is also inevitable; this rage, so generally discounted, so little understood even among the people whose daily bread it is, is one of things that makes history." In contradistinction to the modus operandi of inter-group relations specialists and social scientists, Baldwin is not convinced that infor-mation and education are sufficient to alter the effects of rage. "Rage can only with difficulty, and never entirely, be brought under the domination of the intelligence and is therefore not susceptible to any arguments whatever."[71] Baldwin transports rage, a subject in psychological studies of prejudice, into the realm of historical forces.[72]

Although Wright is often characterized as the midcentury writer who examined rage, "Stranger in the Village" shows how Baldwin staked a claim to the same territory, expanding on the subject of rage as a psychohistorical phenomenon. "Also, rage cannot be hidden, it can only be dissembled. This dissembling deludes the thoughtless, and strengthens rage and adds, to rage, contempt. There are, no doubt, as many ways of coping with the resulting complex of tension as there are black men in the world, but no black man can ever hope to be liberated from this internal warfare—rage, dissembling, and contempt having inevitably accompanied his first realization of the power of white men." Although Baldwin views racialized social relations as based in power, their most significant and dramatic dimension lies in the psychological forces they generate, and in the ways these forces in turn affect history. The essay makes clear that white identity, or whiteness, is a pivotal subject in any investigation of racial ideology. "One of the ironies of black-white relations [is] that, by means of what the white man imagines the black man to be, the black man is enabled to know who the white man is."[73]

"Stranger in the Village" makes clear that beyond narrating instances of racial conflict, Baldwin wishes to say something about racial categorization. Baldwin had argued that the protest novel tradition inadequately explored dialectical relation-ships between racial categories, and the same idea informs "Stranger in the Village," which departs from the Swiss mountaintop of the title to reflect more broadly on black and white in Europe and America. Emphasizing the "tremendous effects the presence of the Negro has had on the American character," Baldwin surmises that the "evolution of [Negro] identity was a source of the most intolerable anxiety in the minds and lives of his masters." Commenting on the interrelationships between racial meanings, Baldwin contends that as African Americans were kept beyond the limits of American-ness, it was increasingly "impossible for Americans to accept the black man as one of themselves, for to do so was to jeopardize their status as white men." The historical result of such racialized social dynamics has been a society marked by psychological disease. "But not to accept him was to deny his human reality, his human weight and complexity, and the strain of denying the overwhelmingly undeniable forced Americans into rationalizations so fantastic that they approached the pathological."⁷⁴

As in Lillian Smith's cultural criticism, racial designations calcify and produce cultural maladies, the historical weight and psychological costs of which can be difficult to assess. Focusing on the dehumanization that accompanies race thinking, Baldwin points to a broader cultural failure among Americans to understand the interracial past and present, connecting that failure to the indulgence of a "state of innocence."⁷⁵ In the words of one critic, Baldwin concludes his collection by putting innocence "on notice that its days are numbered."⁷⁶ The essay's final line seems to confirm the impossibility of avoiding the "interracial drama" of American history: "This world is white no longer, and it will never be white again."⁷⁷ By pointing to a "reality" that has not yet been grasped and an innocence that is waning, Baldwin calls upon the maturity discourse of the early Cold War. But rather than serving as an occasion for accommodation with American institutions and social life, Baldwin's realist commentary deliberately renders "interracial drama" the pressing American story, the main tragedy of the American scene.

Themes of maturity and innocence were useful and adaptable within the polarized political environment of the early Cold War. Such themes were certainly present in the work of Baldwin's fellow critic, Leslie A. Fiedler, whose book, *An End to Innocence* (1955), straddled literary and political topics in such chapters as "Hiss, Chambers, and the Age of Innocence" and "Adolescence and Maturity in the American Novel." Expressing a view that Baldwin would likely have shared, Fielder maintained that the "years since 1940 have been for writers and critics in America a time of disenchantment, marking, one hopes, the passage from the easy enthusiasms and approximate ambitions of adolescence to the juster self-appraisal of maturity."⁷⁸ In Fiedler's essays, as in the writings of the New York intellectuals more generally, innocence and maturity represented opposite poles on a continuum, a continuum that could effectively evaluate political allegiances no less than aesthetic value. Fiedler believed that American novelists were beginning to grow into "maturity" as they posed a central question about "Western literature and its future": "Can the lonely individual, unsustained by tradition in an atomized society, achieve a poetry adult and complicated enough to be the consciousness of its age?"⁷⁹

The idea of innocence, which had figured prominently in accounts of American history since the nineteenth century, became something of a foil in the work of many of the New York intellectuals. For them, a move away from notions of American innocence was the necessary price for a mature reappraisal of American life. Such a conceptual scheme brought the idea of a diminishing attachment to innocence into the discursive terrain of anticommunism. But such political reworking of the notion of American innocence did not appeal to critics and writers who wished to historicize the cultural resonance of stories of innocence. In *The American Adam: Innocence, Tragedy, and Tradition in the Nineteenth Century* (1955), R. W. B. Lewis examined the cultural power of the American as a figure of innocence and the vast historical potentialities implied in that characterization. A major starting point for Lewis's analyses was that the "vision of innocence and the claim of newness were almost entirely misleading."[80] For his part, Baldwin presents the psychological meanings of racial categories as a crucial area of exploration for a process of intellectual renewal that might transform the logic of American innocence from a set of representations and commonplaces into a cultural problem. Lewis and Baldwin seemed to agree that American innocence could not simply be traded in for American maturity without doing the difficult work of investigating the historical and psychological needs that it met.

Baldwin identified with the notion of the mature writer and certainly adhered to the tenet that an emphasis on subjectivity could help to bring about more responsible and independent writing. Nevertheless, his "Stranger in the Village" redirects the language of vaunted maturity and burdensome innocence not to pronounce on the communist threat to freedom but instead to assert that race problems call for greater intellectual attentiveness and that a turn to problems of race in American thought could engender a salutary end to innocence. Baldwin did not feign commitment to the discourses of the cultural Cold War in a bid to one day substitute those discourses with an alternative agenda; a much more complex kind of intellectual labor was at work. In developing his voice as a public intellectual, Baldwin found ways to leverage his identification with anticommunist rhetoric in ways that conferred intellectual credibility on the literary-historical analysis of American race thinking. Without a doubt, Baldwin presented his most penetrating accounts of race problems during a moment of rapprochement with American culture and American institutions among many intellectuals. Yet if much of the broader political culture of the postwar period took "un-American activity" to be the major subject of the day, Baldwin's essays supplied an implicit rejoinder to that Cold War logic by way of a persistent revisiting of the terrain of "race."

Such subjects were not often among the priorities of postwar literary intellectuals taking part in a "rediscovery" of America. That rediscovery involved much more sanguine assessments of American institutions and economic arrangements than had been offered by the New York intellectuals prior to the postwar period. One place where the language of rediscovery was brought to public life was the *Partisan Review*—

organized "Our Country, Our Culture" symposium held in New York in 1952. The symposium organizers drew attention to the "affirmative attitude toward America" many postwar intellectuals seemed to share, though they were careful to note that such affirmation was not necessarily "unequivocal." In his contribution to the symposium, Trilling lent his considerable support to the idea of a rediscovery and affirmation of America when he proposed that an "avowed aloofness from national feeling is no longer the first ceremonial step into the life of thought."[81] In his essays, Baldwin also made use of collective expressions such as "our culture" and "our country." But the pictures of American life he presented, and the tone of detached analysis he created, did not suggest long-delayed affirmation or satisfying rediscovery. In a kind of twist on the title of the famous symposium, he wrote in the "Autobiographical Notes" of *Notes of a Native Son* that "I love America more than any other country in the world, and, exactly for this reason, I insist on the right to criticize her perpetually."[82] Baldwin's words exceed the sense of affinity for America presented in the symposium. At the same time, he intrinsically declines the language of rediscovery and insists upon critical distance from American social and cultural life.

Baldwin and the "Post-Freudian Age"

If Baldwin had begun to secure credentials as an important writer among the New York intellectuals by the late 1940s, the publication of *Notes of a Native Son* in 1955 brought him many more readers. The young journalist Dan Wakefield recalled that the collection arrived on the New York intellectual scene as something of a revelation. The paperback edition included a cover photograph of Baldwin; Wakefield remembered being "as quickly transfixed by the writing as I had been by the eyes on the cover." Baldwin's writing stood out for what Wakefield and others often described as its "intensity" and for the authority of the prose, "the sureness of it." Among writers making their way in the 1950s, Wakefield was likely not alone in feeling that Baldwin's essays augured something large. "I sensed it could change my own thinking and writing, my very life," Wakefield recalled.[83] The process of writing the essays in *Notes of a Native Son* had a similar effect on Baldwin. They were of crucial importance, he wrote, because "I was trying to decipher my own situation, to spring my trap."[84]

Notes of a Native Son received high praise among reviewers. "Few American writers handle words more effectively in the essay form than James Baldwin," Langston Hughes famously wrote in the *New York Times*. In the essays, the "thought becomes poetry, the poetry illuminates the thought," he added.[85] "Make no mistake about it, this is one of the most important works yet written on the Negro in America and abroad," wrote Thomas D. Jarrett in *Phylon*. Jarrett emphasized the Myrdalian strain in Baldwin's "penetrating realism," pointing to Baldwin's assertion that at "the root of the American Negro problem is the necessity of the American white man to find a way of living with the Negro in order to be able to live with himself."[86] Race thinking and racial antagonisms had created a world that allowed whites to exert "gratuitous humiliation" on blacks, a situation that inevitably drove "many people mad, black and white."[87] Baldwin's writing was reminiscent of Myrdal's argument about dissonance in the nation's simultaneous assertion of democratic values and practices of racial oppression, signaling a writer willing to "anatomize the hatred and confusion that separate the races."[88]

Critics noted the "incisiveness and calm objectivity" of Baldwin's prose, which gave his considerations of American life "a precision which is impressively analytical and persuasively sound."[89] A *Time* reviewer called *Notes of a Native Son* an "effort to retrieve the Negro from the abstractions of the do-gooders and the no-goods," attributing to Baldwin an ability to locate the "Negro's pent-up hostility" in unexpected places.[90] *Commonweal* commended Baldwin for the "depth, intensity and clarity" he brought to his subjects, going so far as to call him "the most perceptive Negro writing today."[91] Yet another reviewer stressed Baldwin's compelling and novelistic writing style—"dramatic, dense, bitter, swift, and self-absorbed"—and predicted that the book would become an "important chapter in our cultural history."[92] Baldwin's work in the postwar years also gained the admiration of many editors and literary critics. Isaac Rosenfeld, literary editor of the *New Leader,* considered Baldwin one of the rare writers who "can penetrate outward disorder to the inner meaning, where the fact that men suffer degradation, and the significance for human culture of that degradation, are one." Baldwin, he said, arrived at "inner, broader meaning" through "immediate, painful perception."[93] Lionel Trilling wrote that Baldwin revealed a concern with style and an evident "commitment to delicacy of perception," noting that the younger writer had "taken his place in the literary and cultural avant-garde."[94]

Baldwin's modernist artistic sensibilities and fluency with literary-historical varieties of psychoanalytic exploration had certainly helped him to secure a measure of cultural authority among literary intellectuals. Yet his elevated status, particularly among the New York intellectuals, would begin to wane by the mid-1950s. If at one time Baldwin's writings were read as a measure of the value of the literary-historical imagination, his continued reflection on race problems seemed to put him out of step with privileged sectors of intellectual culture. Although "The Harlem Ghetto" had appeared in *Commentary* in the late 1940s, the same magazine was noticeably less enamored of Baldwin in 1956, when Charles H. Nichols reviewed both *Notes of a*

Native Son and Baldwin's second novel, *Giovanni's Room* (1956). Although Baldwin continued to receive praise for his stylistic achievements, Nichols wrote that Baldwin's works were beset by unrelieved "determinism, doom, and feeling of depravity." Nichols, though perhaps not all those associated with the literary culture of the New York intellectuals, recognized an author "tormented by self-hate" and willing to assume the "inferiority of the Negro."[95] Baldwin seemed to exhibit "an anachronistic attitude toward race" and could apparently no longer claim the intellectual currency he enjoyed among literary and cultural critics in the late 1940s and early 1950s. Although it is impossible to think about Baldwin's trajectory without considering his connection to New York intellectual circles, assimilating him entirely to that particular formation of literary culture occludes much about his work, including the ways that his focus on race hierarchy contravened dominant tendencies in cultural criticism.

Notes of a Native Son emerged from what journalist Max Lerner called the "post-Freudian Age," a period in which psychological literacy served as the basis for many forms of writing. *Notes of a Native Son* appeared the same year that Robert Lindner published *The Fifty-Minute Hour,* which showcased the author's work in prisons and mental hospitals through a set of case studies. With his expertise as an analyst, Lindner produced stories about terrible psychological maladies and astonishing cases. By contrast, Baldwin's essays were about more commonplace matters, yet they were extraordinary in a complementary way because Baldwin explored the pervasive and perverse work of racial ideologies with a clear-eyed, even clinical, precision that differed from most discussions of race. If psychoanalytic writers like Lindner were said to bring artistry to depictions of the disorders they treated, Baldwin brought the logic of psychoanalytic inquiry and exactitude to his reflections on social and cultural life. Lerner, who wrote the introduction to Lindner's book, could have been referring to many examples of American writing, not only works by psychoanalysts, when he alluded to the midcentury tendency to create works that were "in part documentary, in part interpretation within the mold of an art form." Lerner's words apply equally to Baldwin's essays, which were artistic interventions intended to bring American life in sharper relief. Lindner had not merely presented "materials for a story but human personalities in deep trouble, each with a little fire of rebellion burning in him, each salvageable and worth salvaging."[96]

Of course, psychoanalytic thinking had never been the exclusive property of literary intellectuals, and it had long traversed political divisions. Conveying views that Baldwin and many literary intellectuals shared, the leftist sociologist C. Wright Mills argued in *The Sociological Imagination* (1959) that psychoanalysis had led to significant revisions in the work of humanistic and social scientific thinkers alike. For

Mills, psychological inquiry was a critical resource for interpreting the workings of culture. "It may well be that the most radical discovery within recent psychology and social science is the discovery of how so many of the most intimate features of the person are socially patterned and even implanted." Biography could no longer be excluded from explorations of the social world since the personal and the historical were intricately related. "The principle of historical specificity holds for psychology as well as for the social sciences," Mills wrote. Like Baldwin and other postwar intellectuals, Mills came to see that even "intimate features of man's inner life" were best understood as "problems within specific historical contexts."[97]

Beyond Postwar America

The exploration of race thinking in the social, cultural, and psychological life of the nation represented an intellectual imperative for Baldwin, who believed that such explorations warranted the widest possible readership. The biographical accounts, dissection of cultural forms, and search for emotional truths in Baldwin's essays cumulatively rendered race thinking a historical problem that encompassed all of these dimensions. Stan Weir, a writer and longtime trade unionist who spent time with Baldwin in the early-to-mid-1940s, likewise recalled that Baldwin came to see his best work as making it "possible for white as well as Black Americans to witness the Black experience—and the white experience—as part of the same societal process."[98] Trilling remarked that Baldwin had brought within his "purview not only the particular anomaly of the Negroes in their disadvantaged situation, but the whole moral life of the nation."[99]

In the 1960s and 1970s, Baldwin's work remained an important resource for making sense of the racist social order because of its psychological concerns. *The Fire Next Time* (1963) emerged during a different historical moment from that of *Notes of a Native Son*. For one cultural historian, *The Fire Next Time* "straddled the line between the integrationist views of civil rights leaders and the angry militance soon to come."[100] But Baldwin's attention to the psychological dimensions of racism would be a mainstay of his criticism, even in the revised context of racial struggle, for, as one critic has argued, "Baldwin's uncompromising negative critique of American political culture extends beyond black nationalist critiques in terms of the complexity of its psychological depth" via a continual return to the question of "how both white and black identities have been constructed in the Americanization process."[101] In interviews in the 1960s, Baldwin presented in more directed and pointed ways key assumptions that had underpinned the essays from the postwar decade. In one interview he told Studs Terkel, "The country doesn't know what it has done to

Negroes. And the country has no notion whatever—and this is disastrous—of what it has done to itself. North and South have yet to assess the price they pay for keeping the Negro in his place; and, to my point of view, it shows in every single level of our lives, from the most public to the most private."[102]

In *Racial Oppression in America* (1972), the sociologist Robert Blauner referred to Baldwin as a writer who "pointed to the deep mutual involvement of black and white in America." Baldwin expressed and dissected the "profound ambivalence" and the "love-hate relationship" that marked that involvement. A growing number of scholars in the 1960s and 1970s found the available social scientific analysis of racial conflict too simplistic. The paradigms for understanding the racially divided society that obtained in the 1940s and 1950s, particularly those organized around the concept of prejudice, no longer seemed capable of providing sufficient insights. There was a basic difference between "racism as an objective phenomenon, located in the actual existence of domination and hierarchy, and racism's concomitants of prejudice and other motivations and feelings," Blauner wrote.[103]

Yet, even as older paradigms gave way to a vocabulary of racism and internal colonization, psychological inquiries related to racial antagonisms and race thinking would continue to inform emerging discourses. Baldwin's body of work, which addressed both material deprivations caused by the racism and the place of race within the psychic economy of American culture, would remain a compelling resource. His writings, which first gained prominence during a period in which great significance was attached to the study of prejudice, retained substantial relevance as the concept of racism achieved that stature.[104] Lines such as those that Baldwin might have penned in the 1940s and 1950s found their way into the scholarship of the 1960s and 1970s. "Blacks as a collective presence have never been invisible or inconsequential to American institutions and white psyches," Blauner wrote. Baldwin, like few others, provided vital ways of thinking about the "still little-understood psychology of racism."[105]

In the 1960s, C. L. R. James reflected on how Baldwin's work had come to serve as a widely recognized emblem of contemporary antiracism. His words evoke the volatility of the 1960s in terms not of student rebellion but instead of the ongoing reckoning with the institutionalized disempowerment that followed slavery. "For a century, the United States had perpetrated against millions of its citizens a civil and psychological brutality of which it itself is now only becoming fully aware," James wrote. "James Baldwin, popularly regarded at home as well as abroad as the effective spokesman against the century old persecution of the Negro Americans, has unequivocally stated that the problem is not a problem of the black skin—it is a sickness in American civilization itself which has expressed and expresses itself in the persecution of the Negro population."[106] The vocabulary of disease and violence that functioned through psychological mechanisms had not, of course, emerged fully formed in the 1960s. Instead it was carried into those years through the discursive labors Baldwin and others undertook and, not least, as a result of the salience the "psychological" continued to carry for those who wished to make sense of the miasma of "race" in the second half of the twentieth century.

For all the ways that Baldwin's arguments entered the mainstream, becoming starting points for reinterpretations of the American past, his greatest contribution for many remained the critical disposition he modeled within literary and cultural criticism. Describing the impact of Baldwin's work, novelist Toni Morrison recalled that he had "made American English honest," a feat akin to creating a language that was "truly modern, dialogic, representative [and] humane." He had replaced "soft, plump lies" with "lean, targeted power," and in so doing created distinctive ways of thinking, new forms of knowledge.[107] Another writer, Colm Toibin, argued that the essays became instantly compelling documents because Baldwin insisted on "being personal, on forcing the public and the political to submit to his voice and the test of his experience and his observation."[108] The words Morrison and Toibin choose to explain Baldwin's work appear incongruous, for even as the writing is personal and dialogic, there is also "targeted power," an active attempt to compel the "political to submit." Yet the essays in particular derived their power from this very incongruity, from the candidness, even amiability, with which they presented personal experience and the palpable anger that they transmuted into a sense of urgency.

Sensitivity to the "large set of opposites" that defined Baldwin allows both Morrison and Toibin to discern the multilayered nature of his dissenting contribution.[109] Baldwin's maverick prose style breathed new life into psychological inquiries related to the racist social order, inquiries that had gained momentum within public commentary beginning in the early 1940s. Baldwin made the psychological exploration of racial discord and race thinking an inescapable topic for the literary and, by extension, moral imagination of the postwar years. As forms of writing, Baldwin's essays could not be dismissed, and as an argument for the relevance of "race" for American culture as a whole, they were likewise difficult to ignore. Working in privileged quarters of literary and cultural criticism, Baldwin indeed extended an argument that Wright had done much to bring into American intellectual life, albeit in his own inimitable way.

In an interview late in his life, Baldwin was asked what major task might serve as an expansive and resonant theme in the work of contemporary black writers. "This may sound strange, but to make the question of color obsolete," he responded, with characteristic quickness.[110] In the late 1940s and early 1950s, when many of Baldwin's most important essays were composed, this assertion would not have seemed strange. After all, with memories of the war as fresh in everyday life as in the world of letters, a midcentury humanism that emphasized the depraved uses to which racial thinking could be put achieved wide credibility. Baldwin's efforts to describe the impact of racial thinking on everyday lives, like his determination to assess the place of racial thinking in the psychological life of the nation, brought his aims within the parameters of that midcentury humanism. The desire to make color obsolete also fits with the general tenor of his essays, which brought to life through compelling prose the despair, distrust, and alienation race hierarchy generated. If Baldwin brought race into the world of postwar literary intellectuals, he did so to emphasize how it implicated the culture as a whole and to present in detail the harms and hazards it carried. Thus, his remark that writers might strive to "make the question of color obsolete" supplies a way to read much of his writing, not least the essays that were in many ways his most creative acts. But Baldwin's words extend even beyond his own work, for they provide a way to recall the dominant rationale that animated the turn to the psychology of race. Beginning in the 1940s with Wright and extending through Baldwin's postwar writings, the move toward the psychology of race became an abiding part of the antiracist imagination as a strategy that looked to a horizon where color lines and racial codes ceased to have cultural and psychological purchase.

In the years between the publication of *Native Son* (1940) and *Notes of a Native Son* (1955), antiracist writers endeavored to renew—not jettison—ideological contestation by returning in novel ways to the longstanding, volatile, and ever mutating racial ideologies of American life. Cultural critics working in relation to modern psychological vocabularies played a pivotal role in devising resonant forms of antiracist commentary, amplifying them well beyond the corridors of social scientific research on race prejudice and in contravention of the constrained discursive bandwidth that had been labeled the Negro Problem throughout the first half of the twentieth century. Contesting racist ideologies, cultural critics rebutted the "end-of-ideology" that presumably characterized all postwar thinking. Indeed, Wright, Smith, Baldwin, and other antiracist thinkers worked in active noncompliance with the professed end-of-ideology. Sociologist Daniel Bell's book, *The End-of-Ideology: On the Exhaustion of Political Ideas in the 1950s,* though not published until 1960, described the "mood" of the postwar era as one in which ideology was increasingly associated with violence and sloganeering.[111] For Bell, disclosures about the inhumanity of the Nazi regime made it necessary to level a somber indictment against movements and forms of radical political thought that could be linked to ideology. In a period of putative intellectual exhaustion, the analysis of ideologies, too, was to be avoided.

The mid-twentieth-century turn to psychology dramatized the inextricable connection of race hierarchy to the daily making of culture, underscoring the necessity of reading the ideological work of racial practices and scripts. The literary work and cultural criticism that followed represented theoretical labors that modeled critical rereading of the racial scripts, discourses, and behavior that suffused social and cultural life. All the writers explored in this study regarded "race" as an invidious abstraction that underwrote social, political, and economic mechanisms of violence. Indeed, much midcentury social and cultural commentary began with the assumption that taken-for-granted beliefs about race were part of the overall race problem and were, for that reason, a subject that all artists, cultural critics, and intellectuals had a responsibility to address. Wright's affinities for psychological inquiry and psychotherapeutic methods enabled his attentiveness to the effects, personal and material, of race as practices of signification. Wright's efforts did not reduce race hierarchy to a psychological problem but instead provided the basis for interpreting the full range of its effects, thereby insisting on race as a political and historical category.[112] Wright and other antiracist writers modeled a form of cultural interpretation both alert to the harms of racism and racist ideology *and* directed toward a time when race no longer served as an emblem for grasping the present or as a means of anticipating the future.

Insofar as the end-of-ideology thesis pointed to changes in the scope and content of writing in the postwar era, the argument helps to explain developments in American intellectual life, including the emergence of conformist or apolitical psychologies and "consensus" accounts of American history and society.[113] Consensus theory, associated with the construction of a benign core American tradition, furnished the basis for a pluralist orientation that influenced much of postwar humanistic and social scientific thought. Psychologists and sociologists played a disproportionately large role in the advance of consensus theory through research in the reduction of intergroup tensions. It is against the backdrop of the end-of-ideology and an emergent consensus theory that posited an exceptional American past that the strands of antiracist criticism explored in this book deserve reconsideration. Far from hastening an end to ideology, Wright, Smith, and Baldwin called attention to the ideological processes through which meanings and sentiments collected around "race." The corpus of antiracist writing they helped create stood in opposition to the intellectual culture denoted by the end-of-ideology in asserting the vital importance of recognizing and reflecting on the material and psychological effects of racial ideologies and the ideological interpolation of varieties of racial logic. For these writers, an end-of-ideology did not seem imminent when it came to racism and race thinking. It was therefore within a contradictory space—a postwar intellectual culture hostile to ideological criticism and the continuing salience of race—that Baldwin and others devised interventions that made U.S. race hierarchy a central, rather than parochial, concern for American writers and Americans at large.

Conclusion

This study has concentrated on the ways modern psychological inquiry figured in Richard Wright's intellectual contribution to U.S. antiracist criticism and helped set its terms more broadly. Wright's commitments to psychological and psychotherapeutic inquiry prompted him to reopen the question of what constituted a valid and viable cultural politics in relation to a racist social order. Locating these commitments in the story of mid-twentieth-century American letters alters available understandings of Wright's significance to U.S. cultural history. By the 1950s, after Wright's reworking of cultural criticism, intellectuals observing race hierarchy and racial antagonisms no longer needed to justify drawing on a psychological vocabulary. Such a vocabulary had acquired a footing within cultural commentary as a resource for narrating and interpreting American life and as a means of nurturing a political imagination predicated on the demise of the racist social order.

American cultural criticism relied on the analytical innovation that Wright, along with Lillian Smith, James Baldwin, and others, set in motion well into the second half the twentieth century. A new generation of authors would build on their insights and strategies by making modern psychological inquiry serve antiracist ends. Two books published in 1970 signal variations on the midcentury antiracism described in this study. "Our racial crisis has made us realize that white racism in America is no aberration, but an ingredient of our culture which cannot be fully understood apart from the rest of our total situation," wrote Joel Kovel in *White Racism: A Psychohistory* (1970). Kovel's approach posited that "psychology alone does not nearly account for the scope of the racial problem," for racism in America involved mechanisms and bureaucratic structures that produced poverty and material disparities. Yet, Kovel argued, unconscious structures and psychological patterns had helped to install racist ideologies in the United States, giving them viability across different political cultures—on "whatever terrain is provided."[1] Kovel explored the psychological compulsions of the historical past to read the ideologies and activities that comprised racism. Just as Wright crafted a critical idiom designed to intervene in the cultural politics of the 1940s, Kovel set out to compose a psychohistory that supplied readers with new ways to understand the historical compulsions and cultural disfigurations related to "present-day racism" in the second half of the twentieth century.

In the realm of literary creativity and cultural criticism, Toni Morrison, for whom Baldwin served as a particular influence, drew upon the antiracist critique of her predecessors. Also appearing in 1970, Morrison's first novel, *The Bluest Eye,* was set in the 1940s and bore the discursive marks of the psychological investigation of racial antagonisms undertaken in earnest in those years. The novel reinvokes "dolls" in ways that bring to mind the Clarks' "doll studies." Morrison's narrator, Claudia, describes the social world as seen by the African American girls in the story. She recalls: "Adults, older girls, shops, magazine, newspapers, window signs—all the world had agreed that a blue-eyed, yellow-haired, pink-skinned doll was what every girl child treasured."[2] The novel depends on assumptions about race as a complex structure consisting of social and psychological dynamics, a strategy that parallels in a distinctive literary idiom the concerted efforts by social scientists and cultural workers in the 1940s to determine the basis of what was then commonly referred to as "race prejudice." Elaborating on the cultural and intellectual forces that shaped her choices as a writer, Morrison has noted that her book was written during the first half of the 1960s, when the "assertion of racial beauty was not a reaction to the self-mocking, humorous critique of cultural/racial foibles common in all groups, but against the damaging internalization of assumptions of immutable inferiority originating in an outside gaze."[3]

Morrison's novel provided ways to explore the nexus of assumptions of inferiority and internalization by focusing on the ordinary settings of transmission within which the pedagogy of race hierarchy occurred.[4] Speaking to the cultural politics and circumstances of the 1960s, Morrison's words also recall the questions and cultural diagnoses presented by Wright, Smith, and Baldwin, suggesting postwar reinventions of the antiracism generated in the 1940s. The intricate borrowings and mutual questions that link Morrison to work from the 1940s should not obscure ways antiracist cultural politics changed in the 1960s and beyond, diverging amid circumstances and demands unforeseen. Yet there is one constant that Morrison's literature and criticism stipulates. In much the way that her precursors in the mid-twentieth century had done through modern psychological thought, Morrison honed her skills as writer and critic to "learn how to maneuver ways to free up . . . language from its sometimes sinister, frequently lazy, almost always predictable enjoyment of racially informed and determined chains."[5]

The antiracism explored in this study interrupted commonsense racial thinking —Morrison's "racially informed and determined chains"—in potent but also partial, incipient ways. And while later writers picked up the intellectual and literary threads developed in opposition to the racist social order and its habits of mind, antiracist criticism in the second half of the twentieth century overwhelmingly followed a trajectory of identitarian concerns. Psychological questions changed dramatically under the rubric of "identity politics," becoming vehicles for the stabilization of personal consciousness. In the process, racial designations became recoded as valuable and reproducible assets to the work of political viability, rather than problems in cultural, social, and political formation. Indeed, the affective problems implicated by race and race hierarchy emphasized in the 1940s later became minimized, as the constitution and rehabilitation of racial identities served, more and more, as the basic means of challenging race hierarchy. In retrospect, the chief characteristic of the antiracist critical moves of the 1940s may well be the attentiveness to the psychological confusions and harms created by attachments to the notion of racial difference and the attendant inability to envision a political order sans "race." When the writers examined in this study return to our contemporary attention, they are sometimes mistakenly relegated to an identitarian framework. They are taken to be concerned primarily with the formation and sustenance of identities rather than the transformation of a social order in which accommodation to racial strictures circumscribes individual and collective existence. Yet reading these writers for how much they diverge from identitarian, or identity-based, frameworks reveals the character of the cultural politics they generated. It recalls that what midcentury antiracist writers modeled above all was a refusal to accede to the common sense of race thinking.

If this model did not always gain traction with subsequent generations of U.S. writers, it nevertheless resonated with, and even impinged on, the work of writers beyond the United States, especially anticolonial critics addressing race thinking in the context of European imperialism. In furthering criticism predicated on the salience not of identity but rather of conditions of domination and practices of racialization, several U.S. writers anticipated the critical idiom of the Martinican psychiatrist Frantz Fanon. When Fanon wrote his classic account of colonialism, *Black Skin, White Masks* (1952), unraveling the "Black-White relationship" was his explicit aim. For Fanon, the starting point for any such project rested on an acknowledgment that the "White man is locked in his whiteness" and the "Black man in his blackness."[6] Fanon intertwined cultural and psychological inquiry, looking across a range of literatures and texts to locate the main dynamics of the Black-White relationship. He endeavored to make sense of twentieth-century metropolitan racism and the psychological violence exercised by ongoing colonial structures. His response to these histories engendered his anticolonial humanism. Fanon at times drew on U.S. black writing to develop his reading of the Black-White relationship. The racial discord on display in the work of Richard Wright, Chester Himes, and Hollywood social-problem films such as *Home of the Brave* (1949) offer occasions for Fanon's critical imagination to recast the question of colonialism in terms of the broader problems of racism, ideology, and modernity. Not coincidentally, Fanon's turn to American writing and the history of racial hierarchy in the American context chronologically follows his exposure to the U.S. military as a World War II soldier in France, where U.S. dictates led to the segregation of soldiers from the French colonies from their white French counterparts. Yet there is more than biography at work in Fanon's immersion in American narratives. Wright and Himes, along with several other black and white authors in the 1940s, prefigured the intensified psychological questioning that characterized *Black Skin, White Masks.* Indeed, the "psychological," as Fanon understood it, mirrors the analytical inflection that Wright and others attached to the category. Fanon foregrounds his psychological analysis but is quick to add that his aim, the "disalienation of the black man," can scarcely proceed without pairing the "psychological" with a "brutal awareness of the social and economic realities."[7] For Fanon, psychological analysis does not obviate social and economic facts on the ground but rather endows them with a renewed relevance.

Wright's work extended into the era of decolonization associated with Fanon. In 1960, he drafted a preface for a second edition of *Black Metropolis.* Fifteen years had passed since he had written the original introduction for the book. As he composed the draft, *Brown v. Board of Education* loomed large in Wright's mind as a crucial moment, one that could not be disentangled from the "most salient change to take place since the publication of *Black Metropolis*": "the emergence of the U.S. as the unchallenged leader and spokesman of the Western world." This development caused "the Negro [to] became a kind of touchstone in the Cold War of ideas and international pressures" as a "minority that took on a kind of symbolic value of the workability of democracy itself." Portentous and global in its implications, *Brown* also mattered because of its validation of psychological interpretation, which encompassed an elaboration of the phenomenon "self-hate" as an "organic part of any system of oppressed peoples' mentality." The Supreme Court decision, Wright wrote, gripped Americans with "emotional tension" and a shock that was still reverberating. Wright agreed with the decision's premise that racist social environments harmed personalities, predicting that the ensuing changes in American life would lie along a path both "psychological" and "painful."[8]

Wright linked *Brown* to several events from the intervening years, not least the 1955 "reaching out that culminated in Bandung," a key moment in the story of decolonization. The meeting of the "representatives of colored mankind" in Indonesia "showed that the marks of oppression went deep, lasted longer, and were to be

noticed, and had to be reckoned with" even after the departure of colonial admin-
istrators. Wright referred to the first Asian-African conference of states, a collective
statement of opposition to colonialism that reconfigured world politics by bolstering
decolonizing, nationalist movements. In lectures delivered in Europe, Wright continually returned to psychological themes as he examined the state of the decolonizing world. Reflecting broadly on the history of imperialism, he held that "Asia and
Africa thus became a neurotic habit that Europeans could forgo only at the cost of a
powerful psychic wound."[9] Wright had long understood African American life as
part of a transnational history of dispossessed minorities. Like the agonizing and
uncertain process of decolonization, *Brown* augured necessary changes, but it also
represented the beginning rather than the culmination of deliberations on race
hierarchy. Those deliberations would require attentiveness to the psychological costs
of race hierarchy—the burden of which the decision itself could not possibly carry.

Much like anticolonial critics whose writings in the 1950s and 1960s posited the
"implacable dependence" that linked colonizer and colonized, guiding the conduct
and shaping the character of each, Wright suggested a post-*Brown* period requiring
mechanisms for the "decomposition of this dependence" among America's racial
camps.[10] He wove his understanding of the mutual implication of black and white
into his work from early on, emphasizing in particular that African Americans shared
"all of the glorious hopes of the West, all of its anxieties, its corruptions, its psychologies maladies."[11] Revisiting *Killers of the Dream* for a 1961 edition, Lillian Smith
similarly expanded the geographical span of her story, reframing her account of
American life through the political idiom of decolonization. Her book acquired new
urgency as challenges to "colonialism's twin brother, segregation" took the form of
bus boycotts and civil disobedience. The protocols of race hierarchy and segregation
began to appear mostly as a "trap in which we were hopelessly caught were it not for
the young and their fine talent for doing the unpredictable."[12] The major anticolonial
writers of the decolonization era saw the colonial relationship as one involving
irreducible affective dimensions, as material and economic forms of domination
maintained through psychological investments and patterns. In marking the relationship between commentary on race hierarchy in the United States and the emergent,
decolonizing world, antiracist writers implicitly indicated the transnational character of
the psychological questions they brought to bear on histories of domination.

Richard Wright, Ralph Ellison, and James Baldwin enter the story told in Barack
Obama's autobiographical *Dreams from My Father* (1995). The works of these authors
cannot resolve the contradictions of his specific situation as the son of a white
American mother and a black African father, what Obama refers to as the "terms of

my birth." Moreover, for all their insights and all of their value as sources of ideas with which he could argue, the books Obama reads fail to bring solace: "In every page of every book, in Bigger Thomas and invisible men, I kept finding the same anguish, the same doubt; a self-contempt that neither irony nor intellect seemed able to deflect." Obama would seek out yet other writers and other models for the modes of "self-creation" that would bring him practical means of assessing his social location and possible trajectories. Yet, despite his admittedly brief mention of Wright, Ellison, and Baldwin, Obama may be said to extend their work in certain respects. One need not adopt a sanguine view of his impact on U.S. political culture to recognize the powerful literary sensibility he brings in his writing to questions of race hierarchy and the strategies that have been devised to respond to its sordid consequences. Obama is perhaps nowhere more like Wright than when he turns his attention to black nationalism and delivers an assessment of its meanings. On the void he sees black nationalism filling, Obama writes that for a "people already stripped of their history, a people often ill-equipped to retrieve that history in any other form than what fluttered across the television screen, the testimony of what we saw every day seemed only to confirm our worst suspicions about ourselves." Drawing upon his familiarity with the political and social circumstances of much of black America, Obama claims to understand the extent to which, "deep down, all blacks were potential national-ists." But, befitting Wright, he finally characterizes such nationalism as a form of "displacement," a historically intelligible morality tale that involved "engaging in self-criticism while removing ourselves from the object of criticism." The critique of black nationalism Obama levels, though itself not beyond critique, evinces the close reading of historical particulars and psychological dynamics that marks much of his writing, which, in its own way and for its own time, delivers perspectives on the worlds bequeathed by race hierarchy. Obama does not write about a vaunted post-racial America but instead makes the continuing, tragic, and "almost mathematical precision with which America's race and class problems [become] joined" one of his main subjects.[13] Yet if Obama expresses alertness to the lingering, mutating forms of race hierarchy, he does not assume a perpetually "racial" America. Notably, he does not submit a future racial ordering as the solution to the contradictions of race hierarchy and the ways it has formed the American scene.

Disenchantment with "race" served as the basis for the cultural criticism that many antiracist writers of the 1940s produced. In the closing pages of *Black Skin, White Masks,* Fanon, too, diverges from a race-centered or identity-based ethic. "My life must not be devoted to making an assessment of black values," he writes, for such a resolution would make him a "victim of the Ruse of a black world." The writers on whose work I have focused were committed to parting with the mystifications of "race" and were governed in their thinking by something like the promise of Fanon's disalienation, a form of liberation possible "for those Whites and Blacks who have refused to let themselves be locked in the substantialized 'tower of the past.' "[14] The existential and psychological rereading of race Wright and others undertook similarly departed from any concern with racialized values and identity-based logic. The rationale for constructing an antiracist cultural politics that deviated from the lure of racialized values had everything to do with banishing the deceptions and harms of the racist social order to the "tower of the past."

Introduction

1. Richard Wright, "Harlem Is Human" (1945–46), Richard Wright Papers, Beinecke Rare Book and Manuscript Library, Yale University, New Haven, CT.

2. Michel Fabre, *The World of Richard Wright* (Jackson: University Press of Mississippi, 1985), 54.

3. Wright, "Harlem Is Human."

4. Carey McWilliams, *The Education of Carey McWilliams* (New York: Simon & Schuster, 1979), 114–15. Michael Denning discusses McWilliams in this period in *The Cultural Front: The Laboring of American Culture in the Twentieth Century* (New York: Verso, 1996), 44–54. On racial conflict during the war, see Harvard Sitkoff, "Racial Militancy and Interracial Violence in the Second World War," *Journal of American History* 58 (December 1971): 661–81, and Richard M. Dalfiume, "The 'Forgotten Years' of the Negro Revolution," *Journal of American History* 55 (June 1968): 90–106.

5. Robert Korstad and Nelson Lichtenstein, "Opportunities Found and Lost: Labor, Radicals, and the Early Civil Rights Movement," *Journal of American History* 75 (December 1988): 786, 788.

6. W. E. B. Du Bois, "Apology," *Phylon* 1 (1940): 3–5.

7. On the "racial-cultural situation," see Denning, *Cultural Front*, 445–53.

8. See Daniel Wickberg, "Homophobia: On the Cultural History of an Idea," *Critical Inquiry* 27 (Autumn 2000): 42–57.

9. Horace R. Cayton, "Race Relations and Negro Morale," Wright Papers.

10. Kenneth Clark, "The Effects of Segregation and the Consequences of Desegregation: A Social Science Statement," 1952, Kenneth Clark Papers, Library of Congress, Washington, DC.

11. Kenneth Clark, "Racial Factors and Effective Psychotherapy," 26 August 1954, Clark Papers.

12. Clark, "Racial Factors."

13. Ellen Herman, *The Romance of American Psychology: Political Culture in an Age of Experts* (Berkeley: University of California Press, 1995), 183.

14. Nat Hentoff, "The Integrationist," in *The Nat Hentoff Reader* (Cambridge, MA: Da Capo, 2001), 165.

15. As Ellen Herman puts it, the public rise of psychology involved a "wide-ranging campaign to infuse society with psychological enlightenment"; *Romance of American Psychology*, 2.

16. Franz Alexander, "Psychology and the Interpretation of Historical Events," in *The Cultural Approach to History*, ed. Caroline Ware (New York: Columbia University Press, 1940), 57, 48.

17. Ware, *Cultural Approach to History*, 199.

18. See Franz Samelson, "From Race Psychology to Studies in Prejudice," in *Journal of the History of the Behavioral Sciences* 14 (1978): 265–78.

19. Alfred Kazin, "The Freudian Revolution Analyzed," in *Freud and the Twentieth Century*, ed. Benjamin Nelson (Cleveland: Meridian, 1957), 13–14.

20. Ibid., 14.

21. Herman, *Romance of American Psychology*, 63.

22. Clark, "Effects of Segregation." Also see Daryl Michael Scott, *Contempt and Pity: Social Policy and the Image of the Damaged Black Psyche, 1880–1996* (Chapel Hill: University of North Carolina Press, 1997), especially "Justifying Equality: Damage Imagery, *Brown v. Board of Education* and the American Creed." As Scott writes, the decision put a premium on the "low level of aspiration and defeatism among segregated groups" and the "hypersensitivity and anxiety displayed by many minority group children about their relation to the larger society." For a counterpoint, see Shelley Eversley, "The Lunatic's Fancy and the Work of Art," *American Literary History* 13 (2001): 445–68.

23. Clark, "Effects of Segregation." See also Helen Leland Witmer and Ruth Kotinsky, eds., *Personality in the Making: The Fact-Finding Report of the Midcentury White House Conference on Children and Youth* (New York: Harper, 1952).

24. Richard Wright, introduction to *Black Metropolis: A Study of Negro Life in a Northern City*, by St. Clair Drake and Horace R. Cayton (1945; reprint, Chicago: University of Chicago Press, 1993), xxix.

25. Lionel Trilling, "A Tragic Situation," in *Richard Wright's "Black Boy": A Casebook*, ed. William Andrews and Douglas Taylor (New York: Oxford University Press, 2003), 39.

26. Scott, *Contempt and Pity*, 98, 169.

27. Nikhil Singh, *Black Is a Country: Race and the Unfinished Struggle for Democracy* (Cambridge, MA: Harvard University Press, 2004), 121.

28. Wright, introduction to *Black Metropolis*, xxv.

29. Cedric J. Robinson, *Black Marxism: The Making of the Black Radical Tradition* (1980; reprint, Chapel Hill: University of North Carolina Press, 2000), 352. Robinson writes that Wright did not reject Marxism outright but instead attempted to "locate it, to provide a sense of the boundaries of its authority." See also William J. Maxwell, *New Negro, Old Left: African American Writing and Communism between the Wars* (New York: Columbia University Press, 1999).

30. According to Cedric Robinson, Wright sought a "psychological and intellectual locus unlike anything his experience of Western radicalism and activism" had modeled; *Black Marxism*, 352.

31. Herbert Aptheker, "A Liberal Dilemma," *New Masses*, 14 May 1946.

32. Ellison, *Shadow and Act* (1964; reprint, New York: Random House, 1994), 311, 315.

33. Richard Wright, *Native Son* (1940; reprint, New York: Harper Perennial, 1998), 377.

34. On the "Negro Problem" as a category and its later pluralization, see Susan Gillman, *Blood Talk: American Race Melodrama and the Culture of the Occult* (Chicago: University of Chicago Press, 2003). The phrase, "capitalized and in singular form, makes visible the derogatory grammars of nineteenth century racial science and social policy," Gillman writes (1).

35. Lillian Smith, "Southern Defensive—II," *Common Ground* 4 (Spring 1944): 43–45.

36. Ranjana Khanna, *Dark Continents: Psychoanalysis and Colonialism* (Durham: Duke University Press, 2003), 105.

37. Michel Fabre helpfully points out that Wright's existentialism "should by no means be limited to his contacts with the French existentialist group from the mid-'40s to the mid-'50s." For, as he observes, Wright's "interest in an existentialist world both predates and postdates those contacts"; "Wright and the French Existentialists," in *The World of Richard Wright* (Jackson: University Press of Mississippi, 1985), 159.

38. Michael Rustin, "Psychoanalysis, Racism and Anti-Racism," in *Identity: A Reader,* ed. Paul Du Gay (London: Sage, 2000), 187.

39. See Singh, *Black Is a Country,* and Penny von Eschen, *Race against Empire: Black Americans and Anticolonialism, 1937–1957* (Ithaca: Cornell University Press, 1997).

40. Daryl M. Scott describes Du Bois as among the most important figures in African American letters to set in motion a focus on the "psychological and mental problems of black folk" with the aim of exposing "pathologies that could be healed by progressive social engineering"; *Contempt and Pity,* 6. Scott's specific characterization of Du Bois's work notwithstanding, his argument serves as a valuable reminder of the longstanding varieties of psychological inquiry created to intervene within the culture and politics of the racist social order.

41. Richard Wright, "A World View of the American Negro," *Twice a Year* (New York: Twice a Year Press, 1948), 346.

42. Michael Carter, "Book-of-the-Month Author Talks for AFRO," *Afro-American,* 13 January 1945.

Chapter 1 • Richard Wright Writing:
The Unconscious Machinery of Race Relations

1. Quoted in *Richard Wright: Books and Writers,* ed. Michel Fabre (Jackson: University Press of Mississippi, 1990), 9.

2. Kenneth Clark, "Racial Factors and Effective Psychotherapy," 26 August 1954, Kenneth Clark Papers, Library of Congress, Washington, DC.

3. Ibid.

4. Michel Fabre, *The World of Richard Wright* (Jackson: University Press of Mississippi, 1985), 71.

5. E. Franklin Frazier, "The Pathology of Race Prejudice," *Forum,* June 1927, 856, 862.

6. Robert E. Park, "The Bases of Race Prejudice," *Annals of the American Academy of Political and Social Science* 140 (November 1928): 12.

7. Alain Locke, *Race Contacts and Interracial Relations: Lectures on the Theory and Practice of Race,* ed. Jeffrey C. Stewart (Washington: Howard University Press, 1992), 64.

8. Ibid., 64–65.

9. In 1963, Edward Shils wrote that "Dollard's was the first in a series of studies of the

situation of the American Negro; its psychological sensitivity had never been equaled in the study of the stratification of American white society"; "The Contemplation of Society in America," in *Paths of American Thought,* ed. Arthur Schlesinger Jr. and Morton White (New York: Houghton Mifflin, 1963), 404.

10. Richard Wright, introduction to *Black Metropolis: A Study of Negro Life in a Northern City,* by St. Clair Drake and Horace R. Cayton (1945; reprint, Chicago: University of Chicago Press, 1993), xxxi.

11. Ibid., xxx.

12. Franz Alexander, "Educative Influence of Personality Factors in the Environment," *Environment and Education,* ed. Ernest W. Burgess et al. (Chicago: University of Chicago Press, 1942), 42, 47.

13. William H. Sheldon, *Psychology and the Promethean Will* (New York: Harper, 1936), 51.

14. Richard Wright, introduction to *No Day of Triumph* by J. Saunders Redding (New York: Harper, 1942).

15. Farah Jasmine Griffin notes that Wright emphasized the "urban attack on the migrant's psyche" and the "dehumanizing effect of indifference"; *Who Set You Flowin'?: The African-American Migration Narrative* (New York: Oxford University Press, 1995), 75, 70.

16. Paul Gilroy, *Darker than Blue: On the Moral Economies of Black Atlantic Culture* (Cambridge, MA: Harvard University Press, 2010), 141.

17. Ibid.

18. Horace R. Cayton and Elaine Ogden McNeil, "Research on the Urban Negro," *American Journal of Sociology* 47 (September 1941): 176.

19. Ibid., 178, 180–81.

20. Quoted in Michel Fabre, *The Unfinished Quest of Richard Wright* (Urbana: University of Illinois Press, 1993), 230–31.

21. Ibid., 95, 97.

22. George M. Fredrickson, *Black Liberation: A Comparative History of Black Ideologies in the United States and South Africa* (New York: Oxford University Press, 1995), 180.

23. Ibid., 43.

24. Richard Wright, "Blueprint for Negro Writing," in *Richard Wright Reader,* ed. Ellen Wright and Michel Fabre (New York: Harper and Row, 1978), 37. "Blueprint for Negro Writing" originally appeared in *New Challenge* in 1937.

25. As George Hutchinson puts it, Wright ignored "institutional, aesthetic and ideological continuities between the Harlem Renaissance and later African American social realism"; *The Harlem Renaissance in Black and White* (Cambridge, MA: Harvard University Press, 1995), 277.

26. Wright, "Blueprint for Negro Writing," 41–42.

27. Ibid., 42–43.

28. Ibid., 42–43, 48.

29. Quoted in Fabre, *Unfinished Quest,* 230–31.

30. Ibid., 228–29.

31. Ralph Ellison to Wright, 3 November 1941, Richard Wright Papers, Yale Collection of American Literature, Beinecke Rare Book and Manuscript Library, Yale University.

32. For an extended discussion of Wright and the Chicago sociologists, see Carla Cappetti,

Writing Chicago: Modernism, Ethnography, and the Novel (New York: Columbia University Press, 1993), chapters 8 and 9. Histories of the "Chicago school" include Fred H. Matthews, *Quest for an American Sociology: Robert E. Park and the Chicago School* (Montreal: McGill-Queen's University Press, 1977), and Henry Yu, *Thinking Orientals: Migration, Contact, and Exoticism in Modern America* (New York: Oxford University Press, 2001).

33. Gavin Jones, *American Hungers: The Problem of Poverty in U.S. Literature* (Princeton: Princeton University Press, 2008), 139. Invoking Wright's own words, Jones notes that Wright wanted to understand the behavioral and mental problems of urban blacks as they flowed from "frantic poverty."

34. Robert E. Park, Edward W. Burgess, and Roderick D. McKenzie, *The City* (Chicago: University of Chicago Press, 1967).

35. Ibid., 1, 2, 22, 20.

36. Ibid., xviii.

37. On the focus on urban life among Chicago sociologists, see Rolf Lindner, *The Reportage of Urban Culture: Robert Park and the Chicago School* (Cambridge: Cambridge University Press, 1996).

38. Park, Burgess, and McKenzie, *The City*, 26.

39. Edwin Berry Burgum, *The Novel and the World's Dilemma* (New York: Oxford, 1947), 226.

40. Hugh M. Gloster, *Negro Voices in American Fiction* (Chapel Hill: University of North Carolina Press, 1948), 222, 233.

41. Fanny Butcher, "Negro Writes Brilliant Novel, Remarkable Both as Thriller and Psychological Record," *Chicago Tribune*, 6 March 1940, Wright Papers.

42. Melvin B. Tolson, "Richard Wright: *Native Son*," *Modern Quarterly* 11 (Winter 1939), Wright Papers.

43. Jacque Frederick to Richard Wright, 18 September 1940, Wright Papers.

44. Roy Wilkins, interview by Warren Bower for "The Reader's Almanac," transcript, 15 July 1940, Wright Papers.

45. Edwin R. Embree, *13 against the Odds* (New York: Viking Press, 1944), 25.

46. Louis Menand, "Richard Wright: The Hammer and the Nail," in *American Studies* (New York: Farrar, Straus and Giroux, 2002), 83.

47. Richard Wright, *Native Son* (1940; reprint, New York: Harper Perennial, 2005), 377, 383, 391.

48. Ibid., 383.

49. Ibid., 399–400.

50. Richard Wright, foreword to Paul Oliver, *Blues Fell This Morning: Meaning in the Blues* (1960; reprint, Cambridge: Cambridge University Press, 1990), xvii.

51. Wright, *Native Son*, 403.

52. Ibid., 377, 383, 391.

53. Michael Denning, *The Cultural Front: The Laboring of American Culture in the Twentieth Century* (New York: Verso, 1996), 252–53.

54. Richard Wright, "How 'Bigger' Was Born," in *Native Son*.

55. Harry Slochower, *No Voice Is Wholly Lost: Writers and Thinkers in War and Peace* (New York: Creative Age Press, 1945), 309, 310, 315.

56. Harry Slochower, "In the Fascist Styx," *Negro Quarterly* 1 (Fall 1942): 227–40.

57. As Stacy I. Morgan writes, Wright brought into representation an "*already active* and virulent strain of domestic racism"; *Rethinking Social Realism: African American Art and Literature, 1930–1953* (Athens: University of Georgia Press, 2004), 284.

58. Denning, *Cultural Front,* 11.

59. M. F. Ashley Montague, "Racism and Social Action," *Psychiatry* 9 (May 1946): 143–44.

60. Wright, "How 'Bigger' Was Born," xiv.

61. Ibid., xi.

62. Richard Wright, "Writers and Readers," interview transcript, 23 December 1941, Wright Papers.

63. David L. Cohn, "The Negro Novel: Richard Wright," *Atlantic Monthly,* May 1940, Wright Papers.

64. Richard Wright, "I Bite the Hand That Feeds Me," *Atlantic Monthly,* June 1940, Wright Papers.

65. Ibid.

66. Richard Wright, draft of "I Bite the Hand That Feeds Me" (1940), Wright Papers.

67. Lillian Smith, "A Trembling Earth," in *The Winner Names the Age: A Collection of Writings by Lillian Smith,* ed. Michelle Cliff (New York: W. W. Norton, 1978), 123–24.

68. Wright, introduction to *Black Metropolis,* xxx.

69. As Jerry W. Ward Jr. argues, Wright made "the nemesis of race the subject" of his best-known novel; "Everybody's Protest Novel: The Richard Wright Era," in *The Cambridge Companion to the African American Novel,* ed. Maryemma Graham (Cambridge: Cambridge University Press, 2004), 176.

70. Richard Wright, *12 Million Black Voices: A Folk History of the Negro in the United States of America* (1941; reprint, New York: Thunder's Mouth, 1998).

71. See Khalil Gibran Muhammad, *The Condemnation of Blackness: Race, Crime, and the Making of Modern Urban America* (Cambridge: Harvard University Press, 2010). Muhammad has written convincingly on the historical emergence of the "Negro Problem": "The monumental shift from slavery to freedom meant more than the transformation of slaves into freedmen—the realization of the hopes and prayers and resistance of four million people; it also meant a paradigm shift in the terms used to discuss, debate, and deal with them. The slavery problem became the Negro Problem."

72. Wright, introduction to *Black Metropolis,* xxviii.

73. Wright, *12 Million Black Voices,* 30.

74. Richard Wright, "The Negro and the Parkway Community House" (1941), Wright Papers.

75. Ibid.

76. Wright, *12 Million Black Voices,* 99, 106–11, 109, 108.

77. "The Voice of U.S. Negroes Is Heard," *Dynamic America,* December 1941, Wright Papers.

78. H. C. Nixon, review of *12 Million Black Voices, Nashville [Tennessee] Banner,* 28 January 1942.

79. Cara Green Russell, review of *12 Million Black Voices, Charlotte Observer,* 16 November 1941, Wright Papers.

80. Richard F. Crandell, "Dark Thoughts on Dark Citizens," *Herald Tribune,* 23 November 1941, Wright Papers.

81. Ralph Thompson, review of *12 Million Black Voices, New York Times,* 18 November 1941, Wright Papers.

82. John Pittman, "The Voice of U.S. Negroes in Heard," *People's World,* 19 November 1941, Wright Papers.

83. Esther P. Oliver to Richard Wright, 29 March 1945, Wright Papers.

84. Harry V. Dempsey to Richard Wright, 13 February 1942, Wright Papers.

85. Wright, introduction to *Black Metropolis,* xx, xxv. Subsequent page references appear in text.

86. Drake and Cayton, *Black Metropolis,* 762–63.

87. Hazel Rowley, "The Shadow of the White Woman: Richard Wright and the Book-of-the-Month Club," *Partisan Review* 4 (Spring 1999): 625–34.

88. Walter White, review of *Black Metropolis, PM,* 11 November 1945, Wright Papers.

89. Thomas Sancton, review of *Black Metropolis, New Republic,* 12 November 1945, Wright Papers.

90. Richard H. King, *Race, Culture, and the Intellectuals, 1940–1970* (Baltimore: Johns Hopkins University Press, 2005), 32.

91. Herbert Aptheker, *The Negro People in America: A Critique of Gunnar Myrdal's "An American Dilemma"* (New York: International Publishers, 1946), 62.

92. "Editorial," *Life,* 24 April 1944, quoted in Drake and Cayton, *Black Metropolis,* 760.

93. Richard Wright, *Black Boy: A Record of Childhood and Youth* (1944; reprint, New York: Harper, 1994), 298. Subsequent page references appear in text.

94. Paul Gilroy writes that much of Wright's work treats the "myriad tragedies to be discovered in the systematic inability of racialized groups to communicate, to recognize each other's humanity"; introduction to *Eight Men* (1940; reprint, New York: Harper, 1996), xv.

95. Wright makes available much more than a set of participant observer reports and finally presents a work that refuses to undertake "travels from bondage to bondage forever," as one scholar has portrayed the trajectory of Wright's narrative; Carla Cappetti, "Sociology of an Existence: Richard Wright and the Chicago School," in *The Critical Response to Richard Wright,* ed. Robert J. Butler (Westport, CT: Greenwood, 1995), 90. Rather, as Abdul Jan-Mohamed argues, by "excavating the repressed layers of his consciousness" and "establishing a specular relation with society's attempt to negate him," Wright becomes "an unrelenting and unflinching explorer of human suffering"; "Negating the Negation as a Form of Affirmation in Minority Discourse: The Construction of Richard Wright as Subject," in ibid., 108, 122, 111.

96. Isidor Schneider, "One Apart," *New Masses,* 3 April 1945, Wright Papers.

97. Edward A. Laycock, "Richard Wright Records Rebellion, Horror, and Despair of His Youth," *Boston Morning Globe,* 1 March 1945, 15.

98. Henry Steele Commager, "The Negro Problem in Our Democracy," *American Mercury,* June 1945, Wright Papers.

99. George Seaton, review of *Black Boy, Commonweal* 46 (23 March 1945): 568–69.

100. "This Too Is America," *Common Sense,* April 1946, Wright Papers.

101. Mrs. Joseph Miller to Richard Wright, 7 April 1945, Wright Papers.

102. Raymond Kennedy, "A Dramatic Autobiography," *Yale Review* 39 (Summer 1945): 762–64.

103. William Harrison, review of *Black Boy, Boston Chronicle,* 8 December 1945, reprinted in *Richard Wright: The Critical Reception,* ed. John M. Reilly (New York: Burt Franklin, 1978).

104. J. K. S., "A Searing Picture of Childhood in the South," *Minneapolis Tribune,* 4 March 1945, reprinted in Reilly, *Richard Wright: The Critical Reception.*

105. Richard K. White, "*Black Boy:* A Value Analysis," *Journal of Abnormal and Social Psychology* 4 (October 1947): 157–74, Wright Papers.

106. Horace R. Cayton to Wright, n.d., Wright Papers.

107. Horace R. Cayton, "Frightened Children of Frightened Parents," typescript carbon, 22 February 1945, Wright Papers.

108. Ralph Ellison, "Richard Wright's Blues," in *Shadow and Act* (New York: Random, 1994), 77. For more on Wright's influence on Ellison, see Michel Fabre, "From *Native Son* to *Invisible Man:* Some Notes on Ralph Ellison's Evolution in the 1950s," in *Speaking for You: The Vision of Ralph Ellison,* ed. Kimberly W. Benston (Washington, DC: Howard University Press, 1990).

109. Ellison, "Richard Wright's Blues," 81, 84–85.

110. Daniel Horowitz, *Betty Friedan and the Making of the Feminine Mystique: The American Left, the Cold War, and Modern Feminism* (Amherst: University of Massachusetts Press, 1998), 66.

Chapter 2 • *Richard Wright Reading:*
The Promise of Social Psychiatry

1. Fredric Wertham, *Dark Legend: A Study in Murder* (New York: Duell, Sloan, and Pearce, 1941), 51.

2. Fredric Wertham, *The Circle of Guilt* (New York: Rinehart, 1956), 200, 199, 81.

3. Wertham, *Dark Legend,* 33.

4. Michel Fabre, *The Unfinished Quest of Richard Wright* (Urbana: University of Illinois Press, 1993), 236–37.

5. Quoted in Richard Kluger, *Simple Justice: The History of* Brown v. Board of Education *and Black America's Struggle for Equality* (New York: Vintage, 1991), 442.

6. Fredric Wertham, "An Unconscious Determinant in *Native Son,*" *Journal of Clinical Psychopathology* 6 (1944): 112.

7. Fabre, *Unfinished Quest,* 46–47.

8. Wertham, "An Unconscious Determinant in *Native Son,*" 114.

9. Fredric Wertham, review of *Black Boy, Journal of Clinical Psychopathology* 6 (1945): 643.

10. Wertham to Wright, 16 March 1945, Richard Wright Papers, Beinecke Rare Book and Manuscript Library, Yale University, New Haven, CT.

11. Will Herberg, "Freud, the Revisionists, and Social Reality," in *Freud and the 20th Century,* ed. Benjamin Nelson (1957; reprint, Cleveland: World, 1966), 146, 148.

12. Franz Alexander and Helen Ross, eds., *Twenty Years of Psychoanalysis* (New York: W. W. Norton, 1953), 190, 192.

13. Elizabeth Lunbeck, *The Psychiatric Persuasion: Knowledge, Gender, and Power in Modern America* (Princeton: Princeton University Press, 1994), 306–7.

14. Franz Alexander, "Hostility and Fear in Social Life," *Social Forces* 17 (October. 1938): 27.

15. See John Dollard et al., eds., *Frustration and Aggression* (New Haven: Published for the Institute of Human Relations by Yale University Press, 1939).

16. Robert L. Sutherland, *Color, Class, and Personality* (Washington, DC: American Council on Education, 1942), xiv, xvi.

17. Ibid., 74–75.

18. Kenneth Burke, *The Philosophy of Literary Form: Studies in Symbolic Action* (1941; reprint, New York: Vintage, 1957), xxi.

19. Kenneth Burke, *A Grammar of Motives* (New York: Prentice-Hall, 1945), 339.

20. Ibid., 339–40.

21. Kenneth Burke, *A Rhetoric of Motives* (New York: Prentice-Hall, 1950), 194–95.

22. Ibid., 259.

23. Louis Wirth, "A Review of *Permanence and Change,*" in *Critical Responses to Kenneth Burke, 1924–1966,* ed. William H. Rueckert (Minneapolis: University of Minnesota Press, 1969), 103.

24. Ibid.

25. Kenneth Burke, *Attitudes toward History* (Berkeley: University of California Press, 1984), 93–94.

26. Ibid., 95.

27. Kenneth D. Benne, "Toward a Grammar of Educational Motives" (1947), in Rueckert, *Critical Responses to Kenneth Burke,* 201.

28. Howard Nemerov, "The Agon of Will as Idea: A Note on the Terms of Kenneth Burke" (1947), in Rueckert, *Critical Responses to Kenneth Burke,* 191.

29. Phillip Wylie, *Generation of Vipers* (New York: Rinehart, 1942), xviii.

30. Ibid., xviii, xvi, xv.

31. Ibid., 96–97, 101.

32. Ibid., 97.

33. Ibid., 156–57, 181, 169–70.

34. Wright to Philip Wylie, 10 October 1944, quoted in *Richard Wright: Books and Writers,* ed. Michel Fabre (Jackson: University Press of Mississippi, 1990), 191.

35. Richard Wright, introduction to *No Day of Triumph,* by J. Saunders Redding, reprinted in Fabre, *Richard Wright: Books and Writers,* 234.

36. Ibid.

37. J. Saunders Redding, *No Day of Triumph* (New York: Harper and Brothers, 1942), 39.

38. Richard Wright, "Comment on *Wasteland* by Jo Sinclair," Selected Records of Harper & Brothers, 1909–1960, Princeton University Library, Rare Books and Special Collections, Princeton, NJ.

39. Richard Wright, "*Wasteland* Uses Psychoanalysis Deftly," *PM Magazine,* 17 February 1946, reprinted in Fabre, *Richard Wright: Books and Writers,* 246.

40. Ibid.

41. Ibid.

42. Nathan G. Hale Jr., *The Rise and Crisis of Psychoanalysis in the United States: Freud and the Americans, 1917–1985* (Oxford: Oxford University Press, 1995), 277. As Hale notes, discussions generated by psychoanalysts "created a strong impression of the efficacy of psychotherapy and the scientific status of psychoanalytic theory and practice."

43. Ibid., 245.

44. Kluger, *Simple Justice,* 443.

45. Quoted in ibid., 444.

46. Richard Wright, "Psychiatry Comes to Harlem," *Free World* 2 (September 1946): 49–50, 51.

47. Ibid., 51, 50.

48. Ibid., 51.

49. Ralph Ellison, "Harlem Is Nowhere," in *Shadow and Act* (New York: Random House, 1994), 294–95, 297–98.

50. Arnold Rampersad, *Ralph Ellison: A Biography* (New York: Knopf, 2007), 219.

51. Earl Brown, "Timely Topics," *New York Amsterdam News,* 15 February 1947.

52. S. I. Hayakawa, "Second Thoughts," *Chicago Defender,* 4 January 1947.

53. S. I. Hayakawa, "Second Thoughts," *Chicago Defender,* 11 January 1947.

54. Robert Bendiner, "Psychiatry for the Needy," *Tomorrow,* April 1948, 22.

55. "Psychiatry in Harlem," *Time,* 1 December 1947, 50.

56. Ralph G. Martin, "Doctor's Dream in Harlem," *New Republic,* 3 June 1946.

57. Norman M. Lobsenz, "Human Salvage in Harlem," *Coronet,* March 1948, 133–34, 136.

58. John Hohenberg, "Harlem Clinic Now Official VA Agency," *New York Post,* 24 February 1947.

59. Wright to Aswell, 27 November 1944, Selected Records of Harper & Brothers.

60. Richard Wright, "The Children of Harlem," draft, n.d., Wright Papers.

61. Ibid.

62. Richard Wright, "Harlem Is Human," Wright Papers.

63. Arnold Rampersad, afterword to *Rite of Passage,* by Richard Wright (New York: Harper Collins, 1994), 135.

64. Robert L. Cooper, "The Frustrations of Being a Member of a Minority Group: What Does It Do to the Individual and to His Relationships with Other People?" *Mental Hygiene* 29 (April 1945): 189.

65. Although written in the 1940s, *Rite of Passage* was not published until the 1990s.

66. Ira L. Gibbons, "Character Building Agencies and the Needs of Negro Children and Youth," *Journal of Negro Education* 19, no. 3 (Summer 1950): 363–64.

67. Richard Wright, journal, 10, 11, 13 January 1945, Wright Papers.

68. Wright, *Rite of Passage,* 57.

69. Ibid., 102.

70. Quoted in Richard Wright, introduction to *Black Metropolis: A Study of Negro Life in a Northern City,* by St. Clair Drake and Horace R. Cayton (1945; reprint, Chicago: University of Chicago Press, 1993), xxxii.

71. Ibid., xxxiii.

72. Eli Zaretsky, *Secrets of the Soul: A Social and Cultural History of Psychoanalysis* (New York: Knopf, 2004), 282.

73. Benjamin Karpman to Wright, 6 October 1942, Wright Papers.

74. Benjamin Karpman to Wright, 29 August 1942, Wright Papers.

75. Carey McWilliams, *Factories in the Field: The Story of Migratory Farm Labor in California* (Boston: Little, Brown, 1939).

76. Benjamin Karpman to Wright, 21 April 1945, Wright Papers. See also Charles V. Charles, "Optimism and Frustration in the American Negro," *Psychoanalytic Review* 3 (July 1942), Wright Papers.

77. Karpman to Wright, 21 April 1945.

78. Benjamin Karpman to Alain Locke, 20 December 1937, Alain Locke Papers, Moorland-Springarn Research Center, Howard University, Washington, DC.

79. Karpman to Wright, 21 April 1945; 29 October 1945.

80. On the reception and impact of Myrdal's book, see Walter A. Jackson, *Gunnar Myrdal and America's Conscience* (Chapel Hill: University of North Carolina Press, 1990), and David Southern, *Gunnar Myrdal and Black-White Relations: The Use and Abuse of "An American Dilemma," 1944–1969* (Baton Rouge: Louisiana State University Press, 1987).

81. Benjamin Karpman to Wright, 25 May 1945, Wright Papers.

82. Benjamin Karpman, "The Many and the Few: Psychogenetic Studies in Race Relations," outline, n.d., Wright Papers.

83. Fabre, *Unfinished Quest,* 271.

84. Helen V. McLean to Wright, 2 April 1945, Wright Papers.

85. Helen Ross to Wright, 11 October 1944, Wright Papers.

86. Richard Wright, "Gertrude Stein's Story Is Drenched in Hitler's Horrors" (1946), in Fabre, *Richard Wright: Books and Writers,* 247.

87. Gertrude Stein, "The New Hope in Our 'Sad Young Men,'" *New York Times Magazine,* 3 June 1945, SM3.

88. Richard Wright to Gertrude Stein, 27 May 1945 and 29 October 1945, Gertrude Stein and Alice B. Toklas Papers, Beinecke Rare Book and Manuscript Library, Yale University, New Haven, CT.

89. S. I. Hayakawa, review of *Science and Sanity, American Speech* 18, no. 3 (October 1943): 219–26.

90. Alfred Korzybski, *Science and Sanity: An Introduction to Non-Aristotelian Systems and General Semantics* (Lakeville, CT: International Non-Aristotelian Library Publishing Company, 1958), xxvii, 12, xxix, liii. Korzybski's book was originally published in 1933; a second edition appeared in 1941.

91. Charles I. Glicksberg, "Human Aspects of the Race Problem," *School Review* 54 (November 1946): 523–24, 528.

92. Richard Wright, "Towards the Conquest of Ourselves" draft, n.d., Wright Papers.

Chapter 3 • Race and Minorities from Below:
The Wartime Cultural Criticism of Chester Himes,
Horace Cayton, Ralph Ellison, and C. L. R. James

1. Horace R. Cayton, "An Awakening: The Negro Now Fights for Democratic Rights of All of the World's Peoples," *Pittsburgh Courier,* 27 February 1943.

2. Penny Von Eschen, *Race against Empire: Black Americans and Anti-Colonialism, 1937–1957* (Ithaca, NY: Cornell University Press, 1997), 40–42.

3. Simone de Beauvoir, *The Ethics of Ambiguity,* trans. Bernard Frechtman (1948; reprint, New York: Citadel, 1964), 89, 45, 48, 84.

4. Richard Wright, "Suggestions for the Launching of a Magazine Whose Popular Contents Would Appeal to the White Middle Class," typescript drafts (1943), Richard Wright Papers, Beinecke Rare Book and Manuscript Library, Yale University, New Haven, CT.

5. Nikhil Singh, *Black Is a Country: Race and the Unfinished Struggle for Democracy* (Cambridge, MA: Harvard University Press, 2004), 123.

6. Richard Wright, "The Negro Speaks," proposal for a collection of essays, notes [1944?], Wright Papers.

7. "Chester Himes Direct," in *Conversations with Chester Himes,* ed. Michel Fabre and Robert E. Skinner (Jackson: University Press of Mississippi, 1995), 138–39, 127.

8. Chester Himes, "Now Is the Time! Here Is the Place!" (1942), in *Black on Black: Baby Sister and Selected Writings* (Garden City, NY: Doubleday, 1973), 217.

9. Chester Himes, "Democracy Is for the Unafraid," in *Primer for White Folks,* ed. Bucklin Moon (Garden City, NY: Doubleday, 1945), 482, 481.

10. Chester Himes, "Second Guesses for First Novelists," *Saturday Review of Literature* 29 (16 February 1946): 13.

11. Chester Himes, "The Dilemma of the Negro Novelist in the United States," in *Beyond the Angry Black,* ed. John A. Williams (New York: Cooper Square, 1966), 52–58.

12. Chester Himes, letter to the editor, *Commentary,* May 1948.

13. Christopher Breu, "Freudian Knot or Gordian Knot?: The Contradictions of Racialized Masculinity in Chester Himes' *If He Hollers Let Him Go,*" *Callaloo* 26, no. 3 (2003): 775.

14. Chester Himes, *If He Hollers Let Him Go: A Novel* (1945; reprint, New York: Thunder's Mouth Press, 1986), 38.

15. Ibid., 41.

16. Ibid., 3–4.

17. Hazel Carby, "Figuring the Future in Los(t) Angeles," *Comparative American Studies* 1 (2003): 24–25.

18. Richard Wright, "Two Novels on the Crushing of Men, One White and One Black" (1945), in *Richard Wright: Books and Writers,* ed. Michel Fabre (Jackson: University Press of Mississippi, 1990), 210–13. In addition to reviewing *If He Hollers Let Him Go,* Wright discussed Arthur Miller's novel *Focus,* about the psychology of mob violence and anti-Semitism in urban America.

19. Horace R. Cayton, "The Dark Inner Landscape," *Book Bulletin of the Chicago Public Library* 28 (February 1946): 19–20.

20. Horace R. Cayton, "The Bitter Crop," in *Northwest Harvest: A Regional Stock-Taking,* ed. V. L. O. Chittick (New York: Macmillan, 1948), 186–87.

21. James Baldwin, "History as Nightmare," *New Leader* 30 (October 1947): 11, 15.

22. Frantz Fanon, *Black Skin, White Masks* (1952; reprint, New York: Grove, 1967), 140, 156. Fanon interspersed references to both Himes's novel and Wright's *Native Son* in his first book-length work on colonialism and racism. Fanon misinterpreted aspects of the plot of Himes's novel. Yet his references to the work indicate familiarity with American writing about anti-

black racism. For more on Fanon's misinterpretations, see David Macey, *Frantz Fanon: A Biography* (New York: Picador, 2000), 125, 127, 193–94.

23. Chester Himes, Rosenwald Fund fellowship application, 1947, Rosenwald Fund Papers, Fisk University, Nashville, Tennessee.

24. "Chester Himes: An Interview" (1964), in *Conversations with Chester Himes,* ed. Michel Fabre and Robert E. Skinner (Jackson: University Press of Mississippi), 15.

25. Cayton, "Bitter Crop," 189.

26. Horace R. Cayton, "Race Relations and Negro Morale," Wright Papers.

27. Horace R. Cayton, "The American Negro--A World Problem," *Social Education* 8 (May 1944): 205–8.

28. Horace R. Cayton to Richard Wright, 22 October 1944, Horace R. Cayton Papers, Vivian G. Harsh Research Collection, Chicago Public Library, Chicago, IL.

29. Henri Peretz, "The Making of *Black Metropolis,*" *Annals of the American Academy of Political and Social Science* 595 (September 2004): 168–75.

30. Cayton to Wright, 2 April 1945, Wright Papers.

31. Cayton to Wright, 25 May 1942, Wright Papers.

32. Cayton, "Bitter Crop," 181.

33. Cayton to Marshall Field, 9 April 1945, Wright Papers.

34. Ibid.

35. Cayton to Wright, 2 April 1945.

36. Cayton to Field, 9 April 1945.

37. Horace R. Cayton, "Black Boy," *Pittsburgh Courier,* 10 March 1945.

38. Helen V. McLean, "The Emotional Health of Negroes," *Journal of Negro Education* 18 (1949): 283–90.

39. Horace R. Cayton, "The Psychological Approach to Race Relations," *Reed College Bulletin* 25 (November 1946): 16.

40. Horace R. Cayton, *Long Old Road* (Seattle: University of Washington Press, 1970); see esp. "The Dark Inner Landscape."

41. Helen V. McLean, "Frightened People," transcript of lecture, 2 July 1945, Wright Papers.

42. Ibid.

43. Helen V. McLean, "Racial Prejudice," *Phylon* 6 (1945): 145–53.

44. Cayton to Wright, 9 August 1949, Wright Papers.

45. Horace R. Cayton, "The Psychological Approach to Race Relations," *Reed College Bulletin* 25 (November 1946): 9–10.

46. Ibid., 24–25, 27.

47. Ibid., 25.

48. Ibid., 6.

49. Ralph Ellison, "Remembering Richard Wright," in *The Collected Essays of Ralph Ellison,* ed. John F. Callahan (New York: Modern Library, 2003), 670.

50. Ralph Ellison, "Richard Wright and Recent Negro Fiction," *Direction* 4 (Summer 1941): 12–13.

51. John F. Callahan, introduction to *Collected Essays of Ralph Ellison,* xxv.

52. Ellison, "Richard Wright and Recent Negro Fiction," 13.

53. Ellison, "Remembering Richard Wright," 670.

54. Ralph Ellison, "Beating That Boy," in *Collected Essays,* 148, 146.

55. Ralph Ellison, editorial, *Negro Quarterly* (1943), reprinted as "The Negro and the Second World War," in *Cultural Contexts for Ralph Ellison's "Invisible Man,"* ed. Eric J. Sundquist (Boston: Bedford, 1995), 239.

56. Ibid.

57. Ibid., 239, 235–36.

58. Ralph Ellison, "*An American Dilemma:* A Review," in *Collected Essays,* 335.

59. Ralph Ellison, "Richard Wright's Blues," in *Collected Essays,* 134.

60. Ibid., 140–41.

61. Ralph Ellison, "Twentieth-Century Fiction and the Black Mask of Humanity," in *Collected Essays,* 84, 82–83.

62. Ibid., 96–97.

63. Ibid., 83–84.

64. Ibid., 97, 82.

65. The essay would not appear in print until *Shadow and Act* was published in 1964.

66. Ellison, "*An American Dilemma:* A Review," 328–40.

67. Ralph Ellison, "Perspectives on Literature," in *Collected Essays,* 782–83.

68. John S. Wright, *Shadowing Ellison* (Jackson: University Press of Mississippi, 2006), 83.

69. Ellison, "*An American Dilemma:* A Review," 340.

70. Ralph Ellison, "The Shadow and the Act," in *Shadow and Act* (1964; reprint, New York: Random House, 1994), 280. The essay originally appeared in *The Reporter,* 6 December 1949.

71. Ibid., 276–77, 80.

72. Arnold Rampersad, *Ralph Ellison: A Biography* (New York: Knopf, 2007), 96–97.

73. Kenneth Burke, "The Rhetoric of Hitler's 'Battle,'" in *Terms for Order,* ed. Stanley Edgar Hyman (Bloomington: Indiana University Press, 1964), 95.

74. Ibid.

75. Ibid., 118; emphasis in original.

76. Kenneth Burke, "War, Response, and Contradiction," in *The Philosophy of Literary Form: Studies in Symbolic Action* (1941; reprint, New York: Vintage, 1957), 209.

77. Ellison, "*An American Dilemma:* A Review," 335.

78. Kenneth Burke, "Secular Conversions" (1935), in *Terms for Order,* ed. Stanley Edgar Hyman (Bloomington: Indiana University Press, 1964), 56–57.

79. Kenneth Burke, "Freud--and the Analysis of Poetry," in *Philosophy of Literary Form,* 223.

80. Ralph Ellison, "Working Notes for *Invisible Man,*" in *Collected Essays,* 343.

81. Ibid., 344.

82. Interview with Ralph Ellison, *Preuves* (May 1958), in *Collected Essays,* 295, 299–300.

83. Ellison, "Remembering Richard Wright," 666, 670, 674, 677–78.

84. C. L. R. James to Lyman and Freddie Paine, and to Grace Lee and James Boggs, 24 February 1976, cited in Scott McLemee, introduction to *C. L. R. James on the "Negro Question,"* ed. Scott McLemee (Jackson: University Press of Mississippi, 1996), xiv. See also Bill Schwarz, "C. L. R. James's American Civilization," *Atlantic Studies* 2 (2005): 15–43.

85. See James, *C. L. R. James on the "Negro Question" and American Civilization,* ed. Anna Grimshaw and Keith Hart (Cambridge, MA: Blackwell, 1993).

86. C. L. R. James, "My Friends: A Fireside Chat on the War by Native Son," in *C. L. R. James on the "Negro Question,"* 17–22.

87. C. L. R. James to Constance Webb, n.d. [1944], in *Special Delivery: The Letters of C. L. R. James to Constance Webb, 1939–1948,* ed. Anna Grimshaw (Oxford: Blackwell, 1996), 189–90; emphasis in original.

88. Ibid., 193.

89. C. L. R. James, "On *Native Son* by Richard Wright," in *C. L. R. James on the "Negro Question,"* 55–58.

90. C. L. R. James, "The Revolutionary Answer to the Negro Problem in the United States" (1948), in *C. L. R. James on the "Negro Question,"* 138–47.

91. James, *American Civilization,* 199–260, 211, 208–9.

92. Schwarz, "C. L. R. James's *American Civilization,*" 24.

93. James, *American Civilization,* 234.

94. Oliver Cox, *Race: A Study of Social Dynamics,* Fiftieth Anniversary Edition of *Caste, Class, and Race* (New York: Monthly Review, 1998), 72, 170.

95. Ibid., 230.

96. Alan Wald, *Trinity of Passion: The Literary Left and the Antifascist Crusade* (Chapel Hill: University of North Carolina Press, 2007), 128.

97. Ibid., 126. For Wright and Petry, as for Himes, Cayton, Ellison, and James, antiracism during and after the war revolved around the work of urging readers to "surmount the apprehension of social forces as the fixed forces of nature."

98. Ben Burns, "Portrait of 'The Street'" (1946), in *The Critical Response to Ann Petry,* ed. Hazel Arnett Ervin (Westport, CT: Praeger, 2005), 5.

99. Cayton to Langston Hughes, 22 January 1950, Langston Hughes Papers, Beinecke Rare Book and Manuscript Library, Yale University; Cayton to Wright, 22 January 1950, Wright Papers.

Chapter 4 · Strange Fruit:
Lillian Smith and the Making of Whiteness

1. Richard Wright, "This, Too, Is America," *Tomorrow* 4 (May 1945), in *Conversations with Richard Wright,* ed. Keneth Kinnamon and Michel Fabre (Jackson: University Press of Mississippi, 1993), 68.

2. Lillian Smith, "The Right Way Is Not the Moderate Way," in *The Winner Names the Age: A Collection of Writings by Lillian Smith,* ed. Michelle Cliff (New York: W. W. Norton, 1978), 69.

3. Richard H. King, *Civil Rights and the Idea of Freedom* (New York: Oxford University Press, 1992), 235–36.

4. Paula Snelling, "re: Lillian Smith," n.d., Lillian Smith Papers, George A. Smathers Libraries, University of Florida, Gainesville. For more on Snelling's relationship with Smith, see two essays by Margaret Rose Gladney: "Paula Snelling: A Significant Other," in *Modern*

American Queer History, ed. Allida M. Black (Philadelphia: Temple University Press, 2001), and "Personalizing the Political, Politicizing the Personal: Reflections on Editing the Letters of Lillian Smith," in *Carryin' On in the Lesbian and Gay South,* ed. John Howard (New York: New York University Press, 1997).

5. Lillian Smith and Paula Snelling, Julius Rosenwald Fellowship application, Rosenwald Fund Papers, Fisk University, Nashville, TN.

6. Ibid.

7. Smith to Joan Titus, Thanksgiving Weekend November 1959, in *How Am I to Be Heard?: Letters of Lillian Smith,* ed. Margaret Rose Gladney (Chapel Hill: University of North Carolina Press, 1993), 236.

8. Lillian Smith, *Killers of the Dream* (1961; reprint, New York: W. W. Norton, 1994), 12. Subsequent page references appear in text.

9. Ruth Benedict, "Race Problems in America," *Annals of the American Academy of Political and Social Science* 216 (July 1941): 74.

10. Lillian Smith and Paula Snelling, "Man Born of Woman," in *Winner Names the Age,* 175. The essay originally appeared in *South Today* in 1941.

11. Nelson Antrim Crawford and Karl A. Menninger, eds., *The Healthy-Minded Child* (New York: Coward-McCann, 1930), viii, 17, 13.

12. Lawson G. Lowrey, "The Formation of Habits," in Crawford and Menninger, *Healthy-Minded Child,* 114–15.

13. Hortense Powdermaker, "The Anthropological Approach to the Problem of Modifying Race Attitudes," *Journal of Negro Education* 13 (1944): 299.

14. Elizabeth Lunbeck, *The Psychiatric Persuasion: Knowledge, Gender, and Power in Modern America* (Princeton: Princeton University Press, 1994), 115.

15. Karl A. Menninger, *The Human Mind* (New York: Knopf, 1945), 12, 15.

16. Karl A. Menninger, *Love against Hate* (New York: Harcourt, Brace, 1942), 126–27.

17. Lillian Smith, "Dope with Lime," *South Today* 7 (Winter 1942–43): 62.

18. Gordon W. Allport, *The Nature of Prejudice* (1954; reprint, New York: Doubleday, 1958).

19. Anne C. Loveland, *Lillian Smith: A Southerner Confronting the South* (Baton Rouge: Louisiana State University Press, 1986), 15.

20. Lillian Smith, biographical notes, n.d., Lillian Smith Papers, University of Florida.

21. Margaret Rose Gladney, "A Chain Reaction of Dreams: Lillian Smith and Laurel Falls Camp," *Journal of American Culture* 5 (Fall 1982): 50, 52–53. Gladney's short yet highly suggestive article is the only available scholarly account devoted exclusively to Smith and Laurel Falls.

22. Lillian Smith, "Children and Color," in *Winner Names the Age,* 30.

23. Lillian Smith, "There Are Things to Do," in Helen White and Redding S. Sugg Jr., eds., *From the Mountain* (Memphis: Memphis State University Press, 1972), 116. The essay originally appeared in the Winter 1942–43 issue of *South Today.*

24. Smith and Snelling, Rosenwald Fellowship application.

25. Smith to W. E. B. Du Bois, 22 December 1937, and Du Bois to Smith, 4 January 1938, reels 48, 49, W. E. B. Du Bois Papers, University of Massachusetts (microform version).

26. Pauli Murray to Smith, n.d., Lillian Smith Papers, University of Florida.

27. Lillian Smith, "One More Sigh for the Good Old South," *Pseudopodia* 1 (Fall 1936): 15.

28. Paula Snelling, "Sigmund Freud: An Attempt at Appraisal," in *From the Mountain,* 191–202.

29. W. E. B. Du Bois, "Southern Trauma," in *From the Mountain,* 271–73.

30. Smith, "There Are Things to Do," 3.

31. Lillian Smith, "A Letter from Lillian Smith," open letter to members of Blue Ridge Conference [1944], Lillian Smith Papers, University of Georgia.

32. Ibid.

33. Caroline Ware, *The Cultural Approach to History* (New York: Columbia University Press, 1940), 14, 11, 10. Pauli Murray communicated with Smith about Ware's enthusiasm for Smith's work. See letters from Murray to Smith in the Lillian Smith Papers, University of Florida.

34. Goodwin Watson, "Clio and Psyche: Some Interrelations of Psychology and History," in Ware, *Cultural Approach to History,* 43.

35. Lillian Smith, "Dope with Lime," *South Today* 8 (Spring-Summer 1944): 103.

36. Clyde Kluckhohn, *Mirror for Man: The Relation of Anthropology to Modern Life* (New York: Whittlesey House, 1949), 26–27, 36, 204.

37. Ibid., 291.

38. Smith to Guy B. Johnson, 12 June 1944, in *How Am I to Be Heard,* 86.

39. Smith to Richard Wright, 12 June 1944, in *How Am I to Be Heard,* 84.

40. Lawrence K. Frank, *Nature and Human Nature* (New Brunswick, NJ: Rutgers University Press, 1951), 81.

41. Lillian Smith, "The Mob and the Ghost," in *Winner Names the Age,* 135.

42. Lionel Trilling, *Freud and the Crisis of Culture* (Boston: Beacon, 1955), 54–55, 36–37.

43. Trilling, introduction to *The Life and Work of Sigmund Freud,* by Ernest Jones, edited and abridged by Trilling and Steven Marcus (New York: Basic Books, 1961), x.

44. Nathan G. Hale Jr., *The Rise and Crisis of Psychoanalysis in the United States: Freud and the Americans, 1917–1985* (Oxford: Oxford University Press, 1995), 119.

45. Lawrence Kubie, *Practical and Theoretical Aspects of Psychoanalysis* (New York: International Universities Press, 1950), 232.

46. Ibid., 252.

47. Ibid., 13, 243.

48. Ibid., 351.

49. Fred Hobson, *Tell about the South: The Southern Rage to Explain* (Baton Rouge: Louisiana State University Press, 1983), 314. See also Fred Hobson, *But Now I See: The White Southern Racial Conversion Narrative* (Baton Rouge: Louisiana State University Press, 1999).

50. Quoted in Loveland, *Lillian Smith,* 67, 63.

51. Smith to Lawrence Kubie, 15 May 1943, in *How Am I to Be Heard,* 71.

52. Richard Wright, introduction to *Black Metropolis: A Study of Negro Life in a Northern City,* by St. Clair Drake and Horace R. Cayton (1945; reprint, Chicago: University of Chicago Press, 1993), xxvi.

53. Lillian Smith, *Strange Fruit* (1944; Athens: University of Georgia Press, 1985), 59.

54. Ibid., 88.

55. Ibid., 95.

56. Lillian Smith, "A Personal History of *Strange Fruit:* A Statement of Purposes and Intentions," *Saturday Review of Literature,* 17 February 1945, 10.

57. Smith to Walter White, 14 February 1942, in *How Am I to Be Heard,* 55.

58. W. E. B. Du Bois, "As the Crow Flies," *New York Amsterdam News,* 10 June 1944.

59. W. E. B. Du Bois, "Prospect of a World without Race Conflict," *American Journal of Sociology* 49 (March 1944): 450–56, 454.

60. W. E. B. Du Bois, "Searing Novel of the South," *New York Times Book Review,* 5 March 1944, 1, 22.

61. John Chamberlain, "Books of the Times," *New York Times,* 29 February 1944.

62. Nathaniel Tillman, "*Strange Fruit* in Retrospect," *Phylon* 5 (1944): 288–89.

63. Ben Burns, "Off the Book Shelf," *Chicago Defender,* 15 December 1945.

64. Anna Greene Smith, review of *Strange Fruit, Social Forces* 23 (October 1944): 113–14.

65. "This Too Is America," *Common Sense,* April 1946, Richard Wright Papers, Beinecke Rare Book and Manuscript Library, Yale University, New Haven, CT.

66. Smith to Walter White, 14 February 1942, in *How Am I to Be Heard,* 55.

67. Michel Fabre, *Richard Wright: Books and Writers* (Jackson: University Press of Mississippi, 1990), 147.

68. Marion Thompson Wright, "But the Twain Do Meet," *Journal of Negro Education* 13 (Autumn 1944): 521.

69. Frank, "The Historian as Therapist," in *Society as the Patient,* 301.

70. Ibid., 307

71. Hanns Sachs, *The Creative Unconscious: Studies in the Psychoanalysis of Art* (Cambridge, MA: Sci-Art Publishers, 1942), 100.

72. Ibid., 201–2.

73. Ibid., 47.

74. Erich Kahler, *Man the Measure, A New Approach to History* (New York: Pantheon Books, 1943), 6.

75. Lillian Smith, "Why I Wrote 'Killers of the Dream,'" *New York Herald-Tribune Book Review,* 17 July 1949.

76. Betty Friedan, *The Feminine Mystique* (New York, W. W. Norton, 1963). Friedan's intellectual and political indebtedness to midcentury psychological thought is discussed in Daniel Horowitz, *Betty Friedan and the Making of the Feminine Mystique: The American Left, the Cold War, and Modern Feminism* (Amherst: University of Massachusetts Press, 1998), esp. chapters 3 and 4.

77. Smith, *Killers of the Dream,* 153. See also Philip Wylie, *Generation of Vipers* (New York: Rinehart, 1942).

78. George Kimmelman, review of *Killers of the Dream, Journal of Religion* 30 (October 1950): 290–92.

79. Horace R. Cayton, "The Psychological Approach to Race Relations," *Reed College Bulletin* 25 (November 1946): 24–25.

80. Alain Locke, "Wisdom de Profundis: Review of The Literature of the Negro, 1949: Part II—The Social Literature," *Phylon* 11 (1950): 171–75.

81. W. M. Brewer, review of *Killers of the Dream, Journal of Negro History* 36 (April 1950): 209–10.

82. Joshua Logan, comment on *Killers of the Dream,* Lillian Smith Papers, University of Georgia.

83. William G. Barrett, review of *Killers of the Dream, Psychoanalytic Review* 20 (1951): 129–30.

84. Lawrence Kubie, comment on *Killers of the Dream,* Lillian Smith Papers, University of Georgia.

85. Quoted in Smith to Smith Family, 11 October 1949, in *How Am I to Be Heard,* 130–31.

86. Franz Alexander, *Fundamentals of Psychoanalysis* (New York: W. W. Norton, 1948), 203–5, 149.

87. Lillian Smith, "Wanted: Lessons in Hate," *North Georgia Review* 4 (1939): 12–15.

88. Smith, "Ten Years from Now" (1951), in *Winner Names the Age,* 66.

89. Lawrence K. Frank, *Feelings and Emotions* (Garden City, NY: Doubleday, 1954), 37–38.

90. Smith to Lawrence Kubie, 29 June 1959, in *How Am I to Be Heard,* 225.

91. Smith to Helen Drusilla Lockwood, 28 August 1955, Lillian Smith Papers, University of Georgia.

92. Smith to Arthur Raper, 9 March 1965, Arthur Franklin Raper Papers, Southern Historical Collection, Manuscripts Department, Wilson Library, University of North Carolina at Chapel Hill.

93. Snelling, "re: Lillian Smith."

94. Lillian Smith, "Words That Chain Us and Words That Set Us Free," in *Winner Names the Age,* 152.

95. James Baldwin, interview with Studs Terkel (1961), in *Conversations with James Baldwin,* ed. Fred L. Standley and Louis H. Pratt (Jackson: University Press of Mississippi, 1989), 20.

Chapter 5 • Notes of a Native Son:
James Baldwin in Postwar America

1. James Baldwin, "Alas, Poor Richard," reprinted as "Richard Wright," in *The Nonconformers: Articles of Dissent,* ed. David Evanier and Stanley Silverzweig (New York, Ballantine, 1961), 149.

2. James Baldwin, Rosenwald Fellowship application, Julius Rosenwald Fund Papers, Fisk University, Special Collections, Nashville, TN.

3. Ibid.

4. Ibid.

5. Mary McCarthy, "A Memory of James Baldwin," *New York Review of Books* 36 (27 April 1989): 48–49.

6. James Baldwin, "Previous Condition," *Commentary* 6 (October 1948): 339. For a persuasive reading of the narrative similarities between "Previous Condition" and Wright's *Native Son,* see Horace A. Porter, *Stealing the Fire: The Art and Protest of James Baldwin* (Middletown, CT: Wesleyan University Press, 1989), 84–95.

7. Baldwin, "Previous Condition," 335, 342.

8. James Baldwin, "Maxim Gorki as Artist," *Nation* 64 (12 April 1947): 427–28.

9. James Baldwin, "Everybody's Protest Novel," in *Notes of a Native Son* (1955; reprint, Boston: Beacon, 1984), 15.

10. James Baldwin, "Many Thousands Gone," in *Notes of a Native Son,* 40, 32.

11. Ibid., 40.

12. Ibid., 39.

13. Morris Dickstein writes that "neither Baldwin nor [Ralph] Ellison ever challenged one essential tenet of Wright's—that the experience of African Americans was deeply conditioned by the traumatic facts of racial separation and discrimination"; *Leopards in the Temple: The Transformation of American Fiction, 1945–1970* (Cambridge, MA: Harvard University Press, 2002), 181.

14. Blyden Jackson, "The Continuing Strain: Resume of Negro Literature in 1955," *Phylon* 17, no. 1 (1956): 39–40.

15. Baldwin, "Richard Wright," 145, 149.

16. James Baldwin, interview with Julius Lester (1984), in *Conversations with James Baldwin,* ed. Fred L. Standley and Louis H. Pratt (Jackson: University Press of Mississippi, 1989), 223.

17. Alan Wald, *The New York Intellectuals: The Rise and Decline of the Anti-Stalinist Left from the 1930s to the 1980s* (Chapel Hill: University of North Carolina Press, 1987), 10.

18. James Gilbert, "Literature and Revolution in the United States: *The Partisan Review,*" *Journal of Contemporary History* 2 (April 1967): 169.

19. Frances Stonor Saunders, *The Cultural Cold War: The CIA and the World of the Arts and Letters* (New York: New Press, 1999), 160.

20. For two treatments of this subject, see Richard Pells, *The Liberal Mind in a Conservative Age: American Intellectuals in the Forties and Fifties* (New York: Harper and Row, 1985), and Andrew Ross, "Containing Culture in the Cold War," in *No Respect: Intellectuals and Popular Culture* (New York: Routledge, 1989).

21. Lionel Trilling, in the symposium on "Our Country, Our Culture," *Partisan Review* 19 (May–June 1952): 2–5.

22. "Manifesto of the Congress of Cultural Freedom" (1950), quoted in Nathan Abrams, "A Profoundly Hegemonic Moment: De-Mythologizing the Cold War New York Jewish Intellectuals," *Shofar: An Interdisciplinary Journal of Jewish Studies* 21, no. 3 (2003): 78.

23. Robert Gorham Davis, "American Writing and the Academy" (1948), in *The New Partisan Reader, 1945–1953,* ed. William Phillips and Philip Rahv (New York: Harcourt, Brace, 1953).

24. Frederick J. Hoffman, "Psychoanalysis and Literary Criticism," *American Quarterly* 2 (1950): 144.

25. Baldwin, "Autobiographical Notes," in *Notes of a Native Son,* 6.

26. Frederick J. Hoffman, *Freudianism and the Literary Mind* (1945; reprint, New York: Grove, 1957), 330.

27. Paul Goodman, preface to *Freud: On War, Sex, and Neurosis,* ed. Sander Katz, trans. Joan Riviere et al. (New York: Arts and Science Press, 1947), 8–9.

28. Sigmund Freud, "A Difficulty of Psycho-Analysis" (1917), in *Freud: On War, Sex, and Neurosis,* 17.

29. Lionel Trilling, "Contemporary American Literature and Its Relation to Ideas," *American Quarterly* 1 (Autumn 1949): 204.

30. Davis, "American Writing and the Academy."

31. Hoffman, "Psychoanalysis and Literary Criticism," 144.

32. Quoted in Hans Meyerhoff, "Freud and the Ambiguity of Culture," *Partisan Review* 24 (Winter 1957): 117.

33. Ibid.

34. Hoffman, *Freudianism and the Literary Mind*, 19.

35. Ernest van den Haag, "Of Happiness and of Despair We Have No Measure," in *Mass Culture: The Popular Arts in America*, ed. Bernard Rosenberg and David Manning White (New York: Free Press, 1957), 532.

36. Lionel Trilling, "The Situation of the American Intellectual," *Perspectives USA* 3 (1953): 39, 41.

37. Ibid., 116.

38. Philip Rahv, in "Our Country and Our Culture: A Symposium," *Partisan Review* 19 (May–June 1952): 308.

39. Ross, *No Respect*, 54–55. See also Geraldine Murphy, "Romancing the Center: Cold War Politics and Classic American Literature," *Poetics Today* 9 (1988): 737–47.

40. Murphy, "Romancing the Center," 741.

41. Ross, *No Respect*, 54–55.

42. Geraldine Murphy, "Subversive Anti-Stalinism: Race and Sexuality in the Early Essays of James Baldwin," *ELH* 63, no. 4 (1996): 1025.

43. Baldwin, "Harlem Ghetto," 71.

44. William Phillips, "The Intellectuals' Tradition" (1941), in *The Partisan Reader: Ten Years of "Partisan Review," 1934–1944*, ed. William Phillips and Philip Rahv (New York: Dial, 1946), 491, 493.

45. Lionel Trilling, "James Baldwin," in *Company of Readers*, ed. Arthur Krystal (New York: Free Press, 2001), 154.

46. Philip Rahv, "Notes on the Decline of Naturalism," *Perspectives USA* 2 (1953): 40.

47. Saunders, *Cultural Cold War*, 140.

48. Quoted in ibid.

49. Lionel Trilling, "Editor's Commentary," *Perspectives USA* 2 (1953): 5.

50. James Baldwin, "The Harlem Ghetto," in *Notes of a Native Son*, 51–64.

51. Kenneth Clark, "Candor about Negro-Jewish Relations," *Commentary* 4 (February 1946): 14.

52. Ibid.

53. Kenneth Clark, *Dark Ghetto: Dilemmas of Social Power* (New York: Harper and Row, 1965), 70.

54. Baldwin, "Harlem Ghetto," 57, 71.

55. Ibid., 71.

56. James Baldwin, "Journey to Atlanta," in *Notes of a Native Son*, 66.

57. Baldwin, "Harlem Ghetto," 69.

58. Ibid., 68.

59. Baldwin, "Autobiographical Notes," 8.

60. Ralph Ellison, "Harlem Is Nowhere," in *Shadow and Act* (1964; reprint, New York: Random House, 1964), 295, 297, 299. Lawrence Jackson has written that "Ellison's essay advanced the argument that black people had been psychologically disfigured—temporarily—by white racism. In this, he was involved in an intellectual movement along with fiction

writers Richard Wright, Chester Himes, Ann Petry, and the social scientists Horace Cayton,
St. Clair Drake and E. Franklin Frazier, which aimed to overcome segregation by demonstrat-
ing its deleterious effects." Despite his emergence within a distinct intellectual environment,
Baldwin, in his early essays, can be seen as part of the intellectual movement Jackson describes.
Lawrence Jackson, *Ralph Ellison: Emergence of Genius* (New York: John Wiley, 2002), 374.

61. Baldwin, "Harlem Ghetto," 61.

62. James Baldwin, "The Image of the Negro," *Commentary* 5 (April 1948): 378, 380.

63. Lionel Trilling, *The Opposing Self: Nine Essays in Criticism* (1950; reprint, New York:
Viking, 1959), x.

64. Baldwin, "Autobiographical Notes," 11, 6.

65. Ibid., 6–7.

66. Porter, *Stealing the Fire,* 25.

67. Baldwin, "Everybody's Protest Novel," 15.

68. Baldwin, "Notes of a Native Son," 94, 86–92, 89.

69. Ibid., 93–94.

70. Frantz Fanon, *Black Skin, White Masks* (New York: Grove, 1967), 140.

71. James Baldwin, "Stranger in the Village," in *Notes of a Native Son,* 162, 165.

72. See Abram Kardiner and Lionel Ovesey, *The Mark of Oppression: A Psychosocial Study of
the American Negro* (New York: W.W. Norton, 1951).

73. James Baldwin, "Stranger in the Village," 165–67.

74. Ibid., 170–72.

75. Ibid., 175.

76. Ross Posnock, *Color and Culture: Black Writers and the Making of the Modern Intellectual* (Cambridge, MA: Harvard University Press, 1998), 225.

77. Baldwin, "Stranger in the Village," 175.

78. Leslie A. Fiedler, *An End to Innocence: Essays on Culture and Politics* (Boston: Beacon,
1955), 191.

79. Ibid., 210.

80. R. W. B. Lewis, *The American Adam: Innocence, Tragedy, and Tradition n the Nineteenth
Century* (1955; reprint, Chicago: University of Chicago Press, 1958), 9.

81. Trilling, "Our Country, Our Culture" symposium, 284, 318.

82. Baldwin, "Autobiographical Notes," 9.

83. Dan Wakefield, *New York in the Fifties* (1992; reprint, New York: St. Martin's Griffin,
1999), 137–38.

84. Quoted in James Baldwin and Sol Stein, *Native Sons: A Friendship That Created One of
the Greatest Works of the Twentieth Century: "Notes of a Native Son"* (New York: Ballantine,
2004), 9–10.

85. Langston Hughes, "From Harlem to Paris," *New York Times Book Review,* 26 February
1956, 14.

86. Thomas D. Jarrett, "Search for Identity," *Phylon* 17 (1956): 87.

87. Baldwin, "Notes of a Native Son," 112.

88. Jarrett, "Search for Identity," 88.

89. John Lash, "A Long, Hard Look at the Ghetto: A Critical Summary of Literature by and
about Negroes in 1956," *Phylon* 18, no. 1 (1957): 17.

90. "In the Castle of My Skin" (review of *Notes of a Native Son*), *Time,* 5 December 1955, 112.

91. Dachine Rainer, "Rage into Order," *Commonweal,* 13 January 1956, 385–86.

92. Robert W. Flint, "Not Ideas but Life," *Commentary* 21 (May 1956): 495.

93. Issac Rosenfeld, letter of reference, in Baldwin, Rosenwald Fellowship application.

94. Trilling, "James Baldwin," 153–54.

95. Charles H. Nichols, "The New Calvinism," *Commentary* 23 (January 1957): 94–96.

96. Max Lerner, introduction to *The Fifty-Minute Hour: A Collection of True Psychoanalytic Tales,* by Robert Lindner (1955; reprint, New York: Holt, 1973), vii, ix.

97. C. Wright Mills, *The Sociological Imagination* (New York: Oxford University Press, 1959), 161, 163.

98. Stan Weir, "Meetings with James Baldwin," *Against the Current* 17 (1989): 35–41, 35.

99. Trilling, "James Baldwin," 153–54.

100. Dickstein, *Leopards in the Temple,* 193.

101. Will Walker, "After *The Fire Next Time:* James Baldwin's Postconsensus Double Bind," in *Is It Nation Time?: Contemporary Essays on Black Power and Black Nationalism,* ed. Eddie S. Glaude Jr. (Chicago: University of Chicago Press, 2002), 230.

102. James Baldwin, interview with Studs Terkel (1961), in Standley and Pratt, *Conversations with James Baldwin,* 15.

103. Robert Blauner, *Racial Oppression in America* (New York: Harper and Row, 1972), 165, 10.

104. See Stephen Steinberg, *Turning Back: The Retreat from Racial Justice in American Thought and Policy* (Boston: Beacon, 1995), esp. chapter 3, "The 1960s and the Scholarship of Confrontation."

105. Blauner, *Racial Oppression in America,* 165.

106. C. L. R. James, "Lenin and the Problem," (1964), in *The C. L. R. James Reader,* ed. Anna Grimshaw (Oxford: Blackwell, 1992), 331.

107. Toni Morrison, "Life in His Language," in *James Baldwin: The Legacy,* ed. Quincy Troupe (New York: Simon and Schuster, 1989), 77.

108. Colm Toibin, "The Henry James of Harlem: James Baldwin's Struggles," *Guardian,* 14 September 2001.

109. Ibid.

110. Standley and Pratt, *Conversations with James Baldwin,* 231.

111. Daniel Bell, *The End-of-Ideology: On the Exhaustion of Political Ideals in the Fifties* (New York: Collier, 1961), 344.

112. Paul Gilroy, *"There Ain't No Black in the Union Jack": The Cultural Politics of Race and Nation* (Chicago: University of Chicago Press, 1991), 39.

113. See Russell Jacoby, *Social Amnesia: A Critique of Conformist Psychology from Adler to Laing* (Boston: Beacon, 1975).

Conclusion

1. Joel Kovel, *White Racism: A Psychohistory* (1970; reprint, New York: Columbia University Press, 1984), 3, 34, xxv.

2. Toni Morrison, *The Bluest Eye* (New York: Penguin, 1994), 20.

3. Toni Morrison, afterword to *The Bluest Eye,* 210.

4. Ibid.

5. Toni Morrison, *Playing in the Dark: Whiteness and the Literary Imagination* (Cambridge, MA: Harvard University Press, 1992), xi.

6. Frantz Fanon, *Black Skin, White Masks,* trans. Richard Philcox (1952; reprint, New York: Grove, 2008), xiii.

7. Ibid., 20, xiv.

8. Richard Wright, draft for second edition of *Black Metropolis,* n.d. (unpublished), 1–2, 9, 14, Richard Wright Papers, Beinecke Rare Book and Manuscript Library, Yale University, New Haven, CT.

9. Ibid., 1, 5.

10. Albert Memmi, "On the Colonizer and the Colonized," in *Dominated Man* (Boston: Beacon, 1969), 45.

11. Richard Wright, introduction to *Black Metropolis: A Study of Negro Life in a Northern City,* by St. Clair Drake and Horace R. Cayton (1945; reprint, Chicago: University of Chicago Press, 1993), xxv.

12. Lillian Smith, *Killers of the Dream* (rev. ed. 1961; reprint, New York: W. W. Norton, 1986), 18.

13. Barack Obama, *Dreams from My Father* (New York: Random House, 2004), 85–86, 198–99, 121.

14. Fanon, *Black Skin, White Masks,* 204, 201. On related themes in strands of American and European intellectual life, see Ross Posnock, "The Politics of Nonidentity: A Genealogy," *Boundary 2* 19 (Spring 1992): 34–68.

The Unfinished Quest of Richard Wright (Urbana: University of Illinois Press, 1993), Michel Fabre's biography (translated from the French by Isabel Barzun), remains a key resource for information on Wright as literary artist and intellectual. The book records the range of Wright's contacts with writers, literary agents, editors and associates, and others throughout his career. In *Richard Wright: Ordeal of a Native Son* (Garden City, NY: Doubleday, 1980), Addison Gayle devotes attention to Wright's relationships with other black writers and discusses documents obtained through the Freedom of Information Act related to U.S. government tracking of Wright. Fabre's *The World of Richard Wright* (Jackson: University Press of Mississippi, 1985) brings together several rich essays on Wright's work and intellectual trajectory, including "Wright's First Hundred Books." For the full list of the books in Wright's library and an appendix including book reviews and blurbs by Wright, see Fabre's indispensable *Richard Wright: Books and Writers* (Jackson: University Press of Mississippi, 1990). Edited by Keneth Kinnamon and Michel Fabre, *Conversations with Richard Wright* (Jackson: University Press of Mississippi) collects interviews conducted with Wright in the United States and Europe. *Richard Wright: Impressions and Perspectives* (Ann Arbor: University of Michigan Press, 1973), edited by David Ray and Robert M. Farnsworth, gathers primary and secondary sources in an early effort to historicize Wright's cultural impact. *Richard Wright's Black Boy (American Hunger): A Casebook* (New York: Oxford University Press, 2003), edited by William L. Andrews and Douglas Taylor, also brings together key primary documents and important scholarly essays. Arnold Rampersad's sharp afterword to Richard Wright's *Rite of Passage* (New York: Harper Collins, 1994) describes Wright's connection to the Wiltwyck School for Boys. Hazel Rowley's *Richard Wright: The Life and Times* (New York: Henry Holt, 2002) offers descriptions of Wright's personal life, which she interweaves with discussions of his public and literary achievements. Stylistically romantic, Constance Webb's *Richard Wright: A Biography* (New York: Putnam, 1968) nevertheless contains valuable discussions about Wright's relationships and literary impact, much of it culled from writing by Wright himself and conversations Webb conducted with her subject when he returned to the United States from Paris in 1947. Wright supplied Webb with unpublished autobiographical writing in the 1940s. Additional sources on Wright's work include *Richard Wright: Critical Perspectives Past and Present* (New York: Amistad, 1999), edited by Henry Louis Gates Jr. and Kwame Anthony Appiah; Yoshinobu Kakutani's *Richard Wright and Racial Discourse* (Columbia: University of Missouri Press,

1996); Keneth Kinnamon's *The Emergence of Richard Wright: A Study in Literature and Society* (Champaign: University of Illinois Press, 1973); and Edward Margolies's *The Art of Richard Wright* (Carbondale: Southern Illinois University Press, 1969).

Much of the biographical and critical commentary on Wright written during his lifetime remains a valuable source of insights. Edwin R. Embree's portrait of Wright in *13 Against the Odds* (New York: Viking, 1944), a collection that profiled thirteen African American public figures, is the first significant published biographical piece on Wright. A general treatment, Embree's profile records the sense of momentum and change that Wright's arrival on the literary and cultural scene precipitated. Carl Milton Hughes's *The Negro Novelist* (New York: Citadel, 1953), is the first study to reflect on the impact of Wright's "psychological technique" on African American letters. "Richard Wright: An Evaluation," an essay by J. Saunders Redding, written soon after Wright's death, emphasizes the importance of the introduction to *Black Metropolis:* "an annotation to Wright's entire development." Saunders's evaluation is collected in *A Scholar's Conscience: Selected Writings by J. Saunders Redding* (Lexington: University Press of Kentucky, 1992), edited by Faith Berry.

Historical work on Wright has expanded dramatically over the last decade and a half. Paul Gilroy's " 'Without the Consolation of Tears': Richard Wright, France, and the Ambivalence of Community," in *The Black Atlantic: Modernity and Double Consciousness* (Cambridge, MA: Harvard University Press, 1993), makes a strong historical and theoretical case for reading Wright's work before and after his departure for France as a continuum, and for interpreting Wright's career, in part, as that of a "European intellectual." For a corresponding and informative reevaluation of Wright and other black writers, see Ross Posnock, *Color and Culture: Black Writers and the Making of the Modern Intellectual* (Cambridge, MA: Harvard University Press, 1998). On Gertrude Stein's influence on Wright, see Eugene E. Miller's "Richard Wright and Gertrude Stein," *Black American Literature Forum* 16, no. 3 (Autumn 1982). In *Gertrude Stein and Richard Wright: The Poetics and Politics of Modernism* (Jackson: University Press of Mississippi, 1998), Lynn M. Weiss pairs "visible and audible philosophers of modernity," expanding the available literature on the common preoccupations that defined the relationship between Wright and Stein. Arnold Rampersad's *Ralph Ellison: A Biography* (New York: Knopf, 2007) carefully and informatively recovers the intellectual affinities and congruent aspirations that brought Ellison and Wright together in the 1930s and 1940s. In recent years, transnational work on Wright has led to sophisticated and compelling reinterpretations of his writing and career. Kevin Gaines's *African Americans in Ghana: Black Expatriates and the Civil Rights Era* (Chapel Hill: University of North Carolina Press, 2006) examines Wright's relationship to Ghana. George Cotkin's *Existential America* (Baltimore: Johns Hopkins University Press, 2005) provides a lively account of Wright's relationship to existentialism. Louis Menand's "Richard Wright: The Hammer and the Nail," in *American Studies* (New York: Farrar, Straus, and Giroux, 2002), a trenchant, if short, look at key aspects of Wright work, also emphasizes existentialism. Richard H. King's rich study of *Race, Culture, and the Intellectuals, 1940–1970* (Baltimore: Johns Hopkins University Press, 2004) places Wright's postwar writings alongside those of C. L. R. James, Hannah Arendt, and others and perceptively historicizes the humanist currents running throughout Wright's work. "The *Brown* Decades," *Patterns of Prejudice* 38, no. 4 (2004), also by King, offers a wealth of information on psychological and universalist thought as they impinged on the 1954 decision.

Literary studies bringing historical questions to bear on African American writing have advanced understandings of Wright's work. These include Farah Jasmine Griffin's *Who Set You Flowin'?: The African-American Migration Narrative* (New York: Oxford University Press, 1995) and William J. Maxwell's *New Negro, Old Left: African American Writing and Communism between the Wars* (New York: Columbia University Press, 1999). In *Ethnic Modernism* (Cambridge, MA: Harvard University Press, 2008), Werner Sollors describes Wright's "universalism" and debt to William James. Gavin Jones links Wright's autobiographical work to questions of poverty and literary production in *American Hungers: The Problem of Poverty in U.S. Literature* (Princeton: Princeton University Press, 2008). Recent essays have enriched understandings of the continuing salience of Wright's work. Jerry Ward Jr. brilliantly revisits the subject of Wright's place in the protest tradition in "Everybody's Protest Novel: The Richard Wright Era," collected in Maryemma Graham's *The Cambridge Companion to the African American Novel* (Cambridge: Cambridge University Press, 2004.). Bill V. Mullen's "Space and Capital in Richard Wright's *Native Son* and *Twelve Million Black Voices,*" places Wright's work in dialogue with theories of spatial logic and the racializing effects of capital. Abdul JanMohamed's book-length *The Death-Bound Subject: Richard Wright's Archeology of Death* (Durham, NC: Duke University Press, 2005) builds on his earlier work on Wright, notably "Negating the Negation as a Form of Affirmation in Minority Discourse: The Construction of Richard Wright as Subject," in *The Critical Response to Richard Wright*, ed. Robert J. Butler (Westport, CT: Greenwood Press, 1995). The final two chapters of Carla Cappetti's *Writing Chicago: Modernism, Ethnography, and the Novel* (New York: Columbia University Press, 1993) are devoted to Wright's relationship to the Chicago school of sociology. Cappetti focuses on *Black Boy* and *American Hunger,* works placed in the context of the methods and theory of Chicago sociology, especially the technique of participant observation.

Works addressing mid-twentieth-century cultural politics have posed fresh questions about antiracism and U.S. intellectual and cultural formation. Michael Denning's *The Cultural Front: The Laboring of American Culture in the Twentieth Century* (New York: Verso, 1996) explores Wright's contribution to the ghetto pastoral while also historicizing the antifascist and antiracist strands that emerged from the Popular Front social movement. Denning also recasts the writings of Kenneth Burke as social theory that drew from, and contributed to, the American left. Nikhil Singh's *Black Is a Country: Race and the Unfinished Struggle for Democracy* (Cambridge, MA: Harvard University Press, 2004) brings Wright beyond the realm of literary studies and within a tradition of antiracist theorization. Alan Wald's *Trinity of Passion: The Literary Left and the Antifascist Crusade* (Chapel Hill: University of North Carolina Press, 2007) enlivens literary history through a wide-ranging investigation of the antifascist cultural imaginary of American writers, among them Chester Himes, Ann Petry, and Jo Sinclair. Daryl Michael Scott's examination of antiracist thinkers, *Contempt and Pity: Social Policy and the Image of the Damaged Black Psyche, 1880–1996* (Chapel Hill: University of North Carolina Press, 1997), centers on "damage imagery" and its recurrence in twentieth-century discourses and policy initiatives. Lee Baker's *From Savage to Negro: Anthropology and the Construction of Race, 1896–1954* (Berkeley: University of California Press, 1996) tracks dramatic changes in anthropology, a field closely allied with psychology in the mid-twentieth century. Walter A. Jackson's *Gunnar Myrdal and America's Conscience: Social Engineering and Racial Liberalism,*

1938–1987 (Chapel Hill: University of North Carolina Press, 1990) distills a vast amount of archival material to produce a detailed historical and biographical account of the genesis and meanings of *An American Dilemma,* a product of the midcentury penchant for interdisciplinary work in the social sciences. David Southern's *Gunnar Myrdal and Black-White Relations: The Use and Abuse of an American Dilemma* (Baton Rouge: Louisiana State University Press, 1987) surveys the post-publication reception of *An American Dilemma.* Penny von Eschen's *Race against Empire: Black Americans and Anticolonialism, 1937–1957* (Ithaca, NY: Cornell University Press, 1997) reconstructs the internationalism of African American writers and activists in the 1940s. The specific currents and tensions of postwar intellectual life come into view in Andrew Ross, *No Respect: Intellectuals and Popular Culture* (New York: Routledge, 1989); Richard Pells, *The Liberal Mind in a Conservative Age: American Intellectuals in the Forties and Fifties* (New York: Harper and Row, 1985); Morris Dickstein, *Leopards in the Temple: The Transformation of American Fiction, 1945–1970* (Cambridge, MA: Harvard University Press, 2002); and James Gilbert, "Literature and Revolution in the United States," *Journal of Contemporary History* 2 (April 1967). Historical fluctuations in U.S. racial ideology, including major mid-twentieth-century reconfigurations, are mapped in Matthew Jacobson's *Whiteness of a Different Color: European Immigrants and the Alchemy of Race* (Cambridge, MA: Harvard University Press, 1998). On the history and vicissitudes of the Negro Problem, see Susan Gillman, *Blood Talk: American Race Melodrama and the Culture of the Occult* (Chicago: University of Chicago, 2003), and Khalil Gibran Muhammad, *The Condemnation of Blackness: Race, Crime, and the Making of Modern Urban America* (Cambridge, MA: Harvard University Press, 2010).

Several works have contributed markedly to our understanding of the impact of psychology and various forms of psychological theory on American history and intellectual life. Looking beyond the disciplines and professional organizations to broader larger and more consequential varieties of knowledge production, political culture, and social life, these works have directed scholars toward the multiple and shifting valences of psychological thought, demonstrating persuasively how the social status of psychological thought affected the salience it was accorded in governmental and other quarters. James H. Capshew's *Psychologists on the March: Science, Practice, and Professional Identity in America, 1929–1969* (New York: Cambridge University Press, 1999) looks at World War II as a defining moment in the growth of trained psychologists, psychology departments, and various forms of post-Freudian and humanistic psychologies. Ellen Herman's *The Romance of American Psychology: Political Culture in an Age of Experts* (Berkeley: University of California Press, 1995) surveys political and governmental changes brought about by the work of psychological experts working in a range of domestic arenas, including the study of race prejudice. *The Psychiatric Persuasion: Knowledge, Gender, and Power in Modern America* (Princeton: Princeton University Press, 1994) by Elizabeth Lunbeck tracks the emergence of psychiatric expertise as a form of broad cultural authority in the first half of the twentieth century through the archive of the Boston Psychopathic Hospital. Although the study centers on the years 1912–21, Lunbeck's informative conclusion surveys the vastly expanded purview of modern psychological thought of the mid-twentieth century. C. P. Oberndorf's *A History of Psychoanalysis in America* (New York: Grune and Stratton, 1953), an early history of the subject, focuses on psychoanalytic psychiatry and speculates about why the American environment led psychiatrists and others to approach psychoanalysis with a pronounced "experimental spirit." Nathan Hale's *The Rise and Crisis of Psychoanalysis in the United States: Freud and the Americans, 1917–1985* (New York: Oxford University Press, 1985) covers major developments in psychoanalytic thought and psychotherapeutic practice in the mid-twentieth-century United States. Eli Zaretsky's *Secrets of the Soul: A Social and Cultural History of Psychoanalysis* (New York: Knopf, 2004) captures the subversive dimensions of the story of psychoanalysis. In *Feminism and Its Discontents: A Century of Struggle with Psychoanalysis* (Cambridge, MA: Harvard University Press, 1998), Mari Jo Buhle reconstructs the intellectual culture of psychological investigation in the 1930s and 1940s and the high stakes of psychology for feminist theorizing. Elisabeth Young-Bruehl's *Anatomy of Prejudices* (Cambridge, MA: Harvard University Press, 1998) explores, among other things, the characteristics of American prejudice discourses. Franz Samelson's "From Race Psychology to Studies in Prejudice," in the *Journal of the History of the Behavioral Sciences* 14 (1978), is a key work on the emergence of the prejudice concept. Daniel Horowitz's *Betty Friedan and the Making of the Feminine Mystique: The American Left, the Cold War, and Modern Feminism* (Amherst: University of Massachusetts Press, 2000) describes Friedan's interests in psychology and her immersion in left-wing politics during the 1930s and 1940s. Perry Meisel's *The Literary Freud* (New York: Routledge, 2007) brings the Freudianisms of Kenneth Burke and Lionel Trilling into view. Several earlier works on the permutations of psychoanalytic thought in American intellectual life remain valuable. Benjamin Nelson's edited volume *Freud and the Twentieth Century* (Cleveland: Meridian, 1957) includes reflections on the impact of psychoanalysis by Alfred Kazin, Reinhold Niebuhr, and many others. Caroline Ware's *The Cultural Approach to History* (New York: Columbia University Press, 1940) provides a useful picture of how midcentury American scholars and intellectuals brought psychological inquiry into historical and cultural analysis.

African American antiracist criticism from the World War II period has been profitably historicized in works such as the aforementioned *Race against Empire* and *Black Is a Country*. Scholarship on this period specific to Chester Himes, Horace Cayton, Ralph Ellison, and C. L. R. James has expanded in recent years. On Himes, Edward Margolies and Michel Fabre's *The Several Lives of Chester Himes* (Jackson: University Press of Mississippi, 1997) is an excellent resource, as is *Conversations with Chester Himes* (Jackson: University Press of Mississippi, 1995), edited by Michel Fabre and Robert E. Skinner. Beyond Himes's own autobiographical works, James Sallis's biographical treatment, *Chester Himes: A Life* (New York: Walker and Company, 2001), provides insights into Himes's career as a writer and thinker. A range of impressive literary and historical approaches to Himes's work appears in Charles L. P. Silet's edited work *The Critical Response to Chester Himes* (Westport, CT: Greenwood, 1999). Christopher Breu offers a sophisticated rereading of Himes's novel in "Freudian Knot or Gordion Knot?: The Contradictions of Racialized Masculinity in Chester Himes' *If He Hollers Let Him Go*," *Callaloo* 26, no. 3 (2003). Horace Cayton's autobiography, *Long Old Road* (Seattle: University of Washington Press, 1970), delivers a detailed picture of his scholarly trajectory and influences. An informative essay on Cayton's best-known book is Henri Peretz's "The Making of *Black Metropolis*," *Annals of the American Academy of Political and Social Science* 595 (2004). Ralph Ellison, the subject of a vast number of literary studies, has garnered more attention of late in terms of his wartime work and thinking in the 1940s more generally. Beyond King's *Race, Culture, and the Intellectuals* and Rampersad's *Ralph Ellison*, there is Lawrence Jackson's

Ralph Ellison: Emergence of Genius (New York: Wiley, 2002), which includes a valuable chapter on the intellectual culture in and around Ellison's *Negro Quarterly*. Shelley Eversley's "The Lunatic's Fancy and the Work of Art," *American Literary History* 13 (2001), offers an examination of Ellison's cultural politics in the lead-up to *Invisible Man*. John S. Wright's *Shadowing Ralph Ellison* (Jackson: University Press of Mississippi, 2006) is an exhaustively researched meditation on Ellison's intellectual origins and impact. The contributors to Kimberly W. Benston's *Speaking for You: The Vision of Ralph Ellison* (Washington, DC: Howard University Press, 1987) deliver a range of perspectives on Ellison's work, including his essays. These include contributions by Charles T. Davis, R. W. B. Lewis, Larry Neal, and Michel Fabre. Eric Sundquist's *Cultural Contexts for Reading Ralph Ellison's Invisible Man* (Boston: Bedford, 1995) brings together a rich set of documents attentive to the wartime era. The essays collected in Ross Posnock's *The Cambridge Companion to Ralph Ellison* (Cambridge: Cambridge University Press, 1995) present original angles on Ellison's corpus. On the American years of C. L. R. James, Scott McLemee's introduction to *C. L. R. James on the "Negro Question"* (Jackson: University Press of Mississippi, 1996), a collection of previously unpublished writings, is excellent. The intellectual transformations in James's work during his period in the United States are also the subject of Bill Schwarz's impressive "C. L. R. James's American Civilization," *Atlantic Studies* 2 (2005). Frank Rosengarten's *Urbane Revolutionary: C. L. R. James and the Struggle for a New Society* (Jackson: University Press of Mississippi, 2008) explores the mechanics of James's political affiliations and the intricacies of his thinking about art and literature. Dennis Dworkin's "C. L. R. James in Nevada," *History Workshop Journal* 63 (2007), is a brilliant exploration of the mix of ideas and practical necessities that marked James's U.S. period. Grant Farred's *Rethinking C. L. R. James* (Cambridge: Blackwell, 1996) includes cogent interpretations of James's work by Andrew Ross and Kenton W. Worcestor, among others.

Historical and biographical explorations of Lillian Smith have been uneven, but there are several places to look for careful and insightful readings of her work and impact on American letters. Anne C. Loveland's biography, *Lillian Smith: A Southerner Confronting the South,* is a fine, if workmanlike, basis for further study. *How Am I to Be Heard?: Letters of Lillian Smith* (Chapel Hill: University of North Carolina Press, 1993), a collection of correspondence intelligently edited by Margaret Rose Gladney, advances research on Smith enormously. Two separate and compelling essays by Gladney expand understandings of Paula Snelling's place in Smith's personal and intellectual life: "Paula Snelling: A Significant Other," in *Modern American Queer History* (Philadelphia: Temple University Press, 2001), edited by Allida M. Black, and "Personalizing the Political, Politicizing the Personal: Reflections on Editing the Letters of Lillian Smith," in *Carryin' On in the Lesbian and Gay South* (New York: New York University Press, 1997), edited by John Howard. The best work locating Smith in literary and intellectual contexts can be found in chapters from two books by Fred Hobson, *Tell About the South: The Southern Rage to Explain* (Baton Rouge: Louisiana State University Press, 1983) and *But Now I See: The White Southern Racial Conversion Narrative* (Baton Rouge: Louisiana State University Press, 1999). Hobson's foreword to an edition of Smith's *Strange Fruit* (Athens: University of Georgia Press, 1985) supplies a nuanced historical account of her most famous work. In her contributions to *Out of Whiteness: Color, Politics, and Culture* (Chicago: University of Chicago Press, 2002), Vron Ware produces a valuable reading of Smith's merger of biographical and cultural criticism.

Scholarship on the early work of James Baldwin is expansive and divergent in analytic orientation. James Campbell's *Talking at the Gates: A Life of James Baldwin* (Berkeley: University of California Press, 1991) is an intellectually satisfying biography that nimbly follows Baldwin's nomadic trajectory. The 2002 edition includes a fascinating afterword about Baldwin's FBI file and the legal case Campbell pursued to make more information about government surveillance of Baldwin publicly available. Other biographical treatments include David Leeming's *James Baldwin: A Biography* (New York: Knopf, 1994) and Henry Boyd's *Baldwin's Harlem: A Biography of James Baldwin* (New York: Atria, 2008). Baldwin himself provides information about his origins as a writer in *Conversations with James Baldwin* (Jackson: University Press of Mississippi, 1989), a set of interviews edited by Fred L. Standley and Louis H. Pratt. Baldwin's interview with Studs Terkel is exceptional. A brief but tantalizing set of pages that cast Baldwin's *Notes of a Native Son* as a work that "locates Baldwin firmly as Wright's literary son" can be found in David Marriott's remarkable *On Black Men* (New York: Columbia University Press, 2000). Many of the essays in *James Baldwin: The Legacy* (New York: Simon and Schuster, 1989), edited by Quincy Troupe, offer ways to think about Baldwin's influence on American writing. "The Welcome Table," by Henry Louis Gates Jr., in *Thirteen Ways of Looking at a Black Man* (New York: Random House, 1997), is an informative and personal rendering of Baldwin. Among book-length studies, Horace A. Porter's *Stealing the Fire: The Art and Protest of James Baldwin* (Middletown, CT: Wesleyan University Press, 1989) is an essential work. Several collections of essays provide insights into Baldwin's career. These collections include Harold Bloom's *James Baldwin* (New York: Chelsea, 2007) and Douglas Field's *An Historical Guide to James Baldwin* (New York: Oxford University Press, 2009).